Michel Faber
Critical Essays

Gylphi Contemporary Writers: Critical Essays

Series Editor: Sarah Dillon

Gylphi Contemporary Writers: Critical Essays presents a new approach to the academic study of living authors. The titles in this series are devoted to contemporary British, Irish and American authors whose work is popularly and critically valued but on whom a significant body of academic work has yet to be established. Each of the titles in this series is developed out of the best contributions to an international conference on its author; represents the most intelligent and provocative material in current thinking about that author's work; and, suggests future avenues of thought, comparison and analysis. With each title prefaced by an author foreword, this series embraces the challenges of writing on living authors and provides the foundation stones for future critical work on significant contemporary writers.

Michel Faber
Critical Essays

edited by
Rebecca Langworthy, Kristin Lindfield-Ott
and Jim MacPherson

A *Gylphi Limited* Book

First published in Great Britain in 2020
by Gylphi Limited

Copyright © Gylphi Limited, 2020

All rights reserved.

No part of this publication may be reproduced, stored in a retrieval system, or transmitted, in any form or by any means, without the prior permission in writing of the publisher, nor be otherwise circulated in any form or binding or cover other than that in which it is published and without a similar condition including this condition being imposed on the subsequent purchaser.

A CIP catalogue record for this book is available from the British Library.

ISBN 978-1-78024-096-1 (pbk)
ISBN 978-1-78024-097-8 (Kindle)
ISBN 978-1-78024-098-5 (EPUB)

Cover photo: 'Michel and roadkill, 2006' © Eva Faber, 2020

Design and typesetting by Gylphi Limited. Printed in the UK by ImprintDigital.com, Exeter.

Gylphi Limited
PO Box 993
Canterbury CT1 9EP, UK

Series Titles

David Mitchell: Critical Essays (2011)
Edited by Sarah Dillon. Foreword by David Mitchell.

Maggie Gee: Critical Essays (2015)
Edited by Sarah Dillon and Caroline Edwards. Foreword by Maggie Gee.

China Miéville: Critical Essays (2015)
Edited by Caroline Edwards and Tony Venezia. Foreword by China Miéville.

Adam Roberts: Critical Essays (2016)
Edited by Christos Callow Jr. and Anna McFarlane. Foreword by Adam Roberts.

Rupert Thomson: Critical Essays (2016)
Edited by Rebecca Pohl and Christopher Vardy. Foreword by Rupert Thomson.

Tom McCarthy: Critical Essays (2016)
Edited by Dennis Duncan. Foreword by Tom McCarthy.

M. John Harrison: Critical Essays (2019)
Edited by Rhys Williams and Mark Bould. Foreword by M. John Harrison.

Nicola Barker: Critical Essays (2020)
Edited by Berthold Schoene. Foreword by Nicola Barker.

Michel Faber: Critical Essays (2020)
Edited by Rebecca Langworthy, Kristin Lindfield-Ott and Jim MacPherson.
Foreword by Michel Faber.

Contents

List of Figures	x
Foreword *Michel Faber*	1
Introduction: Defying Genre *Rebecca Langworthy, Kristin Lindfield-Ott and Jim MacPherson*	5
Chapter 1 'House full of mouses': Genre, Language, and Creaturely Ethics *Timothy C. Baker*	15
Chapter 2 Eating Men Is Wrong: Empathy, Femininity and the Abject in *Under the Skin* *Tomasz Dobrogoszcz*	33
Chapter 3 A Walk into Nature: Self and Nature in the Work of Michel Faber *Rebecca Langworthy*	51
Chapter 4 'Nothing had changed': The Representation of Reality in Michel Faber's 'Fish' *Ian Blyth*	65
Chapter 5 *The Book of Strange New Things*: Letters, Delay and Experiences of Time *Kate Wilkinson*	77

Chapter 6   95
ECHOES OF POE: ABSENCE AND THE UNCANNY IN 'THE FAHRENHEIT TWINS' AND *THE COURAGE CONSORT*
Nicholas Prescott

Chapter 7   113
'IN SEPARATE TIME' AFTER *THE BOOK OF STRANGE NEW THINGS*
Rodge Glass

Chapter 8   127
A COMPASSIONATE FICTIONAL UNIVERSE: MICHEL FABER'S *THE BOOK OF STRANGE NEW THINGS* AND THE ART OF THE CREATIVE RESPONSE
Rodge Glass

Chapter 9   139
DOUBLE VISION: ADAPTING MICHEL FABER'S *THE CRIMSON PETAL AND THE WHITE*
Natalie O'Keeffe

Chapter 10   163
'BRANCHES OF GOTHIC COMPLICATION': READING THE GOTHIC IN MICHEL FABER'S *THE CRIMSON PETAL AND THE WHITE*
Matt Foley

Chapter 11   181
UNDER THE COATS OF SKINS: 'FLESH REMAINS FLESH' AND *UNDER THE SKIN* AS AN INTRODUCTION TO GREGORY OF NAZIANZUS'S ANTHROPOLOGY
Oliver B. Langworthy

Notes on Contributors	195
Index	199

List of Figures

Figure 1. Boarding Card, Dr R. Glass, Belgrade to London Heathrow (2nd July 2016) 135

Foreword
Michel Faber

Vanity, all is vanity. The words of Ecclesiastes seem all the more resonant at this point in human history, when the ecological harm we've inflicted on the planet may soon sweep our civilization into oblivion. Even at the best of times – those bygone centuries when we lacked the technology to foul our nest – art has had a tendency to disappear down the plughole quite soon after it pops up. Masterpieces are like humans: we produce a lot of them, make a great fuss of them, then they vanish into the ground and get forgotten. Dickens and Shakespeare are most definitely the exceptions rather than the rule.

As a non-Brit, I've been observing British authors for decades now and noted their very British relationship with acclaim. Some are self-deprecating because they're genuinely modest. Then there are the ones who are self-deprecating because self-deprecation is the shtick that suits them. *God know why anyone would want to read my stuff*, they wisecrack on the radio. *I'm not worthy to tie Jane Austen's bootlaces.* Meanwhile they lie in bed at nights, gnashing their teeth in frustration at the injustice of being passed over yet again for the James Tait Prize, the Booker, the Nobel.

Let me be non-British about this: I'm a serious artist and I write good books. They're enjoyable to read, but they reward study. Any number of scholarly essays could be written about them. It would be feasible to put on a symposium where academics could discuss issues raised by my work for several days and not run out of things to say.

This is precisely what happened in July 2016, when I was invited to join a community of scholars from all over the world, convening at UHI in Inverness for a conference called *Michel Faber: Defying Genre*.

Revisiting ten of the papers delivered at that conference now, I feel the same mixture of validation and bewilderment as I did then. Validation because I am a deliberate and conscious writer; very little ends up in my work by accident. Therefore, the political, philosophical and aesthetic subtexts that academics identify in my books really do correspond to stuff I take great care to put in. (*The Crimson Petal* as a feminist deconstruction of the patriarchy? Sure!) Bewilderment because academics speak a language that I haven't learned, and are liable to reference Jacques Derrida and other theorists I neither read nor understand.

But that's OK. One of the concerns that runs through all my work is the gulf which separates each human from all others and how valiantly we strive to cross it. People as smart as the contributors to this book appreciate better than most the limitations of our bridge-building. Instead of merely ignoring or failing to notice the gulf, they do what they can to create tools for dismantling alienation. And, just as my work has taken them to places they hadn't gone before, so their scholarly analyses introduce me to connections with a wider world of learning. To put it simply: we learn from each other.

Of course, the conference was lovely and gratifying. There was, undeniably, the ego boost – the vanity-stroking, if you like – of being honoured as a producer of admirable things. But more importantly, it was a communion with passionately engaged readers. I meet readers at literary festivals too, in signing queues, but they're often shy, or self-conscious about hogging too much of my time, or inarticulate about what my books have meant to them. At UHI, highly articulate readers had the leisure and the confidence to tell me exactly what they'd seen in my texts. This is a rare and precious privilege. I will never forget the joy of it.

Whether all of this critical attention will translate into long-term survival of my works is, of course, another question altogether. The vast majority of the most well-loved and discussed authors of past centuries are unknown today. Even the luminaries of what seems like last week are fading fast. In recent years, some of my most loyal and perceptive readers have been struck down by illness; some have died. The march of Time pauses for no-one.

I want to conclude this introduction by reflecting on the career of Gert Hofmann, a German author who wrote *Unsere Eroberung* (translated as *Our Conquest*), a novel I admire very much. It came out in 1991 and is out of print, although you can get second-hand copies of it from Amazon for 58p plus postage (no customer reviews).

Hofmann made his living as a teacher. A refugee from East Germany, he taught in Bristol and Edinburgh among many other places. Few people in the UK have heard of him. The bulk of his oeuvre remains untranslated and his British publishing house, Minerva, is a defunct imprint of a larger company that no longer publishes fiction. Hofmann turned to novel-writing quite late in life, and wrote on the kitchen table after work. He got some nice reviews in our press, and won several awards in Germany. He died of a stroke two years after the publication of *Our Conquest*. He was never invited to attend a symposium in Inverness where clever friendly academics told him why his books were so special. His hands never got to hold a volume like the one you're reading now. His luck was probably average, as fine authors of literary fiction go. I know I have enjoyed extraordinary good luck, for which I'm grateful. I offer my heartfelt thanks to all the writers who share their insights within these pages, and to you, the reader.

Introduction
Defying Genre

Rebecca Langworthy, Kristin Lindfield-Ott and Jim MacPherson

In the summer of 2016, a group of scholars travelled to Inverness to attend the first academic conference devoted to the works of Michel Faber at the University of the Highlands and Islands (UHI). The conference, *Michel Faber: Defying Genre*, sought to bring scholarly focus to Faber's varied corpus of works and to explore how his writing challenges our grasp of fictional modes and genres. Each of Faber's novels conveys his skill at working within and challenging the genre modes and conventions his readership expects, providing thought-provoking texts that have been adapted as film, plays, radio drama and TV shows.

The conference also situated Faber within his local landscape. Faber's Highland home in Fearn is less than an hour north of Inverness, and the UHI Campus is located just off the A9, a road that plays such a significant role in *Under The Skin* (2000). The extent to which the Scottish landscape has influenced Faber's creativity is especially apparent in his direct depiction of Scottish settings for a range of his short stories in addition to the psychologically intense interrelationship in *Under The Skin* between the protagonist, Isserley's route through the Highlands and her increasing mental distress. The clear influence of the Scottish landscape, along with the number of literary accolades directed at authors who are Scottish, and Faber's continued relationship with the Edinburgh-based publishing house Canongate all suggest that Faber can be understood as a Scottish author (Lindfield-Ott, 2016). Faber's place in Scottish literary tradition can be further understood if we analyse the evocative depictions of landscape and the development of ideas and philosophies within that setting that sits at the heart of his texts. For Faber, the concepts and methods of genre writing create space in which his versatile narrative style can develop. Faber's work encompasses both the rural and urban and the terrestrial and extra-terrestrial as settings in addition to a range of historical periods, from the Victorian era to apocalyptic futures. Yet, throughout his work, landscape becomes a frame through which wider concepts and philosophical ideas are projected. Although traceable to the literary influence of Faber's situation in the Highlands, his work moves beyond a Scottish readership. The global appeal of Faber's work speaks to the significance and universality of the ideas which he so carefully crafts.

The wide range of Faber's writings hovers on the edge of critical discussion. Building on and incorporating a number of papers presented at the *Michel Faber: Defying Genre* conference, this collection seeks to provide an initial source of scholarly engagement with Faber's works and support further teaching and research of his corpus. During the course of the conference Faber listened to and responded to each paper, providing fresh insight into his creative process and also displaying his awareness of the ability of literary criticism to move beyond the scope of an author's original intended meaning. The results of Faber's engagement can be traced within the scholarly thought of this collection.

Michel Faber's literary identity stems from diverse roots. Born in the Netherlands, his family emigrated to Australia and it was here that he received his early education, before graduating with a degree in philosophy, English language, and literature from the University of Melbourne in 1980. After a string of casual jobs and the dissolution of his first marriage, Faber trained as a nurse and worked in hospitals around Sydney until he emigrated to the Highlands of Scotland in 1993 with his second wife, Eva. Following his relocation to Scotland

Faber began publishing his short stories, many of which include aspects of the Highland and Ross-shire landscapes in which his family lived. Faber's nationality is fluid. He holds a Dutch passport and is considered a Dutch author within the Netherlands. In Australia, Faber is seen as an Australian author, as he spent his formative years in the country and several of his early short stories are set in Australia. In Scotland, Faber is considered to be a Scottish author, as this is the country where he began publishing his work. He has been the recipient of awards such as the Macallan Short Story Competition that require the winner to be 'Scottish by formation'.

Faber's ability to resist categorization goes beyond the question of his nationality. Faber's works also cover a vast range of genres and often defy genre categories. This versatile range is something which Faber has consciously worked towards: 'I wanted each of my books to be very different from the other, and I feel I have pulled it off as many times as I can before I start to repeat myself' (Kidd, 2014a). The Neo-Victoriana of *The Crimson Petal and the White* (2002), and its associated short story collection *The Apple: Crimson Petal Stories* (2006), contrasts with *Under the Skin*'s skilful combination of horror and science fiction. *The Fire Gospel* (2008) provides a thriller adventure novel in the style of Dan Brown's *The Da Vinci Code*. His *The Hundred and Ninety-Nine Steps* (2001) is a murder mystery combining aspects of gothic, horror, romance and adventure, evoking Bram Stoker's *Dracula* through its Whitby setting and John Buchan's *The Thirty Nine Steps* in its title. *The Courage Consort* (2002) is intensely psychological with its focus upon fear, over-reliance upon others and living with depression. *The Book of Strange New Things* (2014), while predominantly a work of science fiction manages to provide deep reflections upon relationships, faith, and the nature of humanitarian work. This originality and versatility leads to striking pieces of literature which have drawn critical acclaim. The ways in which genre conventions are disrupted by his writing is, to Faber's mind, a rearranging of those categories, as his discussion with David Mitchell illustrates: '"I don't know if it makes you uneasy," Faber asks, "when reviewers talk about the stunning originality of our ideas? We're treading territory that has been trodden before – science fiction, genre, fantasy. It's just that we are cooking those flavours in a different way – that is more likely to appeal to people who would otherwise only read Conrad"' (Kidd, 2014a,b,c,d,e).

The significance of Faber's work and the success of his unconventional approach to literature is highlighted by the number and range of literary accolades he has been awarded. His first published collection of short stories, *Some Rain Must Fall* (1998), includes three prize winning stories. The titular tale won the Ian St James Award, 'Fish' won the Macalllan Prize and 'Half and Million Pounds and a Miracle' the Neil Gunn Award. While from his second collection, *Fahrenheit Twins* (2005), 'The Safehouse' won second place in the inaugural National Short Story Prize. Faber's first full-length novel, *Under The Skin* was shortlisted for the Whitbread First Novel Award and his most recent novel *The Book of Strange New Things* won the Saltire Society Scottish Book of the Year in 2015. In addition to this wide range of literary accolades a number of Faber's texts have been adapted – most notably his, neo-Victorian novel *The Crimson Petal and The White* became a four-part television series produced by the BBC in 2011. *Under the Skin* was adapted by Jonathan Glazer into a feature length film that premiered at the Venice film festival in 2014.

Following the death of Eva, his wife in 2014 Faber announced that he has no further plans to write novels, saying in an interview: 'I think I have written the things I was put on earth to write. I think I've reached the limit' (Page, 2014). This signalled a shift in Faber's output, with the powerfully evocative *Undying* appearing in 2016. This collection of poems records the terminal illness of his wife and the subsequent grieving process Faber experienced. In his foreword to the collection Faber explains this shift away from prose to poetry as being driven by loss: 'I hadn't known such need for poetry before. I wish I'd lived into my nineties, with Eva at my side, and never written these things' (Faber, 2016).

Michel Faber: Defying Genre seeks to provide an intellectual overview of Faber's corpus, focusing upon not only Faber's authorly craft but the reception of his works both in popular culture and in an academic environment. As such, this volume has been divided into three sections. The first focuses on Faber's playful use of genre and the tensions that this allows to develop within his texts. The second section looks as Faber's writerly techniques and the range of creative responses to his work, from fiction writing to adaptation. The third and final section examines the ways in which Faber's texts can be used in a teaching environment.

Genre

The collection begins by focusing upon the conceptual space created by Faber's innovative use of genres. Timothy Baker's '"House full of mouses": Genre, Language and Creaturely Ethics' explores how Faber not only defies genre conventions but also the boundaries of species in the short stories 'Tabitha Warren', 'Sheep' and 'Mouse' and in his most recent novel, *The Book of Strange New Things*. Baker argues that Faber's representation of animals challenges his readers' conceptualization of what it means to be human through his exploration of the boundaries between the human and non-human. Tomasz Dobrogoszcz's 'Eating Men Is Wrong: Empathy, Femininity and the Abject in *Under The Skin*' continues the exploration of human-animal ethics. Dobrogoszcz focuses on the ethical questions raised between binary categories of human/animal, self/other and male/female in *Under the Skin*. All of these binaries are developed and explored in the figure of Isserley who functions as a liminal being in Faber's text. Faber's representation of binaries is discussed further in Rebecca Langworthy's 'A Walk into Nature: Self and Nature in the Work of Michel Faber', which explores tensions between individuals and the natural world displayed throughout Faber's works. Langworthy argues that the discomfort expressed between protagonists and the world they inhabit is symptomatic of an underlying vein of nihilistic thought running through Faber's work, especially in *Under the Skin*, *Undying* and *The Book of Strange New Things*.

Ian Blyth's chapter on Faber's short story 'Fish' picks up on the fundamental inability of fiction to represent the real, explored in Faber's fiction. Blyth argues that there is a 'truth' to Faber's representation of a world on the point of collapse in which fish fly through the air, using this as a stepping stone to broader philosophical discussion about the nature of 'reality' and the impossibility of measuring whether a work can represent the world as it 'truly' is. This, then, gets us to think about categories of 'truth' and 'reality' and questions criticism, which privileges 'realistic' fictional representations of the world over those derived from the genres of science fiction and fantasy.

Literary Craft and Response

This section examines the range of responses to Faber's work, from the examination of his techniques, to how this influences other creative writers, and the adaptation of his work for television. Kate Wilkinson's chapter, '*The Book of Strange New Things*: Letters, Delay and Experiences of Time', looks at the narrative technique Faber uses in *The Book of Strange New Things*. Wilkinson focuses on the delay caused by letters in fiction and how Faber recreates this, changing his readers' experience of time in *The Book of Strange New Things*. Building on the theme of readerly response, Nicholas Prescott's chapter 'Echoes of Poe – Absence and the Uncanny in "The Fahrenheit Twins" and *The Courage Consort*' explores Faber's technique as a writer, and how this elicits an often visceral reaction in the reader. Prescott compares these two examples of Faber's work with Edgar Allan Poe and argues that the two authors share similar approaches to mythology, the macabre and the uncanny. Rodge Glass continues the use of delayed time as a narrative technique through creative writing in his piece '"In Separate Time" after *The Book of Strange New Things*', which provides an account through email messages from a husband to his wife. Glass goes on to explore the processes behind this creative response in his essay, 'A Compassionate Fictional Universe: Michel Faber's *The Book of Strange New Things* and the Art of the Creative Response.' This commentary examines Faber's interaction with creative responses and provides an insight into Glass's writing process. The creative response to Faber's work is also the focus of Natalie O'Keeffe's chapter 'Double Vision: Adapting Michel Faber's *The Crimson Petal and the White*', which examines the process of adapting Faber's novel by the BBC. O'Keeffe highlights the complexity of Faber's work and the significance of visual symbolism in developing aspects of Faber's text in the TV production.

Faber in the classroom

The ways in which Faber's work is being used and taught on university programmes is the focus of this third section and demonstrates the flexibility of Faber's work within a classroom setting. Matt Foley's chapter, '"Branches of Gothic Complication": Reading the Gothic in Michel Faber's *The Crimson Petal and the White*', explores of the use of Faber in higher education. It discusses questions raised by Masters' students who studied *The Crimson Petal and the White* as part of *The Gothic Imagination* module at the University of Stirling. Foley has developed his pedagogical experience into a sustained reading of the gothic iconography presented in *The Crimson Petal and the White* and in so doing provides a clear exemplar of how teaching Faber's work can lead to a reworking of existing Faber scholarship. Continuing the classroom interaction of Faber's work, Oliver Langworthy's chapter 'Under the Coats of Skins: "Flesh Remains Flesh" and *Under the Skin* as an Introduction to Gregory of Nazianzus's Anthropology' uses Faber's short story 'Flesh Remains Flesh' and *Under the Skin* as classroom resources through which to understand Late Antique theological concepts. Langworthy uses Faber's texts as easily accessible conceptual lenses that allow students to approach Gregory of Nazianzus's anthropology.

This collection of essays provides the first substantial academic study of Faber's body of work. It offers an overview of current academic thought about Faber's literary significance, from an international range of scholars many of whom include Faber's work in both their research and teaching. This collection's focus on Faber and builds on themes already developed in the ongoing Gylphi Contemporary Writers' series. Faber's work is often closely associated and compared with that of David Mitchell (Kidd, 2014b). Beyond this association there is a hitherto unexplored literary friendship between the two authors, who are often interviewed together. Mitchell wrote a foreword to Allan & Unwin's 2017 Australian edition of *Under the Skin* and speaks glowingly of Faber's work: 'I like Michel Faber's books very much. He's never written a bad one' (Hocking, 2007). By having collections of scholarship that examine each authors' work the potential for future research into the literary friendship of these two men will have a critical foundation from which to develop. This is of course only one of the potential trajectories for future study that this collection seeks to expose. The ways in which Faber defies genre allows this collection to act as a seeding ground for future criticism. The initial conference at UHI in 2016 and Faber's detailed responses to all papers provided an exciting basis from which this collection has emerged and which, we hope, maps out a number of stimulating avenues for future research into the work of Michel Faber.

Works Cited

Faber, Michel (1998) *Some Rain Must Fall*. Edinburgh: Canongate.
Faber, Michel (2000) *Under the Skin*. Edinburgh: Canongate.
Faber, Michel (2001) *The Hundred and Ninety-Nine Steps*. Edinburgh: Canongate.
Faber, Michel (2002) *The Courage Consort*. Edinburgh: Canongate.
Faber, Michel (2002) *The Crimson Petal and the White*. Edinburgh: Canongate.
Faber, Michel (2005) *The Fahrenheit Twins*. Edinburgh: Canongate.
Faber, Michel (2008) *The Fire Gospel*. Edinburgh: Canongate.
Faber, Michel (2014) *The Book of Strange New Things*. Edinburgh: Canongate.
Faber, Michel (2016) *Undying A Love Story*. Edinburgh: Canongate.
Hocking, Ian (2007) 'Interview with David Mitchell' *Serendipity: Free Online Magical Realism Magazine* 1, URL (consulted May 2018): http://www.magicalrealism.co.uk/issue1/interview.php
Kidd, James (2014a) 'David Mitchell and Michel Faber Interview. Two of this generation's best novelists on love, life and literature', *The Independent*, 22 November, URL (consulted April 2018): https://www.independent.co.uk/arts-entertainment/books/features/david-mitchell-and-michel-faber-interview-two-of-this-generations-best-novelists-on-love-life-and-9875894.html
Kidd, James (2014b) 'Episode 41 David Mitchell and Michel Faber in Conversation: Part 1', *This Writing Life*, URL (consulted May 2018):

https://thiswritinglife.co.uk/e/episode-41-writing-life-special-michel-faber-david-mitchell-part-1/

Kidd, James (2014c) 'Episode 42 David Mitchell and Michel Faber in Conversation: Part 2', *This Writing Life*, URL (consulted May 2018): https://thiswritinglife.co.uk/e/episode-42-1456925355/

Kidd, James (2014d) 'Episode 43 David Mitchell and Michel Faber in Conversation: Part 3', *This Writing Life*, URL (consulted May 2018): https://thiswritinglife.co.uk/e/episode-43-writing-life-special-michel-faber-david-mitchell-part-3/

Kidd, James (2014e) 'Episode 44 David Mitchell and Michel Faber in Conversation: Part 4', *This Writing Life*, URL (consulted May 2018): https://thiswritinglife.co.uk/e/episode-43-writing-life-special-michel-faber-david-mitchell-part-4/

Lindfield-Ott, Kristin (2016) 'Fear in Fearn: Place and Imagination in Michel Faber's Ross-shire Fiction', *Northern Scotland* 7: 64–84.

Page, Benedicte (2014) 'Michel Faber: This is my last novel', *Bookseller*, URL (consulted April 2018): https://www.thebookseller.com/news/michel-faber-my-last-novel

Chapter 1

'House full of mouses'
Genre, Language, and Creaturely Ethics

Timothy C. Baker

Contemporary critical discussions of genre frequently begin with a reference to Jacques Derrida's 'law of genre', which insists that 'one owes it to oneself not to get mixed up in mixing genres' (Derrida, 1980: 57). For Derrida genre is not simply an horizon of expectation, nor a commercial contract with the reader. It is instead a law of purity that insists above all else that genres are distinct. To label something as a genre is to define it in one absolute way. As he goes on to write, however, there is within this law already a 'principle of contamination': the very establishment of the law of genre presupposes and allows its own violation. The act of specification makes room for its opposite. As many of the chapters in this volume show, Michel Faber's work not only mixes genres, but owes much of its value to that act of mixing: the law of genre, Faber's work shows, exists to be defied. While much of Faber's work revels in the defiance of traditional literary genres, however, many of his texts go further in defying another genre seen as natural or pure, that of the creature. In short stories such as 'Tabitha Warren', 'Sheep', and 'Mouse', as well as *The Book of Strange New Things*, Faber investigates not only how non-human animals are represented in art, but also how the limits of this representation can be used to reconceptualize the human. Faber's work challenges the fixity of species boundaries, and suggests the importance of reconsidering the relation between ethics and aesthetics when considering both humans and non-human animals. Looking at the relationship between language and the creaturely in Faber's work foregrounds the way he challenges not only literary genres, but the categorization of different forms of life.

The question of what it is to be a creature is best expressed by Peter Leigh fairly early in *The Book of Strange New Things*, when he counters Grainger's assertion that the Oasans are not 'people' with an extended etymological detour:

> 'Well...' He drew a deep breath. 'Here's an idea, Grainger. How about we agree to use the term 'people' in its extended sense of 'inhabitants'? The original Roman etymology isn't clear, so who knows? – maybe it meant 'inhabitants' anyway. Of course, we could use 'creature' instead, but there are problems with that, don't you think? I mean, personally, I'd love to use 'creature', if we could just take it back to its Latin origins: *creatura*: 'created thing'. Because we're all created things, aren't we? But it's suffered a bit of a decline, that word, through the centuries. To the point where 'creature', to most people, means 'monster', or at least 'animal'. Which reminds me, wouldn't it be nice to use 'animal' for all beings that breathe? After all, the Greek word *anima* means 'breath' or soul', which pretty much covers everything we're looking for, doesn't it?' (Faber, 2014: 104)

The idea of the 'creature' here blurs the line between human and non-human animals, or between people and monsters. Yet here Faber also foregrounds the idea of creation as fundamentally linguistic. Peter's formulations refer back to Greek and Latin roots that may be unfamiliar to his audience, or to the book's, and are certainly irrelevant to the Oasans themselves. That is, language creates categories which are divorced from those they categorize, and which nevertheless can be interrogated by them. The density of questions here is similarly important: Peter speaks from a position of authority, and yet voices his ideas hesitantly. The words refer to living beings, and yet remain abstractions. The relation between linguistic categories and real beings is revealed, simply by this repetition and questioning, as inherently arbitrary. And in a sense, of course, it could not be any other way. Peter, Grainger, and the Oasans are all created beings, not in the divine sense implied by Peter, perhaps, but in the sense that they are nothing more than linguistic constructs themselves: they are created beings by virtue of being figures in a novel.

This self-reflexivity is extended a few pages later, when Peter and Grainger discuss the Oasans' physical appearance, and he expresses surprise about their somewhat humanoid attributes:

> 'All along, I've been telling myself I mustn't assume the human design is some sort of universal standard. So I was trying to imagine…uh… big spider-like things, or eyes on stalks, or giant hairless possums…'
> 'Giant hairless possums?' She beamed. 'I love it. Very sci-fi.'
> 'But why *should* they have human form, Grainger, of all the forms they might conceivably have? Isn't that exactly what you'd expect from sci-fi?' (Faber, 2014: 107)

Science fiction, as both the genre of the novel and a genre in the novel, sets expectations for the type of creaturely life that can be encountered. This is a familiar theme of Faber's work, most notably in the opening of *Under the Skin*, which is made more self-reflexive here. In both of these passages, however, Faber highlights the way genre invites or includes contamination or violation. Science fiction should, perhaps, permit us to consider a wider variety of creaturely life than we encounter on Earth and yet it has traditionally privileged the human, or humanoid, above other forms of creaturely life. Likewise, the very words 'creature' and 'animal' suggest a broader horizon of experience than they have traditionally allowed. The monstrous, the animal, the creaturely, the other: all of these are categories both enabled by language and still bound by it.

The close relation between linguistic and biological categories has been noted as far back as Montaigne, for whom the 'hyperbolic power of language generates a logic of deformation and a deformation of logic; humankind nurtures this monstrous presence through the construction of differences that are merely the effects of rhetorical transformations' (Kritzman, 1986: 170). The creation of a language for the monstrous is what permits the identification of the monster according to pre-determined linguistic principles. The monster, the creature, and the other are always linguistically delineated. This is a question not simply of the monstrous, but of any form of other: the categories into which we put beings are always imposed, and become a form of normative language. This is especially the case, as Derrida among others notes elsewhere, with the question of non-human animals. The category of 'the animal' is a linguistic construct that allows humans to speak for, or in place of, the animal: the animal, in Western thought, is defined by lack of speech or response. That is, 'the animal' is not, as it could be, a shared category pertaining to all creaturely life, but one that is linguistically limited in both senses.

The intersection of the lines between literary, linguistic, and biological categories or genres is one of the hallmarks of Faber's writing not only in *The Book of Strange New Things*, but in his short fiction as well. Throughout Faber's work it becomes clear that the designation 'animal' or 'creature' is itself a genre. Like a genre, it is fixed, absolute; like a genre, it always invites mixing or contamination. This tension can be seen most clearly in the story 'Tabitha Warren', from *The Fahrenheit Twins*, in this context one of Faber's most important texts. The name alone suggests animal stories of an earlier age: it implicitly echoes Beatrix Potter's Mrs Tabitha Twitchet, as well as a rabbit warren. Tabitha Warren is the author of a number of novels featuring animal protagonists, including *Cat's Paw*, which the story's narrator dismisses as 'entertaining but gimmicky – *Watership Down* with Kafka pretensions' (Faber, 2006: 215). The story is framed as a letter by an unnamed narrator to an unnamed newspaper editor, correcting the impression given by that paper's obituary and providing an account of an earlier interview that was never published. From the start, the mixture of genres is clear: while the form of the story may be something with which readers are familiar, it is rarely presented as a particularly literary form. Likewise, the story's presentation in italics immediately differentiates it from the rest of the collection. The reader is plunged into a conversation where much of the context is either already known, or is unknowable. This is more than a simple defamiliarization technique: rather, it points to the inability of fiction to straightforwardly present or explain the world. Faber uses a form associated with journalism and real-world events to challenge the reader's assumptions about how characters are contextualized, and what information is essential.

Warren's animal stories occupy a familiar literary category, but do not appear to be based on any particular real-world author, and the reader has no way to judge their quality or the reasons for their success. Instead, the reader must rely on the narrator's criticism of her first novel, *A Dog's Life*:

> *I admired the way the disintegration of Neil and Catherine's relationship is observed through the innocent eyes of their Jack Russell, but even in the most heart-tugging passages, I was nagged by a sense that the alienness of the dog's perspective is a cop-out, a failure of the author to take responsibility for her own cluelessness about human motivation. This failure cripples all her books; for all her cleverness, we know perfectly well that they are not written by cats, dogs, dolphins, rats, and all the other zoological protagonists she worked her way through, but by a woman who never quite got the hang of being human. It was this basic contradiction that I was interested in addressing when I went to interview her.* (Faber, 2006: 215)

Although this passage seems fairly straightforward, it introduces a number of disquieting notes. In discussing a book that is ostensibly about a dog, the narrator has seen only the human, giving names to the human protagonist but referring to the novel's protagonist only by species name. The dog is not fully autonomous, but 'alien', and this alienness is a failure. And yet Warren herself, the narrator says, is also not fully human. Neither the fictional characters nor the writer measure up to a presupposed idea of what it is to be, or understand, humans. Her apparent failure, that is, is not that she writes in an easily-dismissed genre, but that she fails fully to inhabit the genre of her being: she is the wrong kind of creature.

Warren, surprisingly, agrees with the narrator's opinions about her work: '*My earlier novels are no good, no good at all. False, fake, cowardly. The mind in them isn't an animal mind. It's a human mind dressed up in animal clothes. A human voice with a slight animal accent*' (Faber, 2006:

219). As many critics have noted, this inherent anthropomorphism is perhaps the only possible approach to writing about non-human animals. Given the difficulty of knowing a non-human animal's 'true' nature, as Chris Philo and Chris Wilbert (2000: 19) argue, the only possible option is a conscientious, 'hesitant' anthropomorphism 'which would allow the possibility of insights to be produced from considering *some* non-humans in *some* situations *as if* they could perceive, feel, emote, make decisions and perhaps even 'reason' something like a human being'. There is, from this perspective, no way to write the story of a non-human animal that does not ultimately privilege the human. Warren, however, attempts to do exactly that with a tale, she says, that 'really *is* told by a cat'. It begins:

> Time before, here a mouse was. Time before, here a mouse was. Time before, here a mouse was. Time before, here a mouse was. Time before, here a mouse was. Time before, here a mouse was. Grass rustle. Mouse? Mouse? Not mouse. (Faber, 2006: 220)

This, it might strike the reader, and certainly strikes Warren, is a more authentic version of cat experience. It is in English, she concedes – and in Faber's story it is presented in normal type, thus standing out from the italics of the rest of the text – and yet its sensory world, repetition, and focus, may seem more truly feline to the reader. Rather than presenting a cat that can perceive or reason like a human, Warren's cat perceives or reasons like a cat, or so it seems. The story revels in radical difference. And yet, of course, the question remains: what are we reading when we read Warren's story? The basic format takes us back to Thomas Nagel's famous 1974 paper, 'What Is It Like to Be a Bat?', where he argues that we might be able to imagine what it is like to hang by our toes from a rafter, or have webbed arms, or navigate by echolocation. We can, that is, imagine the behaviour. And yet, he argues, this does not tell us anything about what it is like to be a bat. There is a certain 'batness', as it were, that we have no way of accessing. And so the question becomes, does Warren's story tell us what it is like to be a cat, or what it is like to behave as a cat?

What is immediately obvious is that even if this story is from the perspective of a cat, it is still necessarily mediated. When the cat finally catches a mouse, we read:

> Mouse is mine now. In my mouth, warm pulse. On my tongue, heart beat. Come mouse. Come to my house. My house full of mouses, a place for play. This is the way: the grass, the hard ground, the window. (Faber, 2006: 221)

Passages such as this are difficult to read any way but poetically. If the reader can, perhaps, imagine what it would be like to feel the heartbeat of a mouse on their tongue, their attention is also drawn to the rhyme, alliteration, and assonance. This raises the question of whether the story presents a particularly poetic cat narrator, or whether this is an imposition, and if it is an imposition the reader is making, finding patterns where there are none, or one Warren is making, attempting to channel a consciousness that is fundamentally unlike hers. Focusing on what it is like to be a cat ultimately reinforces the role of language in our understanding of creaturely life. What seems to be a radical attempt to transform the relation between language and creaturely being foregrounds the original relation. We can describe, but we cannot fully inhabit.

After this extract, however, the tone of the frame narrative changes: Warren urinates on herself, and her husband shows the narrator out. The narrator ends the story defending Warren's relationship with her husband, against reported claims to the contrary, and claims that once he died, she never spoke again. The narrator's response to Warren's story, which has occupied so much of the text, is never mentioned. In including it in his letter, he may be trying to show that Warren was a more interesting or experimental writer than she has been labelled. In showing the failure of her body, he might be suggesting a concomitant failure of her mind. Yet a possible resolution can be found in the seemingly unrelated defence of her relationship. Warren, the author of animal stories, is seen by the narrator as unable to understand humans, while as the author of the later text she is seen as more emotionally complex. The story suggests that in her apparent love for her husband she demonstrates a greater understanding of human frailty than was previously imagined. Writing the animal in this way, it is implied, leads to better understanding of oneself. The long excursus into feline consciousness is valuable not because it represents a cat's experience authentically, nor because it resists anthropomorphism, or fails to do so. Instead, Faber implies that changing the genre of a story changes both the author and the reader. Mixing genres is not simply a matter of literary aesthetics, but is fundamentally transformative of creaturely being. As such, as Colleen Glenney Boggs (2013: 189) argues, the literary representation of animals ultimately 'challenge[s] our understanding of textual significance and figuration'. Presenting non-human animals in a new, textually-determined way forces the reader to consider the limits of textual representation more generally.

Such questions of representation have been usefully developed in Jakob von Uexküll's short book *A Foray into the Worlds of Animals and Humans*, which was first published in 1934 but has received far more attention recently. Uexküll influentially argues that the perceptual life-world of different creatures is unique, and should be recognized in its difference. It is not the case that humans perceive the world as it is, and other creatures perceive it in a way that is somehow lesser – whether through limited sight, or colour perception, and so on – but that each creature has their own distinct perceptual world. He writes:

> We comfort ourselves all too easily with the illusion that the relations of another kind of subject to the things of its environment play out in the same space and time as the relations that link us to the things of our human environment. This illusion is fed by the belief in the existence of one and only one world, in which all living beings are encased. From this arises the widely held conviction that there must be one and only one space and time for all living beings. (Von Uexküll, 2010: 54)

From a scientific perspective, then, the existence of a unified world of which humans have a privileged understanding is an illusion; indeed, even the world of human perception is more multi-faceted than many realize. Uexküll's argument clearly applies to the two types of animal stories presented in 'Tabitha Warren'. The first, more conventionally anthropomorphic, stories follow the illusion that there is one and only one world, a world, which operates on human principles and perceptions, a world in which the way a Jack Russell observes a human relationship is paramount. The second accepts that the way in which a non-human animal perceives the world is fundamentally different.

Faber's work, however, expands the horizons of this analogy to suggest that not only each type of creature, but each individual creature, has a different perceptual world, and that each story, or literary text, is also a record of a different perceptual world. Literary genres, that is, present a particular type of world, and the mixing of genres, as well as characters, demonstrates the limit of any one world. This is apparent in an early story of Faber's such as 'Sheep' which, perhaps surprisingly, has relatively little to do with sheep. The story concerns five international artists who have been invited to the 'Alternative Centre of the World', somewhere near Inverness, by an anonymous 'art lover' who dislikes a past exhibition of their work (clearly modelled on the 1997 Sensation exhibition curated by Charles Saatchi). The story largely mocks the pretentiousness of young cosmopolitan artists, while also suggesting that the Highlands themselves are not, perhaps, a boundless source for the imagination. The artists are largely bored, and mostly unchanged. Yet there is a moment of potential integration of these disparate worlds, which takes place when one of the artists sees a small child gathering wool to make a toy sheep:

> This little interaction got June Laboyer-Suk thinking, as she and Fay continued to stare into the fields. She hadn't thought about art since early this morning, but now she began to have an idea for a new show, called 'Reconstruction'... no, 'Reclamation'... no, 'Reconstitution of a sheep'. She would collect all the different cuts of lamb from a butcher, and put them together again, with sheepskin car-seat covers and lambswool slippers wrapped around them. Or maybe it would be better just to lay the bits out loose, with a text inviting the audience to assemble them. More confrontational that way. [...]
>
> June turned back to the sheep, at a loss for what to do or say.
>
> 'Baaaaahh!' said one of the sheep, and June realised all at once that her idea for the 'Reconstitution' show was much less interesting than the fact that these animals were here alive, a different species from her,

existing on a part of the planet she might easily never have seen: an alternative centre of the world. […]

An hour later [she was] sitting in a hotel, marvelling at the inedibility of Scottish food and pining for New York. (Faber, 1998: 237–8)

Most importantly, the story highlights not the apparent superiority of the natural world over the artistic world, but rather the fact that the artist immediately returns to her own perceptual world. The sheep and the human both have a lifeworld, and while it briefly overlaps, that shared recognition cannot be maintained. Unlike many recent novelists looking at the relation between human and non-human animals, Faber does not advocate, for instance, shared suffering as a common and unifying experience. Although Isserley's death at the end of *Under the Skin* can be read as an acceptance of her place in a larger world, for instance, it is also resolutely individual, and does not ultimately demonstrate significant shared understanding. Instead, in Faber's work these moments of mutual experience are fleeting, even if essential. In all of Faber's work, whether fantastic or realist, historical or present-day, concerned with animals or humans only, such moments exist, and yet they cannot be maintained. Instead, Faber's work is filled with individuals with their own perceptual worlds that only briefly overlap.

This overlapping of perceptual worlds is, again, well explained by Uexküll. In his 1940 book *A Theory of Meaning* he gives the example of the stem of a blooming meadow flower and asks the reader to imagine it in four environments: in that of a child picking flowers for a bouquet, that of an ant walking across it, that of a spittle-bug larva inside it, and that of a cow, which eats it. As he explains, '[e]ach environment forms a self-enclosed unit, which is governed in all its parts by its meaning for the subject' (Uexküll, 2010: 144). The environment is determined according to its meaning for the animal at a given stage of its life, as well as its own physiological attributes. That is, the child, the insects, and the cow each experience a full, unitary environment, which they interpret according to its value to them. For Uexküll an anthropocentric understanding of the world is essentially misguided.

Instead, we live in a combination of worlds that share certain features, and which might overlap, but are nevertheless distinct.

This understanding of the world is very much what is presented in 'Sheep'. The sheep's perceptual life-world is quite limited, while the artist's is distinctly larger, and yet they are equally valid. Each is enmeshed in a particular environment. This moment of interaction perhaps gestures to a larger worldview that surpasses that of either individual. Such an approach is suggested by Ralph C. Acampora (2006: 5), who argues that each individual creature exists not in a world of simple, self-centred spectatorship, but 'is always already caught up in the experience of being a live body thoroughly involved in a plethora of ecological and social interrelationships with other living bodies and people'. In 'Sheep', June is forced to recognize her embodiment, and her shared space, in a way that momentarily defeats her solipsism. While Faber suggests throughout his work that such solipsism cannot ultimately be overcome, nevertheless a passing recognition of different perceptual worlds is enabled by an encounter with the creaturely.

Even Acampora's idea of enmeshment, however, where we become aware of being bodies mixed with other bodies, or perceptual worlds mixed with other perceptual worlds, does not adequately explain Faber's depiction of the relation between human and non-human animal worlds. Instead, even as Faber suggests that such a shared perspective cannot hold, he also invites us to rethink the very concept of the animal itself, and consequently the human. After all, as Keri Weil reminds us:

> It has become clear that the idea of 'the animal' – the instinctive being with presumably no access to language, texts, or abstract thinking – has functioned as an unexamined foundation on which the idea of the human and hence the humanities have been built. It has also become clear, primarily through advances in a range of scientific studies of animal language, culture, and morality, that this exclusion has taken place on false grounds. (Weil, 2012: 23)

In 'Sheep' the encounter with 'the animal' as such is replaced by an encounter with an individuated sheep, and to a certain extent this disturbs the artist's conception of herself as human, in the sense of a being set apart. Although this revelation cannot hold, encounters with the creaturely still disturb that world, and force a re-evaluation of both the human and the animal. In the story 'Mouse', for instance, two neighbours are drawn together when one of them asks the other to remove a mouse from her flat. One, a gamer, has a perceptual lifeworld built entirely around computer games, while the other sees the world through the prism of their religion. Yet they are united by their disparate concerns for the welfare of a mouse. The man reflects of the woman at one point that '[a] creature less like him was impossible to imagine' (Faber, 2006: 172), and yet the mouse, as a creature theoretically even more unlike him, becomes a unifying force.

All three stories, to varying extents, present what Anat Pick (2011: 193) calls a 'creaturely ethics' that 'lies in the recognition of the materiality and vulnerability of all living bodies, whether human or not, and in the absolute primacy of obligations over rights'. Pick's move here is essential in understanding Faber's work. Previous studies of animal-human relations have often focused on the question of suffering and vulnerability in terms of rights: if we deem that the animal can suffer, it is right to try to eliminate that suffering. This is the position inaugurated by Jeremy Bentham and most influentially promoted in recent years by Peter Singer. Pick's view is somewhat more nuanced. The question is not suffering as such, nor is it consciousness or theory of mind, but rather it is a question of vulnerability, and what she terms the question of attention. In 'Mouse' the man's recognition that the mouse is vulnerable – specifically that it might suffer from being dropped from a second-storey window – changes the limits of his attention. The story ends not with the two human characters, but with the man looking in the grass for the mouse, finding it unharmed. Encounters with non-human animals change the limits of attention and invite a new conceptualization of ethical behaviour. In Faber's work the idea of the animal as such is frequently discarded, and replaced with a broader conception of the creaturely, where each creature inhabits their own, separate, lifeworld and at the same time the combination of multiple lifeworlds allows for a new form of ethical attention to emerge.

Approaching Faber's work through this perspective raises important questions of how literature, literary genres, and language, can engage in such an activity. The perceptual world of the text, after all, appears to be highly specific, and very much delimited. As 'Tabitha Warren' suggests, translating one perceptual lifeworld into another through language is always going to be a project that lends itself to failure. But the juxtaposition of these different lifeworlds allows for a different approach to literature, which Donna Haraway in a recent interview refers to as 'reworlding'. Haraway (2016: 205) situates her work in terms of her own initial love for science, which illustrates how our knowledge of the world, and ourselves, 'is situated historically in particular apparatuses for knowing'. Insofar as an 'apparatus for knowing' is itself a form of genre, it becomes apparent that for both Haraway and Faber, encounters with the creaturely allows for a rethinking of genre. This idea is clarified in a long passage where Haraway discusses the relation between reworlding and interspecies companionship:

> [My work] is part of a *reworlding* – that science fiction term has been very important to me. It seems to me that it is a term necessary for ordinary thinking, way beyond whatever counts as science fiction, these reworldings. So the 'Companion Species Manifesto' comes at a point of no longer being able to write or think without asking, Who are we here? What are we, Who and what are 'we' that is not only human? What is it to be companion species at this historical conjuncture, and so what? Who lives and who dies, how, and so what? Here, in this conjuncture? (Haraway, 2016: 215)

These are precisely the questions Faber asks throughout his work. All of his work asks who we are, what it means to live with other creatures, how we live and die and, crucially, why does this matter? This is true not only in the stories considered above, and his science fiction novels, but in his more realist and historical fiction. Each of his works creates a perceptual lifeworld, through unique combinations of genre, and offers individuals within it that have their own lifeworlds. This can be seen as a process of reworlding, in that it forces the reader to consider their own perception of the world, and suggests the limits of each individual's own perspective. In other words, Faber uses the mechanics of genre fiction as a way of suggesting to the reader that the world they encountering in the text is not their own – as in the opening of *The Crimson Petal and the White* – but must be taken seriously, because every world is not our own. The depiction of the creaturely in Faber's texts is not so much focused on a human/animal divide, but rather on a more comprehensive picture of all mortal creatures in their individual and collective worlds.

Such a broad questioning of creaturely life is made possible through the mixture of genres in Faber's work. Every genre is a worldview, a perceptual lifespace; it is as they are mixed that their specificity and need for combination become apparent. This sense of characters as mortal creatures with their own perceptual lifeworld is expanded even further in *The Book of Strange New Things*. Peter Leigh draws a sharp division between human and non-human suffering. In his initial interview to go offworld, the interviewer asks him to imagine being in a restaurant where ducklings are immersed live in boiling oil before being served to customers, and asks him what he would do. He replies:

> 'If I was really haunted by what I saw in that restaurant, I suppose I could devote my whole life to re-educating the people in that society so they would kill the ducks more humanely. But I would rather devote my life to something that might persuade human beings to treat *each other* more humanely. Because human beings suffer so much more than ducks.' (Faber, 2014: 33-4)

This comment is essential to understanding Peter, who in the novel can be seen perhaps as fundamentally lacking in empathy. Peter's inability to accept the suffering of others leads him to misunderstand his wife and to wilfully ignore the suffering of other humans, as seen not only in his letters to Bea, but also his inability to understand his cat.

Joshua, the cat, makes an appearance early in the novel when, after Peter and Bea have made love, Joshua intervenes:

> Afterwards, Joshua had jumped back on the bed and tentatively laid one forepaw on Peter's naked shin, as if to say, *Don't go; I will hold you*

here. It was a poignant moment, expressing the situation better than language could have, or perhaps it was just that exotic cuteness of the cat put in a protective furry layer over the raw human pain, making it endurable. Whatever. It was perfection. (Faber, 2014: 6)

The passage begins with a clear example of the anthropomorphic gaze, interpreting the creature's actions as fundamentally relevant to human life, as in Tabitha Warren's earlier books. The cat is then presented as wholly other, exoticized and held apart from human pain. The relation between feline and human pain reappears at the moment of Joshua's death. Bea first lists all the human suffering going on around her, systematic slaughter, mass starvation, and economic collapse, writing: 'None of it will seem real to you up there. You are spooning Bible verses into the hungry mouths of Oasans, I appreciate that' (Faber, 2014: 475). She then details Joshua's protracted, cruel, needless death. First she breaks his leg, accidentally. When he runs away he is tortured by two twelve-year-old children; when Bea takes him to the vet he is instantly euthanized against her wishes. In narrative terms, this is important as it is, more than anything, the point at which Bea truly believes that the split in their relationship is unsolvable: their perceptual lifeworlds and experiences are so different that whatever has tied them together no longer matters, or not to the same extent. These scenes, however, also raise the question of genre. More than almost any of Faber's other characters, Peter does not defy genre. He lives in a science fiction novel where he is, for the most part, a heroic missionary. The vast majority of the text tells his story, and encourages the reader to treat the text as a science fiction novel above all else, or perhaps as a novel about faith or love, the ideas most important to Peter. In Bea's letters, however, the reader also sees all the genres on the outskirts: the dystopian novel, the political novel, the novel about young parents, and the novel about creaturely suffering. All of these different genres, in combination, illustrate the way Peter is unable to see past his own experiences, or past the genre of his life. Peter is not only resolutely human, but imprisoned by narrative genre in a way the novel as a whole ultimately challenges.

Throughout his work, Faber challenges the idea of singular or pure genres not just from a literary standpoint, but from an ethical one as well. Attention to the creaturely allows for a reinvestigation of language, of suffering, and of our place in the world. Mixing genres is not simply a literary trick or technique, but provides a way to ask who and what we are at this historical moment. As such, Faber suggests that attention to language and genre is not fundamentally escapist, but allows us to see ourselves in a more pluralistic context, where we are locked in our own worlds and yet, for fleeting moments, can extend ourselves still further. That these moments cannot be sustained is the tragedy of the world. But as texts that are continually open to the reader, that serve, in Peter's words, as a sort of 'frozen Present' (Faber, 2014: 232), the ethical compulsion is passed to the reader. If the characters cannot transcend the genres they live in, perhaps the reader can. As such, Faber's work invites a rethinking of the relation between world and text: by opening our eyes to the pleasures and limitations of genre, Faber forces us to ask what sort of creatures we are, and what it means to live as mortal creatures in this world.

Works Cited

Acampora, Ralph C. (2006) *Corporal Compassion: Animal Ethics and the Philosophy of Body*. Pittsburgh, PA: University of Pittsburgh Press.

Boggs, Colleen Glenney (2013) *Animalia Americana: Animal Representations and Biopolitical Subjectivity*. New York: Columbia University Press.

Derrida, Jacques (1980) 'The Law of Genre', trans. Avital Ronell, *Critical Inquiry* 7(1): 55–81.

Faber, Michel (1998) *Some Rain Must Fall and Other Stories*. Edinburgh: Canongate.

Faber, Michel (2006) *The Fahrenheit Twins*. Edinburgh: Canongate.

Faber, Michel (2014) *The Book of Strange New Things*. Edinburgh: Canongate.

Haraway, Donna J. (2016) 'Companions in Conversation (with Cary Wolfe)', in *Manifestly Haraway*, pp. 199–296. Minneapolis: University of Minnesota Press.

Kritzman, Lawrence D. (1986) 'Representing the Monster: Cognition, Cripples, and Other Limp Parts in Montaigne's "Des Boyteux"', in Jeffrey Jerome Cohen (ed.) *Monster Theory: Reading Culture*, pp. 168–82. Minneapolis and London: University of Minnesota Press.

Nagel, Thomas (1974) 'What Is It Like to Be a Bat?', *Philosophical Review* 83(4): 435-50.

Philo, Chris and Chris Wilbert (2000) 'Animal Spaces, Beastly Places: An Introduction', in Philo and Wilbert (eds) *Animal Spaces, Beastly Places: New Geographies of Human-Animal Relations*, pp. 1-34. London and New York: Routledge.

Pick, Anat (2011) *Creaturely Poetics: Animality and Vulnerability in Literature and Film*. New York: Columbia University Press.

Uexküll, Jakob von (2010) *A Foray into the Worlds of Animals and Humans* with *A Theory of Meaning*, trans. Joseph D. O'Neil. Minneapolis: University of Minnesota Press.

Weil, Kari (2012) *Thinking Animals: Why Animal Studies Now?* New York: Columbia University Press.

Chapter 2

Eating Men Is Wrong
Empathy, Femininity and the Abject in *Under the Skin*

Tomasz Dobrogoszcz

The turn of the twenty-first century saw the publication of several noteworthy works of fiction concerned with the ethics of human-animal interactions. More specifically, a number of writers chose to engage in the debate on the moral implications of carnivorous culinary practices of *Homo sapiens*. The figure of the human carnivore, traditionally ignored in the cultural output of our species, has provided the key focus for such texts as J. M. Coetzee's *The Lives of Animals* (1999), Yann Martel's *Life of Pi* (2001) or Jonathan Safran Foer's *Everything Is Illuminated* (2002). The unsettling issue of eating non-human animals also lies at the core of Michel Faber's debut 2000 novel, *Under the Skin*. In a dynamic, trenchant and humorous narrative, an amalgam of literary genres, including elements of gothic and science fiction, Faber poses fundamental ethical questions about the nature of power and empathy towards the other. This chapter looks at the means by which the novel destabilizes traditionally established boundaries, not only between species, but also between genders. It investigates the potential of Faber's text to disrupt the binaries which often serve as the basis for identity formation: those of human/animal, human/

alien, self/other and male/female. Finally, it employs Julia Kristeva's notion of the abject in order to examine the feminist aspects of the novel.

Under the Skin imparts its ethical meanings under the guise of speculative fiction. Narrated in the third person, the novel focuses largely on its main character, Isserley, a female member of an alien race who has come to Earth with a special mission. In an unconventional narrative strategy, of which more later, Faber refers to representatives of Isserley's species as 'humans' and labels the specimens of Homo sapiens 'vodsels.' Isserley's assignment allows her to escape the humdrum toils of everyday existence on her home planet and its devastated environment which forces the inhabitants to live in underground shelters. The contrast between this desolate, withered world and the pristine, lively character of the earthly setting – the vast, empty stretches of the Scottish Highlands – allows Faber to slip an ecological message into the text. Isserley has to pay a dire price for partaking in this blissful environmental treat: she has undergone a series of mutilating surgical procedures meant to turn her 'human' body into a passable likeness of a vodsel. The plastic surgeons employed on the task have also attempted to reproduce some features of a vodsel's sexual attractiveness into her new physical shape. For Isserley's job is that of a seductress: day in, day out, she drives along Highland roads in her ancient Toyota, prowling for solitary, male vodsel hitchers. When an unaware victim accepts a lift, and Isserley has made sure his disappearance might go unnoticed, she renders him unconscious by means of anaesthetic injectors fitted into the passenger seat. She then drives the immobilized vodsel to a secluded harmless-looking farm, which is, in fact, a food processing plant: after a fattening procedure, her prey is slaughtered and butchered so that it yields high-quality meat, voddissin, sold at exorbitant prices back on Isserley's planet. Under the Skin is certainly not the first narrative told from the perspective of an alien, or of a predatory killer, but Faber's agenda goes further than experimenting with a controversially attractive point of view.

For the uninitiated reader, Under the Skin begins, quite misleadingly, as an account of a serial killer's spree. Faber's shrewd narrative ploy takes advantage of this initial uncertainty about the text's genre: the mystery of Isserley's real identity, of her extra-terrestrial origin and of the actions which, as it finally turns out, are part of her professional involvement is revealed in very small steps. At the beginning, the story produces an inevitable impression that the woman is treating vodsels as sexual objects. This effect is achieved by a careful choice of phrasing in the descriptions of her lonesome raids:

> She was looking for big muscles. (Faber, 2000/2004: 1)
>
> You'd be able to... undress him and turn him over in your mind in advance. (Faber, 2000/2004: 1)
>
> [She] wasn't interested in females, at least not in that way. (Faber, 2000/2004: 3)
>
> His body had been so good – so excellent – so *perfect*. (Faber, 2000/2004: 3)
>
> Isserley might catch a glimpse of his buttocks, or his thighs, or maybe how well-muscled his shoulders were. [He was] a male in prime condition. (Faber, 2000/2004: 4)
>
> [She was] savouring the thought of how superb he'd be once he was naked. (Faber, 2000/2004: 5)
>
> She imagined herself breathing heavily against him as she smoothed his hair and grasped him round to ease him into position. (Faber, 2000/2004: 7)
>
> The bulge in his jeans was promising. (Faber, 2000/2004: 10)

Since in her enigmatic quest Isserley is distinctly fixated on male bodies, scrutinizing potential victims for signs of virility, the narrative generates a sexual ambiguity. It also reverses traditional gender models of behaviour: in this tale the woman plays the part of a sexual predator preying on men.

When, after just a few pages, the reader ascertains that she is, in truth, a predator, because the abducted men are killed, the novel suggests an interpretation which evokes the image of a psychopathic serial killer. Carefully controlled textual hints, such as, 'Who said she had to bring somebody home every day, anyway? One a week should be enough to satisfy any reasonable person' (Faber, 2000/2004: 25), initially corroborate this reading, but can be rewardingly reviewed later, when we already know what really happens on the farm. Yet this discovery is a piecemeal process: the first indication invalidating the psychopathic murderer scenario is the reference to a group of Isserley's collaborators working on her estate. It is only after almost sixty pages into the story, when one of her associates mentions the name of a dish, 'shanks of voddissin in serslida sauce' (Faber, 2000/2004: 57), indubitably suggestive of its origin, that we realize the seized *Homo sapiens* males are killed for their meat.

This is the point when a principal subject of Faber's narrative becomes at last visible: *Under the Skin* is, in fact, not a horror story, but a voice in a debate on human-animal relations, its sensational plotline serving as a metaphor facilitating the text's critique of our carnivorous habits. Faber inverts the usual power structure between humans and animals in order to win the reader's support for his cause, assuming that it is easier to evoke empathy towards victims when they are of your own species. Therefore, the novel poignantly presents the suffering of human males, 'shaved, castrated, fattened, intestinally modified, chemically purified' (Faber, 2000/2004: 97), in the hope of arousing the reader's compassion for them, if not through a considerate appreciation of the plight of *any* living creature, then at least through the affinity to members of the same species. The uncomfortable explicitness of details warrants a penetrating critique of the torturous routines involved in factory farming. As Wendy Woolward (2010: 53) notes, by means of reversing 'conventions of predator and prey' and by 'the reduction of the human body to its vulnerable animality and to its edibility', Faber interrogates the ethical underbelly of the meat industry.

As a contrast for Isserley and her companions involved in ambushing, fattening and slaughtering vodsels, the novel introduces a character of Amlis Vess, a renegade son of the owner of the corporation which procures voddissin and markets it on the alien planet. Amlis, who briefly visits the Earth, is a sort of animal rights activist, a person highly critical of the practice of killing vodsels and feeding on their meat. His ethical stance, based on the belief that humans and vodsels are 'all the same under the skin' (Faber, 2000/2004: 164), emphasizes the novel's objection to eating other species.

Yet one of the major ethical assertions made by *Under the Skin* is that true compassion should not be merely based on our likeness to the victim, but should occur even if the subject of suffering displays incommensurable otherness. The novel's approach to the issue of the relationship between humans and non-human animals largely relies on Isserley's initial inability not just to acknowledge, but even discern, vodsels' pain and misery. For the main part of the narrative, she dissociates herself ethically from vodsels; otherwise she would not be able to carry out her professional duties. André Alexis (2000) suggests that Faber's text provokes 'the confusion of sympathies' and that 'the reader's sympathy for Isserley almost obscures the sheer cruelty of her behavior.' But this disorientation is not a long-lasting impression: the novel presents the protagonist's efforts to narrow her ethical distance to otherness and recognize its anguish.

Analysing *Under the Skin* from the perspective of Deleuze and Guattari's theory of 'becoming-animal,' Sarah Dillon (2011: 135) argues that literature is a perfect medium to express the resentment of 'the animal other,' as it is able to 'provide a site in which the nonhuman animal might be imagined to respond,' or even, as in the case of Faber's novel, to 'imagine an alien animal perspective through which the human animal might be observed'. She quotes Sherryl Vint (2008: 179), who, in a special issue of *Science Fiction Studies* on animal studies, recalls J. M. Coetzee's conviction that 'literature, by enabling us to imagine the world from another's perspective, enables us also to grasp something of the other's experience and to extend our moral engagement'.

The relation between humans and animals, already hinted at in *Disgrace* (1999), lies at the core of Coetzee's metafictional novella *The Lives of Animals* (1999). In the narrative vacillating between fiction and philosophical discourse, Coetzee has his character, the Australian novelist Elizabeth Costello, functioning as his alter ego, produce a fiery tirade against the meat industry, in which she likens killing animals to the Holocaust crimes. Pointing out that the rhetoric of discourse on concentration camps abounds in abattoir phraseology – the victims of 'the Nazi butchers' 'went like sheep to the slaughter' – she claims that the nature of the crime of Nazi oppressors 'was to treat people like animals' (Coetzee, 1999: 20). Costello makes an irreverent and uncomfortable accusation:

> we are surrounded by an enterprise of degradation, cruelty, and killing which rivals anything that the Third Reich was capable of, indeed dwarfs it, in that ours is an enterprise without end, self-regenerating, bringing rabbits, rats, poultry, livestock ceaselessly into the world for the purpose of killing them. (Coetzee, 1999: 22)

She goes on to insist that most Germans of the WWII generation 'lost their humanity' because of the 'willed ignorance' that enabled them to overlook the atrocities occurring in concentration camps. Pinpointing moral inconsistency inherent in the practices of stockyards and slaughterhouses, Coetzee's argument touches on the nature of human empathy, inasmuch as it manifests through dialogue with otherness. To a large extent, it parallels the line of reasoning presented in Ian McEwan's essay in the *Guardian*, published in the immediate aftermath of the 9/11 events, where he excoriates the perpetrators for lack of moral imagination:

> This is the nature of empathy, to think oneself into the minds of others ... Imagining what it is like to be someone other than yourself is at the core of our humanity. It is the essence of compassion, and it is the beginning of morality. (McEwan, 2001)

For Costello, and Coetzee, the major moral failing of the Holocaust perpetrators was not, or at least not directly, the fact that they treated the sufferers like animals, but that they were unable to compassionately enter their minds: 'The horror is that the killers refused to think themselves into the place of their victims, [and that] they closed their hearts. The heart is the seat of a faculty, *sympathy*, that allows us to share at times the being of another' (Coetzee, 1999: 48). In Costello's reasoning, a similar lack of affinity to otherness underpins the distress brought to animals by humans. Faber's novel follows the development of such a form of empathy towards vodsels in Isserley.

One of the means by which *Under the Skin* engages in the animal rights debate is the novel's approach to the issue of language. The narrative relates to the standard distinction between the human and the animal whereby animals are posited to have no subjectivity on the grounds of having no language. During Amlis's visit to the farm, Isserley takes great effort to hide from him the vodsels' fully operative linguistic system of communication, the information which – as she instinctively understands – would anthropomorphize them and prove his cause. Although at this point in the narrative Isserley is only at the beginning of her spiritual journey towards the recognition that otherness also deserves empathy, she already realizes that vodsels are thinking beings and therefore have some inherent 'dignity' (Faber, 2000/2004: 172). Her attempts to obscure from Amlis that those creatures can speak and write prove futile when he discovers that one of the victims has scrubbed the word 'MERCY' on the floor of his pen. Even though Amlis cannot understand the lettering, and Isserley refuses to explain it to him, claiming it is a meaningless scratch mark, he realizes that the creatures have their own language. When Isserley tries to look for an appropriate translation of this word, she finds that it is 'untranslatable into her own tongue' because 'it [is] a concept that just [doesn't] exist' (Faber, 2000/2004: 171). This observation is one of the most bitter examples of Faber's irony, which of course is ultimately not directed at his imaginary alien race, but at *Homo sapiens*.

More generally, the occurrence of differences and incompatibilities between language systems emphasizes the relational and arbitrary nature of anthropomorphic assessments. This is how Isserley reasons that the inhabitants of the Earth cannot be perceived as human:

> In the end, though, vodsels couldn't do any of the things that really defined a humanbeing. They couldn't siuwil, they couldn't mesnishtil, they had no concept of slan. In their brutishness, they'd never evolved to use hunshur; their communities were so rudimentary that hississins did not exist; nor did these creatures seem to see any need for chail, or even chailsinn. (Faber, 2000/2004: 174)

It seems crucial that the narration, which otherwise uses English, should voice the determinant features of Isserley's race by means of non-English words, which are thus merely empty signifiers. For Dillon (2011: 139), 'the emptiness of these specific signifiers serves as a metaphor for the emptiness of *any* signifier that "human" animals have used to distinguish themselves from nonhuman ones, and hence ethically justify their violence towards them'. Likewise, it might indicate that all the signifiers that we use to legitimize our distinctness from animals, and the consecutive lack of empathy, are equally valueless, because they are rooted in the same language whose possession we deny animals.

In fact, Isserley is perfectly aware that vodsels have a very well-developed linguistic system: after all, she has spent months watching television and reading in order to master it and be able to seduce her hitchers. However, she is in denial about their possible 'humanity' and would not call their speech language. Apparently, though, some vodsel phrases and linguistic structures would seep into her own consciousness, like elements of a foreign language one learns, along with the culture absorbed in the process. At one point, a slip of the tongue reveals her unconscious recognition of their system of communication as language: 'But it was all in the past now. Water under the bridge, as the vodsels ... as she'd heard it said' (Faber, 2000/2004: 207).

In her compelling discussion of the position of language in Faber's novel, Sarah Dillon demonstrates that the difference between humans and animals is not only based on the possession of language, but also, very importantly, is caused by language. She provides clear examples of the text's imagery which continuously depicts vodsels in animalistic terms. As the novel is focused mainly on Isserley, this represents her method of animalizing the vodsels in her consciousness before she is able to treat them as meat, 'the deanimation of the vodsels [which] functions as a strategy of othering' (Dillon, 2011: 143) necessary for eliminating any possible intimation of empathy.

Arguably the most efficient means used by Faber to undermine the distinction between humans and animals, a soothing excuse which rationalizes the meat industry, is the linguistic inversion in naming the species: while the text refers to *Homo sapiens* as vodsels, it retains the name 'human beings' for the members of Isserley's alien race. This narrative ploy deepens the reader's consternation at the outset of the novel and, consequently, intensifies its satirical impact. After all, we realize that although when the text mentions 'humans,' it refers to the alien invaders on a vodsel farm, Faber's obviously targets our carnivorous civilization and its violence to animals.

Moreover, *Under the Skin* also destabilizes our usual anthropomorphic assumptions by showing Isserley's attitude to other Earthly species. To the reader's bewilderment, the protagonist displays much more affinity to other mammals she encounters than to *Homo sapiens*. Driving her car through the fields, she is very cautious and tries not to run over rabbits. When one of the abducted vodsels tells her that he has left a dog locked in his parked van, she callously leaves the hitcher on the farm, indifferent to torture and death awaiting him, but resolves to find his pet animal and release it. Through an ironical presentation of Isserley's sympathy as being rooted in her morphological resemblance to quadrupeds, a distant scornful echo of Orwellian 'four legs good, two legs bad' (Orwell, 1945/2008: 31), Faber demonstrates the shallow arbitrariness of our boundaries between species that do and do not deserve empathy. This is most conspicuous in the protagonist's particular affection for sheep:

> 'Have you tried using them for meat?' asked Amlis. Isserley was dumbfounded. 'Are you serious?'... Isserley blinked repeatedly, fumbling for something to say. How could he even think of such a thing?... 'They're... they're on all fours, Amlis, can't you see that? They've got fur – tails – facial features not that different from ours.' (Faber, 2000/2004: 240)

In her dedication to the idea that sympathy should be built upon similarity, Isserley goes as far as to try to convince Amlis that sheep, unlike vodsels, have their own language. Her particular fondness for sheep stems not only from physicality; Isserley admires their serenity and 'innocence,' which she finds 'worlds away from the brutish cunning and manic excitability of... vodsels' (Faber, 2000/2004: 150). This is Faber at his most sarcastic: it is definitely not the first occasion that the species of *Homo sapiens* is identified as 'brutishly cunning' and 'manically excitable,' but this time the denunciation comes from a member of an alien race which kills our species for food.

The discursive destabilization of the human/animal binary raises ethical uncertainty which concerns Isserley herself. Despite being part of the voddissin processing industry, she has moral doubts about abusing vodsels and must use the aforementioned linguistic 'strategy of othering' to be able to accept her involvement in the practice. But Amlis's visit on the farm, with all his argumentation supporting animal rights, activates Isserley's dormant belief in her victims' subjectivity, and eventually results in her transformation. Her ethical confusion culminates in the decision to leave the farm and renounce her own race, despite being aware that this act will inescapably lead to her death. After an accident, she is trapped injured inside a car and, as she cannot allow earthly surgeons to examine her body, she resolves to commit suicide by means of operating the self-destruct explosion mechanism fitted in her vehicle. In the last moments of her life she finally concedes the subjectivity of the vodsel species: as Dillon (2011: 149) observes, the narrative, clearly filtered through the protagonist's focalizing consciousness, repeatedly refers to another driver who comes to her rescue as 'the woman,' or even 'the other woman' (Dillon, 2011: 294–5), which emphasizes their common status. However, what Dillon seems to downplay is that the protagonist finds this common status with the *female* member of the *Homo sapiens* race. Arguably, Isserley's gender is a momentous factor in the process of her ethical transformation.

Apart from Amlis's influence, there are two events that even more directly trigger Isserley's conversion and her decision to abandon the farm. The first meaningful incident is an assault of a hitcher, when the protagonist only narrowly escapes rape. The attack proves to her, as Dillon rightly maintains, that vodsels are not just passive victims but can consciously do harm to her, so there is 'a two-way exchange [between them], an ethical relationship' (Dillon, 2011: 147). The realization that the creatures can also cause her own suffering contributes to the development of her empathy towards the species. Clearly, the assault sparks in her the desire for violent revenge, but the nature of the revenge, besides its racial dimension, is also related to gender.

The other straightforward motive of Isserley's decision to give up working for the voddissin company, Vess Incorporated, is its plan to introduce a new, more economical scheme of obtaining meat for their market. The corporation intends to start breeding vodsels on their home planet, and therefore Isserley is asked to modify her abduction strategy. The employers wish her to supply them with 'a vodsel female, preferably one with intact eggs' (Faber, 2000/2004: 272), for reproduction purposes. This arouses some form of gender solidarity in the protagonist, who will not follow the instruction and soon disappears from the farm. Another signal of this unity is recognizing a vodsel female as 'the other woman.'

In point of fact, abducting a fertile female vodsel for her company would be the first act of violence perpetrated by Isserley against the creature of her own sex: so far, she has been concentrating her hunts on males. Most essentially, *Under the Skin* is a story of a woman who brings death upon men; but this elemental reading, paradoxically, suggests that approaching the text from the feminist perspective can facilitate effective interpretation. A number of ostensibly marginal details concerning acts of violence inflicted on male *Homo sapiens* can acquire a new sense if we look at the narrative not just through the prism of the human/animal or human/alien binaries, but complement it with the binary of male/female, not so readily spotted by the novel's critics and reviewers.

First and foremost, the novel never – not even once, neither directly nor indirectly – explains why Isserley hunts for male vodsels only. Explaining it simply with the question of more substantial muscle tissue size does not seem sufficient. Then, there is an issue of specific circumstances of the procedures that the victims are subject to on the farm. Immediately after they are brought to their pens, the vodsels undergo two simple surgeries: they are castrated and their tongues are cut out. Apparently, the castration is supposed to facilitate the fattening process, while removing the tongues is meant to leave them speechless. Yet, looking at the procedures figuratively, they are meant to deprive the subjects of two dominant attributes of their maleness: the phallus and the logos. Perceived in this way, Isserley's enterprise might be metaphorically understood as a woman's revenge on phallocentric, male-oriented culture.

As the protagonist recalls, a major means by which she acquires knowledge about vodsel culture is television. Faber's narrative gives the reader the sense of what Isserley might have learned, presenting several programmes she watches when she flips through the channels. First of these is an adaptation of *Hamlet*, and she chances upon, of all fragments, the scene of Ophelia's funeral. Her ignorance of the *Homo sapiens* is testified by the fact that she recognizes Yorick's skull as a small sculpture which looks like 'a three-dimensional version of the danger symbol' displayed on the farm (Faber, 2000/2004: 144). Understandably, she finds Shakespeare's English obscure and, consequently, the original line 'And now my Lady Worm's, chapless and knocked about the mazard with a sexton's spade' (*Hamlet*, V.i.82–3) becomes warped into '...and now my lady worms. Chapless, and knocked about the muzzard with a sexed unspayed' (Faber, 2000/2004: 144–5). The distortion produces an aura of nonsensicality, but at the same time it rings with possible phallocentric undertones: 'lady worms' *may* connote female creepy-crawlies, 'chapless, and knocked about the muzzard' *may* hint at an act of violence against a single, man-less woman, while 'sexed' and 'unspayed' are clear references to the animalistic dimension of femininity. Subsequently, Isserley watches other random fragments of TV programmes, which include: a procession of women in niqabs, obviously in support of some women's rights cause since the protesters are holding a placard with a picture of a niqab-enshrouded woman; a crowd of male aggressive football supporters; a horror movie in which a male saves a hysterically screaming big-breasted female from a giant insect. All scenes are imbued with unambiguous signifiers of a male-centred sexist culture of the vodsel race.

Consequently, the interrelation between Isserley and her abductees can be viewed differently: their status as others is derived not only from their animality but also from their masculinity. In such a context, the already mentioned textual strategy meant to represent Isserley's interest in the hitchers' physicality should perhaps be re-examined: the reader, initially guessing from the 'sexual' hints that the protagonist is a maniacal sex-killer, and then dismissing them as the text's purposeful trickery, finally recognizes them for what they really are: the signs of male attractiveness. By means of accentuating Isserley's focus on the indicators of her victims' carnality, the narrative objectifies the vodsels' bodies, presenting them, simultaneously, as chunks of meat and as potential sources of sensual excitement. At this point Faber disquiets the reader by reversing a long-ingrained, and patriarchally induced, cultural stereotype: while the objectification of the female body has been a frequently observed phenomenon, the perception of the male body in the same categories is much less common. This reversal strategy of the male/female distinction parallels the narrative's treatment of the human/animal binary discussed above.

At the same time, *Under the Skin* continuously objectifies Isserley's own body. Her physicality is surgically modified not only to conceal her extra-terrestrial morphology, but also to make her, as much as it is at all possible, alluring for the hitchers, in order to facilitate their seduction. The main attraction is her oversized breast implants, which she emphasizes by wearing very low necklines. The strategy works for most of the vodsels, who fail to notice numerous abnormalities of her body, irremovable remains of her alien origin. Yet, although they regard her as 'half Baywatch babe, half little old lady' (Faber, 2000/2004: 12), they are still sexually attracted to her, and her seductive looks dim their vigilance. In fact, the surgeons who formed Isserley's implants in the shape of female vodsel's breasts were using the pattern derived from pictures in men's magazines. Hence, Isserley's body is a product of male gaze in more than one way.

The novel represents the sexist perspective of the male gaze fixed on Isserley by means of temporary shifts in focalization. Generally, most of the narration follows the main protagonist's point of view, and the focus of the narrative on her is accentuated: in all thirteen chapters her name appears in the opening sentence, while in half of them it is the first word. However, each subsequent hitcher is allowed some narrative space –a paragraph, or a page – focalized on him. This enables the reader to follow the stereotypical perspective of a series of males who see Isserley as a sexual object:

> That's why this car was heated like an oven, of course: so she could wear a skimpy black top and air her boobs for all to see – for *him* to see. (Faber, 2000/2004: 11)

> Maybe he should mention something about bad hair days, to show her he had some idea about these things. Women liked to think there wasn't a hopeless divide between the sexes; it was a real leg-opener, he'd found. (Faber, 2000/2004: 122)

> No wonder the army wasn't happy about women soldiers. Would you trust your life to someone who went out in the snow with an acre of tit showing? (Faber, 2000/2004: 134)

The only hitcher who is an exception is the last: the narrative presentation of his point of view clearly shows that he does not treat Isserley as a sexual object, but shows some genuine sympathy towards her as a person. His attitude might be considered yet another motive for the protagonist's decision to abandon the farm.

It also appears important that Isserley is the only *female* member of her race who participates in the mission on planet Earth; this makes her an estranged other. The men working on the farm seem to be courteous, sympathetic and helpful; they ostensibly admire her courage and the sacrifice she has made for Vess Incorporated: the surgeries have irreparably transformed her body into an unsightly likeness of a vodsel. Despite the fact that they 'treat her as if there was nothing odd or ugly about her at all' (Faber, 2000/2004: 152), Isserley senses their patronizing attitude and pretentiousness of their affinity to her. In essence, she is an object of the male gaze also within her own race.

Her position of otherness is reinforced by the distortions of her body. Although coming to Earth gives her the benefit of experiencing pristine natural surroundings, it comes with a price: the loss of her innate corporality and transformation into a bodily shape which is not only hideous, but also highly uncomfortable, even painful. The surgical procedures, meant to make her a biped, involve the amputation of a significant part of her backbone, along with her tail, and the insertion of metal pins into her spine. She feels she is 'transformed into a beast, with hunched back, scarred flesh, crumbling teeth, missing fingers, cropped hair' (Faber, 2000/2004: 64). As a result of the changes which make her capable of walking on two legs and sitting upright in a car, she is doomed to constant pain, which can be slightly alleviated by everyday exercise. What is more, she is no longer able to sleep in a proper, 'human' fashion, lying on the ground, curled into herself, but must utilize a bed, a disgraceful animal habit. In order to resemble a vodsel, Isserley also has to regularly shave her beautiful copious fur, continuously tense her muscles so as not to bend arms at joints which vodsels do not have, wear vodsel clothes (while her race does not use apparel at all) and terribly uncomfortable custom-made shoes that conceal her long un-vodsel-like feet and allow her to walk.

Yet the direst price she pays concerns her femininity most directly, disrupting its corporal dimension. The amputation procedures undertaken on her body involved the removal of her genitals. Between her legs, there is merely scar tissue, a 'tangle of knotted flesh' (Faber, 2000/2004: 252). On top of all sacrifices, then, Isserley is denied her sexuality, not only by being deprived of any possibility of striking up a relationship, but, more radically, by surgery. This is most harrowing for her during her contacts with Amlis, who she finds glamorous, with his thick, soft, lustrous fur, four shapely limbs, a prehensile tail and a 'vulpine snout' (Faber, 2000/2004: 110). Although she is highly attracted to him, she has to suffer his apparent disgust caused by her looks:

> When he set eyes on her, he would see her the way any normal person from home would see her, and he would be shocked, and she would helplessly have to watch him being shocked. She knew from experience what this felt like; would do anything to avoid feeling it again. The men she worked with on the farm had been shocked too, at first, but they were used to her now, more or less; they could go about their business without gawping (though if there was a lull in activities she always felt their eyes on her). No wonder she tended to keep to her cottage... Being a freak was so wearying. (Faber, 2000/2004: 75)

Isserley's awareness that her body is an anomaly, an animalistic abomination which is being constantly examined by the male gaze of her companions, is more excruciating for her than physical pain.

The presentation of Isserley's mutilated body in *Under the Skin* relates to the condition of abjection introduced by Julia Kristeva. On the grounds of the psychoanalytical theory, especially Sigmund Freud's concept of repression and Jacques Lacan's theory of the mirror stage, Kristeva defines her notions of the abject and abjection in her 1980 study *Powers of Horror*. She locates the abject on the territory between the object and the subject, inasmuch as it represents that which 'cannot be assimilated' (Kristeva, 1980/1982: 1), which 'is radically excluded' and draws one 'toward the place where meaning collapses,' 'a weight of meaninglessness, about which there is nothing insignificant' (Kristeva, 1980/1982: 2). Although the process of ego formation requires that this unassimilable element be expelled as 'improper' and 'unclean' (Kristeva, 1980/1982: 2-3), its traces remain as 'a burden both repellent and repelled, a deep well of memory that is unapproachable and intimate' (Kristeva, 1980/1982: 6). Within the domain of the unclean, Kristeva situates mostly the substances that traverse the boundaries of the body, food, faeces, vomit, blood, pus, but also the ultimate signifier of death, the corpse. Importantly, drawing from the biblical semiotics of defilement, she also finds the abject in incest and the female body (Kristeva, 1980/1982: 93), especially in the indicators of sexual difference, menstrual blood and breastmilk.

The formation of the ego and the subject's later existence within the symbolic order (of language, law and culture) depends on the elimination of defiled elements, which are inherently related to its corporality. Certainly, the stability of the symbolic order demands that the abject be controlled; this, however, is never entirely possible. The condition of abjection results from the inability to permanently exile the abomination which inspires one's horror, leaving in the subject 'a deep anxiety over the possibility of losing one's subjectivity' (McAfee, 2004: 49). Kristeva suggests that the unceasing danger constituted by the abject makes the subject aware of 'the risk to which the very symbolic order is permanently exposed' (Kristeva, 1980/1982: 69). Inasmuch as the unified identity of the subject is threatened, abjection constitutes a wayward form of protection against it.

Yet this 'protection' can also mean the suppression of the feminine. Kristeva often links female oppression with the confused, misogynist form of abjection: given that this condition itself originates in the subject's early separation from the mother, and that the 'rejected' maternal body acquires the status of the abject, the sense of defilement is transferred collectively onto women. The patriarchal culture finds in it a convenient symbolic excuse of the post-Platonic, and Christian, for that matter, perception of the material body as corrupt. For Kristeva (1980/1982: 70), 'the masculine, apparently victorious, confesses through its very relentlessness against ... the feminine that it is threatened by an asymmetrical, irrational, wily, uncontrollable power'.

In *Under the Skin*, Isserley is driven to experience her own disfigured and castrated female corporality as abject. The surgical procedures performed on her body are supposed to accentuate its animalistic qualities and, in effect, make it disgracefully abhorrent for other members of her species. Clearly, the aforementioned false empathy of the men on the farm, whose gaze instates Isserley as a freak, expels her into the territory of absolute and unconditional otherness: as a symbolic subject she is transferred into the category of the abject. Furthermore, Kristeva maintains that the proper functioning of the symbolic order demands the repression of the female body, and likewise Isserley's femininity is stifled in the novel; the text emphatically represents this with the removal of her genitals. The surgical modifications of the protagonist's body acutely disturb her identity: her physiology is transformed into that of an abhorrent animal, but, more importantly, she is deprived of her sexuality and denied the prospect of maternity. In this way, Isserley is represented not merely as a cultural, but also as a biological abject.

In general terms, Faber's narrative positions Isserley as a liminal being. Her hybrid corporality situates her on the borderline between the human and the vodsel. Yet the novel not only destabilizes the ever-too-convenient binary of human/animal, but it also questions the long-established gender stereotypes. Isserley's involvement in the actions legitimized by Vess Incorporated fulfils two objectives simultaneously: as a predatory agent of meat industry, she brings suffering and death on animals, and, as an oppressed woman, she wreaks feminine revenge on patriarchal misogynist culture. Thus, *Under the*

Skin, which manifestly engages in the animal rights debate, can also be perceived as a text which carries feminist undertones.

Works Cited

Alexis, André (2000) 'Funny, You Don't Look Scottish', (a review of *Under the Skin*) *New York Times*, 30 July, URL (consulted November 2017): http://www.nytimes.com/books/00/07/30/reviews/000730.30alextt.html

Coetzee, J. M. (1999) *The Lives of Animals*. London: Profile Books.

Dillon, Sarah (2011) '"It's a Question of Words, Therefore": Becoming-Animal in Michel Faber's *Under the Skin*', *Science Fiction Studies* 38(1): 134–54.

Faber, Michel (2000/2004) *Under the Skin*. Edinburgh: Canongate.

Kristeva, Julia (1980/1982) *Powers of Horror: An Essay on Abjection*, trans. Leon S. Roudiez. New York: Columbia University Press.

McAfee, Noëlle (2004) *Julia Kristeva*. New York: Routledge.

McEwan, Ian (2001) 'Only Love and Then Oblivion. Love Was All They Had to Set against Their Murderers', *Guardian*, 15 September, URL (consulted September 2016): http://www.theguardian.com/world/2001/sep/15/september11.politicsphilosophyandsociety2

Orwell, George (1945/2008) *Animal Farm: A Fairy Story*. London: Penguin Books.

Shakespeare, William (1982) *Hamlet*, in *The Illustrated Stratford Shakespeare*. London: Chancellor Press.

Vint, Sherryl (2008) '"The Animals in That Country": Science Fiction and Animal Studies', *Science Fiction Studies* 35(2): 177–88.

Woolward, Wendy (2010) 'Persian Sheep, Hawksbill Turtles and Vodsels: The Ethics of Eating in Some Contemporary Narratives', *Australian Literary Studies* 25(2): 48–59.

Chapter 3

A Walk into Nature
Self and Nature in the Work of Michel Faber

Rebecca Langworthy

Michel Faber's works often include figures leaving cities or other human-dominated spaces and walking in the 'natural' world.[1] This chapter explores how this movement from the urban to the natural is developed in a selection of Faber's texts, arguing that, as a theme within his work, the disjunction between self and place is an essential and enduring one for Faber. Depictions of the natural world function in opposition to the representations of 'civilization'.[2] Faber develops an underlying sense of nihilism which comes to the fore in the act of walking away from civilization and into the natural world. This movement also transforms figures into animals who intrude upon the permanent features of landscape within nature. Through this transformation, during the transition from civilization to the natural environment, the tensions between animals and landscape are exposed, just as starkly as the divide between the human and natural worlds that Faber depicts. Faber's writing often expresses a deep-seated discomfort between the protagonist and the world they inhabit. This dynamic between Faber's representation of the human and natural worlds discernible across his writing, *Under The Skin*, *The Book of*

Strange New Things, *The Fire Gospel* and his poem 'The 13th' in the collection *Undying* all explore this representation. This chapter looks at two aspects of this dynamic, firstly the disjunction between society and nature as is demonstrated in *The Book of Strange New Things* and *The Fire Gospel* in addition to a selection of Faber's short stories and the recent Amazon Prime adaptation of *The Book of Strange New Things*, 'Oasis'. The second section focuses on the destruction of self and immolation of being in *Under the Skin*, the film adaptation *Under the Skin* by Jonathan Glazer and Faber's poem 'The 13th'. The destruction of self ultimately becomes the rejection of social and urban aspects of the world and affirmation of the natural world, highlighting the dichotomy between humans and nature within Faber's works.

The discomfort of being and nature: landscape and society

Faber's novel *The Book of Strange New Things* is the focus of this initial section exploring how the representation of natural landscape and the social constructs of civilization are juxtaposed to develop a tension from which a sense of discomfort at existing within either place. This sense of existential alienation from the characters context, be that understanding of self, location social structure or faith, can be established through examination of *The Book of Strange New Things* alongside the philosophical concept of nihilism.

The Book of Strange New Things expresses the discomfort of consciously existing within a landscape. In a setting split between apocalyptic urban space and a newly colonized planet, Faber examines the alien and human within nature. Throughout the *Book of Strange New Things*, there is a struggle for meaning – the novel revolves around the messages between Peter, a missionary sent to an alien world, and his Wife, Bea, who remains on earth and witnesses the disintegration of society. The ability of personal faith to respond to the various challenges the couple encounter becomes a prevalent theme which ultimately degrades into a nihilistic realization of their insignificance, and by extension humanity's insignificance.

Faber's approach to nihilistic thought as a reaction to religious belief echoes the work of Friedrich Nietzsche, who argues that faith in God provides meaning for life but that this meaning is false; religion functions for Nietzsche as a form of idealism. He says that humanity has moved beyond Christianity 'not because we lived too far from it, rather because we lived too close' (Nietzsche, 1968: 200). The rejection of or the lack of meaning present within Peter's religious beliefs leads him towards a nihilistic state, what Nietzsche defines as:

> A man who judges of the world as it is that it ought *not* to be, and of the world as it ought to be that it does not exist. According to this view, our existence (action, suffering, willing, feeling) has no meaning: the pathos of 'in vain' is the nihilists' pathos – at the same time, as pathos, an inconsistency on the part of the nihilists. (Nietzsche, 1968: 200)

The trajectory of meaning in *The Book of Strange New Things* reflects this shift away from finding purpose through belief in religion towards a rejection of any meaning ascribed to existence. This rejection of purpose is itself inconsistent as Peter continues to exist beyond the moment of this realization. The continuation of the narrative beyond this point allows the tension between sentience, with its associated sense of self, and the omnipresent natural landscape to become the subject of further examination.

The tension between self and nature is apparent in an examination of the two groups of sentient beings who live within the ecology of the alien planet, Oasis. First, the indigenous tribe whom Peter has been sent to minister to and secondly Tartaglioni, a linguist, who has left the base and attempts to live on the planet unassisted having suffered a breakdown. Both sentient life forms try to move outside their existence, one through the discovery of faith and the other through the abandonment of social structures. However, for both groups, it is their relationship to the landscape of Oasis which becomes the grounding force in their uncertainty.

Human and Oasian communities attempt to resolve their crisis of doubt, at least in part, by attempts to inhabit, yet shape, the natural world of Oasis. A contained example of this is the meeting between

Peter and Tartaglioni. The meeting happens when Peter, having been told that his cat on earth has died, leaves the base and walks out into the wilderness of Oasis. He discovers an abandoned settlement in which Tartaglioni has been hiding. In moments of intense emotional crisis, the protagonists' response is to walk into the natural world; a theme which recurs throughout Faber's work. The tension between nature and the artificial construction of a building becomes an extension of the tension between humans and nature in the description of Tartaglioni's house:

> Oasan interiors usually smelled of nothing much except food and the honeydew air currents that continually flowed through the windows and lapped around the walls, but this room managed to reek of human uncleanness and alcoholic ferment. (Faber, 2014: 419)

This description of Tartaglioni's home reveals underlying tensions between the natural and native landscape and the human approach to these spaces. Tartaglioni has corrupted the room with his 'Human Uncleanness'. The human aspect of this taint is within the air of the room; this corruption is contrasted not with the scent of an Oasan occupant but with the purity of the natural environment as air flows through the space and the vegetation of the planet (the foodstuff of the Oasans, whose diet is vegetarian). The food of the Oasans becomes contrasted with the alcohol of humans, while Oasan food in fresh or lightly processed forms of natural material, the alcohol is brought out of a fermenting process – it is rotting rather than fresh. Humans are shown starkly as figures of corruption, their usage of the natural resources of the planet contrasts with the practised by the native Oasans which leave the natural resources close to their original state when producing food. Tartaglioni's use of the Oasan building emphasises the artificial nature of the construction of buildings from natural materials. This interaction of sentient lifeforms, the natural world and the development of artificial structures is also significant in how Peter interacts with the Oasans. Just as Tartaglioni has sought solace in the landscape from his crises of being so, the Oasans use the local environment to attempt to escape their crises.

For the Oasans, their existential crisis revolves around a fear of death and injury, which is countered by their ostensible conversion to Christianity and the project of building a church. There is a considerable degree of ambiguity regarding what the Oasans think they are doing. Faber maintains this by giving them a language which is illegible to the human reader, the symbolic representation of their speech in the novels highlights the lack of clear communication between the Oasans and Peter when he attempts to explain the purpose of religion to them. The extent of this divide is apparent in the Oasan's attempts to build a church under Peter's direction.

> Just before his departure, Peter had hinted that the roof should be put on as soon as possible, but there was no roof. Nor had any progress been made on the windows, which were still just holes in the walls.
> Standing here reminded him of childhood visits to medieval ruins, where tourists would potter around the remains of a once-thriving abbey abandoned to the elements. (Faber, 2014: 238)

Peter's hints have not been recognized highlighting the semantic disjunction between him and his congregation. The building is not weather tight- it is left still part of the nature Oasis; the elements interact with the church space rather than being barred from it. While Peter sees the church as a ruin, a destroyed structure stripped of meaning, he is unable to comprehend the prioritization and approach to the world which the Oasans take. This disjunction only grows as the novel progresses until Peter realizes that the Oasans have a fear of mortality which has driven them to faith. However, Peter, in a crisis of faith, recognizes that death is a universal element beyond the control of himself and his faith.

> [H]e looked around several times at his church silhouetted against the brilliant sky. No one emerged from it but him. Belief was a place that people didn't leave until they absolutely must. The [alien people] had been keen to follow him to the kingdom of Heaven, but they weren't keen to follow him into the valley of doubt […] After all, their souls dreamt so ardently of a longer stay in the flesh, a longer spell of consciousness. It was natural: they were only human. (Faber, 2014: 490)

There are several significant features within this scene, firstly the church building has been created from mud under Peter's guidance, and he has been living within that building, literally within the mineral earth of this alien world. This shaping of raw nature mimics the shaping of his congregation's beliefs. The alien's faith in God stems from their physiological inability to heal (they will die from a bruise or scrape) the ultimate aim of imposing these artificial systems upon nature is to allow for a 'longer stay in the flesh'. By rejecting this Peter moves towards a nihilistic position in which he no longer sees the elongation of life as a goal. He also positions himself slightly outwith the category of Human, his lack of faith separating him from a human fear of death. The rejection of religion is a core concept within all schools of Nihilistic thought from Nietzsche's statement that 'God is Dead' (Nietzsche, 1882: 108) onward. The textual categorization of the aliens' shifts from non-human to 'only human' when they refuse to accept death's role in their existence and the futility of their belief system, preferring to cling to their artificial system of religious understanding. Their nature forces them to struggle towards the unattainable in their pursuit of resurrection and healing from Jesus. Thus, Peter's moment of Nihilistic crises is left unresolved within the text. He decides to return to earth to try and find his wife. However, he has been warned that there is nothing there for him by Tartaglioni, the most firmly Nihilistic character of the tale. 'What you wanna go back there for? What's the point? Everything's gonna be history soon. History will be history.' (Faber 2014: 421.) Peter's return is not to seek a better or longer life but becomes a form of self-destruction as he returns to a broken society full of uncertainty. He is enacting the intrinsic flaw of nihilism which Nietzsche identified. Although existence is in vain Peter by choosing to return to earth is seeking to find a purpose and meaning in reuniting with Bea. *The Book of Strange New Things* refuses to provide the reader with certainty regarding the protagonist's purpose. This refusal allows the natural world to become a prominent aspect of the tension between the uncertainty of self-direction and the immutability and incomprehensibility of the natural world. The tension between self and nature becomes central to the text because of its nihilistic approach to the exploration of religion and the social constructs associated with civilization.

The Fire Gospel is an enlightening example of how the natural world interacts with civilization in Faber's work. The natural world functions as a threat to personal safety and identity, while also uncovering a further facet of Faber's nihilistic outlook. Owing to its terrestrial setting and characters' human identity is not directly challenged in the way that the inclusion of aliens in *The Book of Strange New Things* allows for. In *The Fire Gospel*'s first scene a carved lion's head almost falls upon Theo, the protagonist, as he enters a museum in Iraq. The lion has been attacked 'with axes crowbars, even guns' it is being treated like a live animal, a predator that is part of the natural world. (Faber, 2008: 1) As such, it is hunted by looters in the attempts to bring down the carving. The Lion is a piece of the building, part of the artificial environment; it becomes dangerous to Theo when it falls. As an animal, the lion is a victim, but as a part of the environment, it is a threat. It is the fabric of the museum which provides the impetus for the tale as a new gospel is discovered in a statue, damaged during an attack. By the end of the tale, Theo is attempting to hide within society and musing upon the concept that 'we are dust [...] But we are dust with a mission.' (Faber, 2008: 192) This mission is the advancement of the Christian faith. When Theo has been shot it is clear that without faith, Faber offers a bleaker view of humanity's place in the cosmos: 'He was a small puppet of meat from Canada, with a hole blasted in it, twirling in the void like any other particle of debris' (Faber, 2008: 192). Both of these approaches to self-perception see the individual as insignificant: either particles or dust.

Both *The Fire Gospel* and *The Book of Strange New Things* explore the underlying tension between their protagonists and the physical environment in which they find themselves. *The Fire Gospel* depicts the relics of civilization (gathered in the museum) as a physical threat and the impetus for the narrative's development throughout the tale. By hiding within the urban landscape, Theo is afforded the chance to gain insight regarding his purpose and place in the universe. *The Book of Strange New Things* also depicts a physical landscape which acts as a threat to the protagonist via its harsh environment and offers the conceptual space for deep reflection upon Peter's purpose. The use of religion within both novels allows for these reflections to become increasingly nihilistic as the artificial constructs of human society and topography are slowly rejected in favour of the natural world. Peter returns to certain death on an apocalyptic planet, and for Theo, he recognizes that he will become the constituent parts of his physical self 'twirling in the void' (Faber, 2008: 192).

Destruction of self and the immolation of being

The nihilistic approach to the world demonstrated in *The Book of Strange New Things* and *The Fire Gospel* continues in *Under the Skin*. However, by not overtly discussing religious beliefs, the tensions between self and nature become ever more apparent. As Sarah Dillon convincingly argues, *Under the Skin* uses the science fiction genre to explore the boundary between human and non-human animal. She suggests that ultimately Isserly enacts Derrida's theory of Limitrophy moving beyond the limits of the categories of human or animal imposed upon her by the reader (Dillon, 2011: 150). In 'The Animal That Therefore I Am (More to Follow)', Jacques Derrida defines the term Limitrophy as follows:

> Limitrophy is therefore my subject. Not just because it will concern what sprouts or grows at the limit, around the limit, by maintaining the limit, but also what feeds the limit, generates it, raises it, and complicates it. Whatever I will say is designed, certainly not to efface the limit, but to multiply its figures, to complicate, thicken, delinearize, fold, and divide the line precisely by making it increase and multiply. (Derrida, 2002: 397–8)

What 'feeds' this limit and all surrounding it is for Derrida, the tensions between human and animal. For this discussion, this tension is extended. Within Faber's work, the limits go beyond the human and animal dynamic to encompass sentient life as an intrusion upon the natural world. In exploring this dichotomy within *Under the Skin* when Faber discovers the limits of these tensions, I suggest that they morph into a form of nihilistic reflection upon the role of self and nature. While accepting Dillon's argument I wish to examine how Isserley is alienated from the natural world in both her human and non-human animal forms because of the tension between the natural world and sentient life which Faber develops in *Under the Skin*.

The tension between sentience and the natural world is, as with *The Book of Strange New Things*, brought to the fore in moments of crisis where Isserley removes herself from the social interaction and moves into nature. Following a sexual assault, she goes to an isolated jetty at Tarbat Ness: '*This* was the place she'd decided to go when she'd still had the spirit to make decisions; now that spirit was gone. She would stay here. The sea would either take her or it would leave her be. What did it really matter?' (Faber, 2000: 190). Isserley's crisis is not solely about artifice and nature and this becomes apparent through her decision to remain in her car while the tide rises. Her car becomes an extension of self, set against the sea. This scene parallels death with the removal of spirit and an abandoning of self to the natural world. Underlying this is the question 'What did it really matter?' The nihilistic abandoning of self to nature is enacted on a small scale here. The removal of Isserley's decision-making spirit is akin to a rejection of her consciousness and as the scene continues her awareness of time grows distorted while her view of nature becomes increasingly vivid; 'the night passed in seconds' (Faber, 2000: 191). This view of nature collapses as the tide recedes and Isserley feels anger at its inability to overwhelm her. '"If that's the way you want it," she said aloud. Her voice shook with rage' (Faber, 2000: 191). The interplay of consciousness and sentience comes to the fore in this vocalization. Isserly in addressing the natural world displays an underlying assumption that she is speaking to something it is this act of speech, an interjection into the natural world, which pulls her away from her stupor.

This idea of meaning beyond consciousness is explored within Faber's work, often focusing on the boundary between sentient and non-sentient life. The struggle between human and non-human animal, as previously identified, is a precursor to this greater nihilistic struggle to reveal the underlying structure of the world. The tension is most clearly expressed at the end of *Under the Skin* when Isserley decides to kill herself.

> The aviir would blow her car, herself, and a generous scoop of earth into the smallest conceivable particles […]
> And she? Where would she go?
> The atoms that had been herself would mingle with the oxygen and nitrogen in the air. Instead of ending up buried in the ground, she would become part of the sky: that was the way to look at it. Her invisible remains would combine, over time, with all the wonders under the sun. When it snowed, she would be part of it, falling softly to earth, rising up again with the snow's evaporation. When it rained, she would be there in the spectral arch that spanned from firth to ground. She would help to wreathe the fields in mists, and yet would always be transparent to the stars. She would live forever. All it took was the courage to press one button, and the faith that the connection had not been broken.
> She reached forward a trembling hand.
> 'Here I come,' she said. (Faber, 2000: 295–6)

This moment is Isserley's final crisis of identity. Dillon ties this to her non-human identity: 'Isserley's becoming-animal leads not just to a becoming-woman but to a becoming-molecular and a becoming-imperceptible.' (Dillon, 2012: 149). Dillon's conception of Isserly's identity leads her to argue for the novel as an example of Limitrophy. However, I suggest that Isserly's final state rejects human, alien, and animal states. Throughout the novel, she has gone for walks at times of crisis in an attempt to discover her place in the world. At this moment she discovers that that place is not as a human, alien or animal but involves complete immolation and disintegration to a molecular level if she is to integrate into the world she wishes to inhabit. This act of self-destruction is also the end of consciousness but even in these final moments Isserley is unable to fully embrace the lack of consciousness within the environment through her final words 'here I come'.

In Glazer's film adaptation we are also presented with a crisis moment when Isserley attempts to integrate into the natural world. Due to the different medium, it is harder to encapsulate the crisis of consciousness which is intrinsic to the transcendent nihilism of the novel. However, there are still clear parallels within Glazer's adaptation. Isserley's crisis has three distinct stages, within the final ten minutes of the film, which demonstrate the evolution of this nihilistic progression of integration with nature. Glazer shows Isserley's image superimposed upon the landscape in the first stage of her crisis. She sleeps in the forest, having moved away from civilization. However, this is an imposition into the forest and nature – she (and her image) are still separate from the natural world she attempts to inhabit.

The second stage of Isserley's crisis sees her physically removing her skin making her both alien and animal within the forest. Her newly revealed form is ant-like, recalling the opening images of the film which feature a close up of an ant. This removal of the representation of her human-self functions both to align her with the non-human animal and yet also defines her as an alien intruder who does not belong in the landscape. This alien aspect brings about the third stage of crisis: Isserley's unfamiliar appearance prompts a forestry worker to douse her with fuel and set her alight. This scene is highly reminiscent of the atomization which ends the novel. There is a muted colour pallet throughout the film. However, the fire which enables Isserley's final transformation brings a brightness to the screen which highlights the enclosed nature of the forest. As she moves beyond the trees, the landscape opens up.

In a final image lingering shot, the forest is removed from the screen with the focus placed upon the sky and falling snow, symbolic of her transformation into atoms. While the novel ends with the removal of Isserley's consciousness, the film's focus upon the snow and silence moves the viewer beyond the narrative's internal consciousness. This focus opens up a significant contemplative space beyond direct consciousness – showing the viewer that there is some enduring structure to the world beyond thought. The development of this conceptual space appears at first to be antithetical to the notion of nihilism as a rejection of the worth of anything however as the philosopher Ray Brassier argues in *Nihil Unbound*:

Ultimately, nihilism's consummation in the affirmation of eternal recurrence rescinds the privilege traditionally ascribed to knowing in favour of a premium on creative affirmation. For only the will that affirms indifference (recurrence as meaningless iteration of the 'in vain') is capable of making a difference by producing being, not as an object of representation, but as a creative power worthy of affirmation. (Brassier, 2007: 215)

Thus, the destruction of the self (or the conscious being) allows access to, and affirmation of, the creative power of nature in *Under the Skin*. The effect of this transcendent nihilism is the acceptance of nothing and the lack of purpose in revealing the creative power of the universe on a molecular level. The rejection of consciousness allows access to this larger reality of matter on a cosmological scale.

Faber's poem 'The 13th' offers a further reflection upon this. In the first stanza, Faber says that snowflakes are: 'Thoughtless, Weightless, / they've come from nothing' this creation ex-nihilo imbues the snow with a power to change the world and, making the 'known unknown' the snow is nihilistically unsettling to the natural world. It removes the order imposed by belief in the known. This concept links to the physicality of Faber's wife, Eva. In the second stanza, Eva is physically described as being 'solid as the landscape'. Through the occlusion of the landscape by the snow, in the ultimate nothingness of her after death, Faber suggests that 'the snowflakes fall right through you' the creation from nothing of the snow is not accessible for Eva who has transcended beyond the scope of creative power. This change is at odds with the affirmation of creative power found in the representation of snow at the end of *Under the Skin* as it divides the self from the natural world at an atomic level.

The atomization of self is a theme which appears in *The Fire Gospel*, *Under the Skin* and in 'the 13th'. The span which these works encompass with *Under the skin* as Faber's first published work in 2000 and 'the 13th' forming part of his latest publication, *Undying*, published in 2016 is of note as it suggests that this a concept which deeply underlies Faber's literary practice. All of Faber's works examined here have crisis moments where the protagonist moves into nature and attempts to remove their agency or consciousness in favour of envelopment by the natural world. These moments indicate the extent to which Faber explores transcendent nihilistic concepts throughout his corpus.

Conclusion

Within the two core texts explored in this essay, there are superficially very different approaches to escaping self-identity. In *The Book of Strange New Things* Peter escapes back to earth, and civilization while in *Under the Skin* Isserley escapes away from humanity and its structures. Peter's trajectory is down – landing back on Earth – while Isserley is propelled up into the atmosphere as atoms. In *Under the Skin*, Isserley's destruction brings her closer to nature while in *The Book of Strange New Things*, Peter is seeking destruction within Humanity. These two texts offer contrasting approaches towards a Transcendental Nihilism – meaning can be found within annihilation, and that meaning exists beyond the scope of consciousness and human thought. Isserley embodies this nihilistic Transcendence through her desire to become atoms which can mix with the non-sentient nature of planet earth and for Peter to return to apocalyptic earth, ensuring his destruction within a planetary monument to humanity. Beyond these superficial disparities, the texts echo each other: both are about aliens on strange planets, both are about the disjunction when communicating with others, and both use landscape to emphasize the reconceptualization of the protagonists' place within the universe.

The role of the natural world is essential to Faber's brand of nihilistic thought. Even within the *Fire Gospel*, a tale set firmly within society it is the natural world which provides the impetus for the plot line. The natural world not only surrounds but intrudes into the narrative at key moments, such as the discovery of the scrolls and the shooting of Theo. The natural world plays an even larger role in Faber's poem 'The 13th' where it is placed in opposition to the consciousness of being while also offering the only point of contact between the living and the dead. What Faber puts forth is more than a reiteration of traditional nihilistic philosophy. His focus upon conscious, sentient beings' interaction with the inanimate landscape questions the boundaries between sentience and being. As Derrida argues in relation to the boundaries between human and animal categories, exploration of these boundaries is not a pursuit into nothingness but is rather a way to 'multiply its figures, to complicate, thicken, delinearize, fold, and divide the line precisely by making it increase and multiply.' (Derrida, 2002: 398) Thus, within Faber's work the examination of nihilism transcends its usual boundaries and locates a non-sentient creation within nature.

Notes

1 For this discussion, the term natural refers to environments that are not processed or developed by sentient life. The natural world in Faber's work is most commonly composed of landscape, weather and flora. Animal life when present, acts as an intrusion into this natural world.
2 In this chapter, the term civilization encompasses any form of artificially developed structure. Civilization includes cities, buildings or vehicles in addition to the social structures which govern the behaviour of Faber's protagonists (both human and alien sentient life forms).

Works Cited

Brassier, Ray (2007) *Nihil Unbound*. Basingstoke: Palgrave Macmillan.
Derrida, Jacques (2002) 'The Animal That Therefore I Am (More to Follow)', trans. David Wills, *Critical Inquiry* 28(2): 369–418.
Dillon, Sarah (2011) 'It is a Question of Words, Therefore': Becoming-Animal in Michel Faber's *Under the Skin*', *Science Fiction Studies* 38(1): 134–54.
Faber, Michel (2000) *Under the Skin*. Edinburgh: Canongate.
Faber, Michel (2008) *The Fire Gospel*. Edinburgh: Canongate.
Faber, Michel (2014) *The Book of Strange New Things*. New York: Hogarth.
Faber, Michel (2016) *Undying*. Edinburgh: Canongate.
Glazer, Jonathan (2013) *Under the Skin*. BFI/Film4.
Nietzsche, Friedrich Wilhelm (1882) *The Gay Science; with a Prelude in Rhymes and an Appendix of Songs*. New York: Vintage Books.
Nietzsche, Friedrich Wilhelm (1968) *The Will to Power*, trans. Walter Kaufmann and R. J. Hollingdale. New York: Vintage Books.

Chapter 4

'Nothing had changed'
The Representation of Reality in Michel Faber's 'Fish'

Ian Blyth

Fiction has always had a problem with reality. In one of Plato's early dialogues, Socrates questions the eponymous Ion about who would be better qualified to lead a Greek army – a rhapsode who sings in the voice of a general, or an actual general? When Ion attempts to convince Socrates that there is in fact no difference between 'the rhapsode's art and the general's', Socrates points out that this could only be the case if the rhapsode was in actuality also a general – and, if this was indeed the case: 'Then why on earth, Ion, being the best rhapsode *and* the best general in Greece, do you go round performing as a rhapsode but not commanding as a general?' (Plato, 2008: 12; emphasis in original). This question about the relationship between poetry and knowledge, and the related questioning of the usefulness of poetry in and of itself, comes to the fore again in the later dialogue, *Republic*, where Socrates and Glaucon discuss poetry and other forms of 'representation' and reach the conclusion that 'a representer knows nothing of value about the things he represents; representation is a kind of game, and shouldn't be taken seriously' (Plato, 1993: 354).

Poetry, which is excluded from the Republic until it can be proved 'that there is more to [it] than mere pleasure' (Plato, 1993: 362), is therefore dismissed as merely an imitation or 'mimesis' of the thing. It is not the thing itself. In many respects, traditional literary criticism has been trying to close this gap between the mimetic and the actual ever since. In Erich Auerbach's iconic study *Mimesis*, for example, he begins his epilogue by stating:

> The subject of this book, the interpretation of reality through literary representation of "imitation," has occupied me for a long time. My original starting point was Plato's discussion in book 10 of the *Republic* – mimesis ranking third after truth – in conjunction with Dante's assertion in the *Commedia* that he presented true reality. (Auerbach, 1953/2013: 554)

Notice that phrase at the end there – 'true reality'. Even today, there is a widely held notion that words such as 'truth' or 'real life' or 'realistic' carry serious critical weight – especially when used in conjunction with each other. We can see this as they are used, again and again, in reviews, promotional materials and other such things, seemingly as a way of reassuring us that what we are being offered has genuine aesthetic value. Whether it be 'golden age' Hollywood epics or modern-day supermarket 'misery memoirs', the truth-telling qualities of a work are asserted and we are told that this is a good story, a good book or film or whatever because it is 'true to life', because it is 'based on a true story', because the people who feature in it are 'real'. The opposite or negative also applies. Again and again, we are told that so-called 'non-realist' or 'non-mimetic' genres, that is genres such as fantasy and science fiction, are somehow lacking the appropriate sense of gravitas, and that their lack of connection to the 'truth' and the 'real' diminishes them: it is just 'made up', it is said, it is trivial, not worthy of serious attention, et cetera. Or, as a certain British actor recently remarked after he had given away details of what was going to happen in a certain HBO series in which he had had a guest role, 'I just think, get a fucking life. It's only tits and dragons' (Anon., 2016). This is a not uncommon view of the often interconnected genres of science fiction and fantasy. Let's be polite and say that it is the word 'dragons' that is the telling part of the put down here (although the show's disturbingly casual use of sexual violence and a narrative device that has been dubbed 'sexposition' has quite rightly often been called into question). Whatever else they may be, so the argument goes, dragons are not true to life – they don't 'exist'. The same, so the argument continues, can be said of any literary genre that represents such things. Science fiction and fantasy are not real, they are not realistic – and fiction has always had a problem with reality.

It will, perhaps, be of no great surprise if I confess that I take a very different view when it comes to these supposedly 'non-mimetic' genres of fiction, and I'd like to say a few things about this difference of view with reference to 'Fish' (Faber, 2000). 'Fish' is one of those stories that sticks with you. I first read it when it won The Macallan/*Scotland on Sunday* Short Story Competition in 1996, and one of the things that struck me on that Sunday morning several decades ago, and one of the things that has struck me whenever I had reread 'Fish' since that day, was just how 'everyday' or 'normal' a story this was. For all of its supposedly 'surreal' qualities (to quote from the website blurb for *Some Rain Must Fall*) and the way in which it 'projects a futuristic world' where 'sharks hover in abandoned corners and human zealots […] loose their fanaticism on the innocent' (Anon, n.d.), my feeling then and now is that 'Fish' makes this all seem remarkably unremarkable – true to life, even. Yes, marine animals swim through the air and human civilization has all but collapsed, but aside from that … Consider for example the opening of the story, and where the emphasis of the narrative voice appears to fall:

> THESE DAYS, Janet let her daughter sleep in bed with her. It wasn't what child psychologists would have said was best, but there weren't any child psychologists anymore, and her daughter needed help just the same.
> Janet had tried forcing Kif Kif to sleep alone, but the little girl would scream with nightmares about God knows what – sharks, probably. Now she was sleeping dreamlessly, cradled in the curve of Janet's waist.
> All around the bed, the flywire was stretched taught from floor to ceiling, the support struts and entrance zipper glowing in the can-

dle-light. Janet shut her eyes against the tick-tick-ticking on the wire and tried to drift off, but it was no use; there was always the anxiety that something was eating through the wire, through the canvas of the zipper, and you would open your eyes to find...
She opened her eyes. Nothing had changed.
There were still the same thirty or forty little fish [...] hovering in the air, bumping against the flywire, trying to get in. (Faber, 2000: 19)

If we look beyond the specifics in this extract, and think instead about what is happening in general, its quotidian ordinariness shines through: there is a mother and daughter; the daughter has trouble sleeping; they are plagued at night by things analogous to mosquitoes, in protection against which they have erected something analogous to mosquito netting. If you focus in on the details, then yes, there are things in these opening paragraphs that do not ring 'true to life'. But, if you take a step back and think of these troublesome things as signs that have an arbitrary association with their 'real life' referents, then these difficulties go away. Replace the 'unfamiliar' with the 'familiar' and structurally what the text says, and what it is saying about what is says, remains unaltered. Everything is different but, also, on a very fundamental level, nothing has changed.

Things are left unsaid, since there is no need for the characters to say them. There are no 'info dumps' in 'Fish' – that is, there are no moments at which one or more characters discuss things they already know for the benefit of the reader. There is no need – the characters already 'know' these things (compare this, for example, with the experience of attending a cricket match on a Sunday: there might be the need for some of the rules of cricket to be explained, in order to know what is actually 'going on' in the match, but the fact that 'tomorrow' = 'Monday' needs no such discussion). Much else is left unexplained. We don't know for instance how it is that these airborne fish came to be; what the origins were of 'the Church of Armageddon' (Faber, 2000: 20); who runs the Soup Kitchen; or why, 'When Kif Kif had suggested that [the fish she had killed when keeping guard] should perhaps be taken to the Soup Kitchen for use as food, Janet had hugged her fear-shaken little girl and wept' (Faber, 2000: 20–1). We are also never told what it is, exactly, that Kif Kif is frightened of

– all we know is what it is *not*. After a near fatal encounter with killer whales, Janet is dumbfounded when Kif Kif expresses her delight and amazement:

> 'I thought you were terrified of sharks and big fish like that,' she said lamely, hugging the slightly alien child tight to her side. 'You have nightmares every night …'
> Kif Kif pawed sleepily at an itchy cheek and nose.
> 'I have nightmares about other stuff,' she said. (Faber, 2000: 26)

This is Janet's and Kif Kif's life, this is what they know. Janet remembers a time before, but Kif Kif knows nothing else – for her, the world of 'Fish' is all that there is as it is all that there has ever been. This is what they have, this is what it is. Fish swim in the air – but hey, fish do that. This is Janet's and Kif Kif's reality, and who are we to say that it isn't real?

Writing in the *London Review of Books* in 2003, in response to the fiftieth anniversary of the US publication of Auerbach's *Mimesis*, Terry Eagleton notes that 'realism is one of the most elusive of artistic terms' – 'If realism is taken to mean "represents the world as it actually is"', he explains, 'then there is plenty of room for wrangling over what counts in this respect' (Eagleton, 2003). Eagleton considers the main problem to be one of representation. Partly this is to do with the archaeological perspective. Eagleton invites us to imagine the position of 'Literary critics in the distant future' and, to adapt his example a little, we might say that these futuristic literary critics 'would not be able to tell that ['Fish'] was non-realist unless […] they had historical evidence that [fish did not in fact swim through the air in the late twentieth century]' (Eagleton, 2003). There is nothing intrinsically non-realist about 'Fish', in other words, it is only the historical evidence that can tell us that this is the case. Janet has this evidence, as does the reader, but Kif Kif does not. Eagleton's other main objection is that there are surely more important considerations than whether or not 'art […] portrays life as it is', considerations such as a work's 'radical content', for instance, or that 'part of the point of art [is to create] things such as the Gorgon, or a grin without a cat, which do not exist in nature' (Eagleton, 2003). Sharks that swim through the air? Dragons? They are much of a muchness – neither 'exists in nature'. This is fair enough, but there is one constant in all of this – in both Auerbach and Eagleton, and in the discussions about what is real and what has never been – and that is the notion that we can in fact know the world as it actually is, or that things actually *do* 'exist in nature'. Eagleton refers to this as 'philosophical realism' (Eagleton, 2003). But philosophy has always had a problem with reality.

In Plato's 'Allegory of the Cave', which can be found in Book VII of the *Republic*, our view of the world is compared to that of prisoners chained up and watching a succession of shadows pass by as they are projected upon a wall. We never see things as they truly are, it is argued, instead what we see are merely degraded copies, faint echoes of unknowable transcendental Forms: 'the shadows of artefacts would constitute the only reality people in this situation would recognize' (Plato, 1993: 241). In Descartes' brilliant but fatally flawed *Mediations*, he attempts to establish a rational justification for the reliability of our sense experience:

> I shall pursue my way until I discover something certain; or, failing that, discover that it is certain only that nothing is certain. Archimedes claimed, that if only he had a point that was firm and immovable, he would move the whole earth; and great things are likewise to be hoped, if I can find just one little thing that is certain and unshakeable. (Descartes, 2008: 17)

Descartes appears to achieve the first step with the so-called 'second formulation' of the '*cogito*', the self-authenticating proposition 'I am, I exist, this is certain' (Descartes, 2008: 19) – although Russell and others have subsequently argued that even this might not the case (see Newman, 2016). However, the implications of Descartes' failure to achieve the rest of his aims can be summarized thus: I am certain that I exist, but I cannot deny that I have some serious doubts about the existence of this book, or indeed you the reader. A century or so later, Kant drew a distinction between objects we perceive 'as appearances' through sense experience, to which he gave the name 'beings of sense (phenomena)', and 'other possible things, which are not objects of our senses at all but are thought as objects merely through the understanding', to which he gave the name 'beings of understanding (noumena)' (Kant, 2007: 258). The problem Kant identified is that we can only ever experience the phenomenal world of appearances, and we can never gain access to the underlying 'actual' reality of the noumenal world of the understanding:

> I cannot, therefore, perceive external things, but can only infer their existence from my own inner perception, by taking the perception as the effect of which something external must be the proximate cause. An inference, however, from a given effect to a definite cause is always uncertain, because the effect may be due to more than one cause. Therefore in referring a perception to its cause, it always remains doubtful whether that cause be internal or external; whether in fact all so-called outer perceptions are not a mere play of our inner sense, or point to actual external objects as their cause (Kant, 2007: 341, emphasis in original).

Again and again, the 'true nature' of the external world proves to be elusive. Hilary Putnam's 1981 'brain in a vat' thought experiment posits a reality in which our physical existence is merely that of a brain attached to a supercomputer that simulates a world indistinguishable from the one in which we think we are living. Putnam explains that 'the purpose' behind this 'is to raise the classical problem of scepticism with respect to the external world in a modern way. (*How do you know you aren't in this predicament?*)' (Putnam, 1981: 6, emphasis in original). Putnam feels that the solution lies in the impossibility of this being true since, if we are all brains in vats, then saying 'I am a brain in a vat' is a self-refuting proposition – 'although the people in that possible world can think and "say" any words we can think and say, they cannot (I claim) refer to what we can refer to. In particular, they cannot think or say that they are brains in a vat' (Putnam, 1981: 8). However, subsequent challenges and responses to Putnam's hypothesis have raised the possibility that, in at least some of the multiple other versions of this sceptical argument, it cannot always be established that an individual (in particular) is *not* a brain in a vat (Brueckner, 2012). Nick Bostrom's 2003 paper, 'Are We Living in a Computer Simulation?', takes things a step further. Bostrom's argument is that if it is possible for a highly advanced post-human civilization to run a hyperrealistic ancestor simulation, then the probability is that they have already done this, and we are in fact currently living in such a simulation:

> A technologically mature 'posthuman' civilization would have enormous computing power. Given this empirical fact, the simulation argument shows that *at least one* of the following propositions is true: (1) the fraction of human-level civilizations that reach a posthuman stage is very close to zero; (2) the fraction of posthuman civilizations that are interested in running ancestor-simulations is very close to zero; (3) the fraction of all people with experiences who are living in a simulation is very close to one.
>
> [...] In the dark forest of our current ignorance, it seems sensible to apportion one's credence roughly evenly between (1), (2), and (3).
>
> Unless we are now living in a simulation, our descendants will almost certainly never run an ancestor-simulation (Bostrom, 2003: 255, emphasis in original).

Again, like the respondents to Putnam, Bostrom is not saying here that we definitely *are* living in a computer simulation, but he is suggesting that we cannot be certain that this is *not* the case.

The point of all of this is that there is a strong consensus that we don't know, and quite possibly cannot know, the truth about reality. And if we don't know what is actually 'real', how can we ever claim to be able to judge whether or not a work 'truly' represents the world 'as it is'? This can go two ways: first, we might say that nothing is real, nothing exists (but such extreme sceptical doubt arguably falls into the trap of becoming a self-refuting proposition – if nothing exists, we cannot say that 'nothing exists'); or second, we could argue, as Markus Gabriel has recently done, that 'everything exists' – 'even unicorns on the far side of the moon', to give but one of his examples (Gabriel, 2015: 1). If a thing can be thought of, Gabriel contends, it possesses its own object domain, its own reality; thus, everything exists. The only exception to this, he argues, is the world itself. For Gabriel, 'existence = appearance in a field of sense' and therefore '[in] order for something to be able to exist it must belong to a field of sense' (Gabriel, 2015: 73). The world is defined as 'the field of sense of all fields of sense, that field of sense in which all other fields of sense appear, and for this reason it is the domain to which everything belongs' (Gabriel, 2015: 73). In other words, the world = reality. However, if this is the case then it follows that the world (or indeed reality) cannot exist: 'We cannot grasp the world conceptually because there is no field of sense to which it belongs' (Gabriel, 2015: 76). As Gabriel explains: 'If the world existed in our thoughts, our thoughts could not exist in the world. Otherwise there would be a second world, which would consist of our thoughts and "the world" (in the sense of the object of our thought). Thus, we would not have succeeded in picking out the real world after all' (Gabriel, 2015: 79). Everything that exists, Gabriel contends, exists because it appears in a field of sense 'in' the world, but it is impossible for the world to appear 'in' the world since that would then require an additional field of sense which was not in the world, and thus the world wouldn't contain all fields of sense and therefore (by definition) could not be the world:

> The world in which we live shows itself as a single continuous transition from field of sense to field of sense, as a coalescence and interweaving of them. It does not reveal an altogether universal cold home [i.e. a cosmos], because such a thing does not exist. [...] All worldviews are false, because they assume that there is a world about which we can have a view (Gabriel, 2015: 97–8).

The conclusion we might draw from this is that if the basis of our judgment on how a text 'participates in' (but does not 'belong to') a particular literary genre (see Derrida, 1980: 65) relies on its relation to or representation of so-called 'true reality', then it needs to be acknowledged that this reality-reliant judgement might require a good deal of further thought, as indeed might the very notion of 'genre' itself – that is, while we can think of texts participating 'in' genres (as we can think of things existing 'in' the world), that does not necessarily confirm the existence of such genres (or the world). If it is the case that a proper understanding of the nature of reality is not attainable, any distinction between the mimetic and the non-mimetic falls apart. Dragons, sharks that swim in the air, unicorns that live on the far side of the moon and other such phenomena can be said to 'exist' after all.

The name of Janet's daughter, Kif Kif, seems relevant in this context. 'Kif' ('the same') is Algerian in origin, and it has passed into common usage in French in the phrase 'c'est kif-kif' – 'it's all the same', 'it doesn't make any difference' (Larousse, n.d., my translations). At the conference, Michel Faber noted that he had used the name Kif Kif in 'Fish' as a reference to a musician in one of his favourite bands from the 1970s, but this other symbolically significant linguistic resonance in 'Kif Kif' is still nevertheless present in the text, whether or not the author intended for it to be there (the author, after all, is only one of many 'readers' of the text – see Barthes, 1977). If we follow through on some of the possible implications of this name Kif Kif, and on our apparent lack of knowledge about actual 'true reality', then we might read the presence of this name in 'Fish' as a suggestion that the whole question of genre distinctions could be redundant. It's all the same thing, or it's always other things. Saying that Monday follows Sunday carries the same quality of 'truth' or 'object reality' as the notion that fish swim through the air. If we cannot be certain that reality is 'real', then all bets are off. Literary realism, philosophical realism, archaeological realism – who is to say? Is 'Fish' literary fiction or is it science fiction? Is it realist or non-realist? Is it mimetic or non-mimetic? Is it the world as it is, or the world as it is not? Well … c'est kif-kif.

Works Cited

Anon. (n.d.) 'Some Rain Must Fall', URL (consulted June 2020): https://www.worldcat.org/title/some-rain-must-fall/oclc/608102260

Anon. (2016) 'Pass Notes – Game of Thrones spoilers: how much damage can Ian McShane do?', *Guardian*, 15 March. URL (consulted June 2016): https://www.theguardian.com/tv-and-radio/shortcuts/2016/mar/15/ian-mcshane-game-of-thrones-season-six-tits-and-dragons

Auerbach, Erich (1953/2013) *Mimesis: The Representation of Reality in Western Literature*, trans. Willard R. Trask. Princeton, NJ: Princeton University Press.

Barthes, Roland (1977) 'The Death of the Author', in *Image, Music, Text*, pp. 142–8, trans. Stephen Heath. London: Fontana.

Bostrom, Nick (2003) 'Are We Living in a Computer Simulation?', *The Philosophical Quarterly* 53(211): 243–55.

Brueckner, Tony (2012) 'Skepticism and Content Externalism', *Stanford Encyclopedia of Philosophy* (Spring 2012 Edition), Edward N. Zalta (ed.). URL (consulted June 2016): https://plato.stanford.edu/archives/spr2012/entries/skepticism-content-externalism/

Derrida, Jacques (1980) 'The Law of Genre', trans. Avital Ronell, *Critical Inquiry* 7(1) 55–81.

Descartes, René (2008) *Meditations on First Philosophy: with Selections from the Objections and Replies*, trans. Michael Moriarty. Oxford: Oxford University Press.

Eagleton, Terry (2003) 'Pork Chops and Pineapples – Mimesis: The Representation of Reality in Western Literature by Erich Auerbach', *London Review of Books* 25(20), 23 October. URL (consulted June 2016): https://www.lrb.co.uk/v25/n20/terry-eagleton/pork-chops-and-pineapples

Faber, Michel. (2000) 'Fish' in *Some Rain Must Fall*, pp. 19–26. Edinburgh: Canongate.

Gabriel, Markus (2015) *Why the World Does Not Exist*, trans. Gregory S. Moss. Cambridge: Polity.

Kant, Immanuel (2007) *Critique of Pure Reason*, trans. Marcus Weigelt. London: Penguin.

Larousse (n.d.) *Dictionnaire de français*. URL (consulted June 2016): https://www.larousse.fr/dictionnaires/francais/kif-kif/45518

Newman, Lex (2016), 'Descartes' Epistemology', *The Stanford Encyclopedia of Philosophy* (Winter 2016 Edition), Edward N. Zalta (ed.). URL (consulted June 2016): https://plato.stanford.edu/archives/win2016/entries/descartes-epistemology/

Plato (1993) *Republic*, trans. Robin Waterfield. Oxford: Oxford University Press.

Plato (2008) 'Ion' in D.A. Russell and M. Winterbottom (eds) *Classical Literary Criticism*, pp. 1–13. Oxford: Oxford University Press.

Putnam, Hilary (1981) *Reason, Truth and History*. Cambridge: Cambridge University Press.

Chapter 5

The Book of Strange New Things
Letters, Delay and Experiences of Time

Kate Wilkinson

Why do twenty-first-century novelists still use letters in their novels? What relationship does the persistence of letters have with the contemporary world of instantaneous digital communications? These questions, which fascinate me, were hovering as I read *The Book of Strange New Things*. This novel, I think, suggests one possible answer: here the communications technology of letters is part of a distinctively contemporary exploration of time. Michel Faber's work shows a long-standing interest in letters: his 2001 novella *The Hundred and Ninety-Nine Steps* concerns an ancient found letter, for example, and a short story in letter form features in his 2005 collection *The Fahrenheit Twins*. However, the effects of the virtual 'letters' in *The Book of Strange New Things* are very different from those of the epistolary elements in his earlier fiction. This novel's intriguing pairing, of a future world more technologically advanced than our own with aspects of a historical form of the novel, points to its concern with our experiences of time: letters, unlike digital messages, texts and apps, must involve delay. Here I look at some of the connections between the different kinds of delay at work in this novel and at work on us as readers. I explore, first, the notion of delay in relation to letters and how they work in fictional narrative; second, some contemporary ideas about how delay is vanishing from our experience of time and the dangers this presents; and third, how delay is significant for reading *The Book of Strange New Things*.

Letters and their time-structure

Michel Faber's fiction is alive to the lure of letters. The archaeologist Siân in *The Hundred and Ninety-Nine Steps* sees a two-hundred-year-old letter rolled up in a bottle and is inarticulate with longing for it. All she can think is '*I want, I want, I want*' (Faber, 2010: 48). Later, as she painstakingly unfurls the letter, it gives up its story to the reader, but only piece by tantalizing piece. In *The Fire Gospel*, Theo Grippin smuggles nine ancient scrolls from Iraq to Canada, driven by an overwhelming desire to possess what he has found. The illicit treasures whisper to him, 'burning a hole in his briefcase'; they are 'like a stash of pornography' (Faber, 2009: 16). These letters are a truly sensational find, written in Aramaic by a convert who 'knew two of Jesus's disciples personally!' and who gives an eye-witness account of the crucifixion (Faber, 2009: 38). But in this satirical story Faber undermines any reverence, either academic or spiritual, that such letters might inspire: they are written by a crashing bore, stolen by a grasping academic, and their contents are offensive to many Christian believers. Faber's treatment of letters exploits their potential to disrupt stories and unsettle readers, whether as archival objects, as narratives reinterpreted beyond their own time, or as partial narratives. In his short story 'Tabitha Warren' Faber uses the form of the letter to present a partial and disconcerting portrait of a highly unusual author (Faber, 2006: 214–22). The letter itself is a response to an obituary, another narrative of Tabitha Warren's life that this story does not include, and the letter's implications are improbable enough to leave open the question of its writer's reliability. Faber's interest in letter forms and their potential is evident too in his earlier work and ideas. In one unpublished novel, a man, who believes he is a reincarnation of Jesus, begins to receive genuine letters from would-be disciples, for example. In another story, a man conducts a one-sided 'correspondence' with a woman he harasses with nuisance phone calls: she is driven to suicide while he imagines that their relationship is deepening.[1]

Letters and their properties are also significant in *The Book of Strange New Things* but with strikingly different effects. In the speculative near-future world of the story, correspondence travels between planets: Peter Leigh is on the planet Oasis, recruited by the corporation USIC to be a Christian pastor, not to the colonists but to the planet's original inhabitants, while his wife Bea remains on earth. They communicate in writing using a technology nicknamed 'the Shoot' (Faber, 2014). There are echoes here of the epistolary novel form (novels written entirely in the form of letters) and also of the narratives of nineteenth-century imperial colonists, whose explorations in others' lands took them beyond the reaches of their familiar structures of time.

The 'Shoot' technology on Oasis is not instantaneous, in spite of its nickname, and because of this its messages function less like electronic messages and more like letters on paper. Peter and Bea refer to them as letters, in fact, and as 'missives', and even, when they are reminding themselves of St Paul, as 'epistles'. Letters on paper have a particular logic of delay, a time structure that derives from their materiality. A paper letter has to travel and so it has to take time; there is a delay between sending a letter and its delivery. There has to be a delay too, between the moment of delivery and the recipient sending a reply, if he or she decides to send one, and another delay until that reply arrives, and another until it is opened. Janet Gurkin Altman discusses these characteristics and their narrative potential in epistolary novels, focusing on letters' discourse and letters as a form of dialogue. A 'triple register' of time routinely operates in this discourse, Altman argues, based on the moment of the narrated event, the moment of writing and the moment of reading. The gaps between these moments, which she calls 'time lags', are productive (Altman, 1977: 303).

Letter-writers are bound in the present but preoccupied with the future, Altman suggests; epistolary discourse is 'vibrant with future-orientation' and with the 'expression of promises, threats, hopes, apprehensions, anticipation, intention, uncertainty, prediction' (Altman, 1982: 124). The 'now' of a letter is defined in relation to either an anticipated or a retrospective 'then': its narrative present must postdate or anticipate the events narrated (Altman, 1982: 127). For Altman, this narrative present is tangled up with impossibilities: the narrative cannot be simultaneous with the event it relates (can any writing?), and while it seems to offer the opportunity of dialogue in the present, it cannot deliver it. If a writer writes 'I feel now', she points out, the reader has no option but to read this as 'you felt then.' Altman calls this phenomenon 'temporal polyvalence'. The meaning of a letter's narrative is multiple and it depends on relationships between points in time: the time of the event described and the times at which a letter is written, posted, received, read and reread (Altman, 1982: 129). Epistolary discourse is marked by hiatuses and gaps: by the time lag between an event and the recording of it, by the time lag between the transmission of a message and its reception, and by the spatial separation of the writer and the addressee. But the language of letters also tries to close these gaps, speaking as if the addressee were present (Altman, 1982: 140). Material letters simultaneously emphasize their logic of delay and work to collapse it. Altman's study focuses on epistolary novels but her idea of 'temporal polyvalence' also applies to letters that are embedded in narrative, as they are in *The Book of Strange New Things*. Embedded letters can produce further complexities: in the temporal relationships between letters and the narratives in which they are embedded; in the order in which letters are written, shown as text, received and read; and in discrepancies between a letter's narrative and a narrator's.

Peter and Bea, corresponding through the Shoot, work hard to collapse the interstellar distance between them. 'My dear Bea,' Peter writes.

> No reply from you yet, and maybe it's a bit soon for me to be writing you another letter. But I couldn't wait to tell you – I've just had a most eye-opening conversation [...] Anyway, are you sitting down? – because I have some amazing news that may knock you flat. (Faber, 2014: 140–1)

'I'm upstairs in our study,' Bea writes to Peter later.

> It's six o'clock in the evening, still full daylight [...] I only just arrived home from work – bliss to be sitting down at last. Too tired to have a shower yet. Your message was waiting for me when I rushed upstairs to check. (Faber, 2014: 172)

In these familiar letter-writing conventions, Peter and Bea imagine when their letters will be read and they note the present moments of their own writing and reading. They give details of where they are and when, and they acknowledge the time lag in their exchanges. Peter and Bea 'are preoccupied with the compensatory creation of present-ness,' to use a phrase of Altman's; their letters 'are the product of temporal absence (from events, from the addressee)' (Altman, 1977: 302–10). Peter's sense of separation from Bea is sharpened by his sense that he is now in a different sphere of time. On his journey to Oasis, with 'no such thing as afternoon, morning or night,' he tries to imagine what Bea might be doing and realizes 'what his watch was for'. It is 'not to tell him anything useful about his own situation, but to allow him to imagine Beatrice existing in the same reality as himself' (Faber, 2014: 43–4). Peter fantasizes that his letters can close the temporal gap between himself and Bea, perhaps not only in their minds as they recreate each other's situations, but also in actual time. 'Evidently, when she wrote this, she hadn't yet received his most recent message,' Peter reflects as he reads. 'Maybe she was reading it right now,' his thought continues, 'at exactly the same moment as he was reading hers. Unlikely, but the thought of such synchronous intimacy was too seductive to resist' (Faber, 2014: 157). What Peter experiences as 'synchronous intimacy' has become part of our contemporary understanding of communication in its near-instantaneous forms. Today we can track, if we choose to, the precise moment that a message we send is received and read on another person's phone. We have come to expect that communications technology collapses vast physical distances and eliminates delay.

Contemporary time-sickness?

What are the implications of the 'synchronous intimacy' that Peter longs for? Many contemporary accounts of our experience of time argue that technology is changing it, and for the worse. Theorists diagnose a kind of time-sickness: we now live in an age in which time is increasingly without structure; the accelerated tempo of computerized communications is unnatural; and we are disorientated by instantaneity. In fact we are damaged, these accounts suggest, by the disappearance of delay. In this section I draw on contributions to this discussion from three contemporary thinkers: Paul Virilio, Jonathan Crary and Bernard Stiegler. Their work suggests some different ways to think about delay, an idea that is significant both for the narrative of *The Book of Strange New Things* and for our experience of reading it.

The philosopher Paul Virilio, who was interested from the 1970s onwards in speed and its social effects, focused in his later work on the timescales of global financial trading systems. In *The Great Accelerator* (2012) he considers the speeds at which these systems operate and the minuscule time intervals in which they make decisions. To describe these time structures, he coins the term 'nanochronology' (Virilio, 2012: 3). (A nanosecond is one billionth of a second: a millionth of a millisecond.) Companies known as 'high frequency traders' use technology that can exploit the split-second delay between the placing of an electronic trading order and its arrival, in order to compare prices across different stock exchanges within thousandths of a second.[2] Markets and trading systems operate according to these timings, far beyond the limits of human perception, and Virilio sees significant consequences in these speeds. These are anticompetitive time structures: they set an 'astronomical TEMPO of an instantaneity and an interactivity that once and for all spurn the old laws of a competitive market.' When the felony of insider trading 'was still committed within the common historical TEMPO of the chronology of days, hours and seconds', he suggests, it was at least possible that humans could detect it (Virilio, 2012: 8–9). Virilio fears that nanotechnology and 'nanochronology' are replacing the chronology of days and hours; they are undermining the temporal structures that we understand and have lived by for generations. 'Surely we can't fail to see the enormous time difference that exists, today, between our at once untimely and interactive practices,' he suggests, 'and our daily life, now so exhausted, so deprived of the intervals of time needed for reflection and responsible action' (Virilio, 2012: 29).

There is a fundamental opposition in Virilio's analysis between technologically-produced time and human time, and the dominance of the first produces problems. First, a culture of constant connection is threatening our capacity to reflect, threatening to do away with the time intervals we need for our memory and understanding to work effectively. We are in a 'culture of CONNECTION and EVERYTHING, NOW. There is no more space to wait in, no more space in which to desire the infinite. In this culture, waiting is always negative' (Virilio, 2012: 57). Delay has effectively become nothing more than a source of impatience. Second, 'real-time' communications are loosening our sense of past, present and future, creating a strange inertia because we now think in terms of virtual connections rather than physical places. Everything happens 'at the speed of light' and there is no need for anyone actually to travel anywhere; this promotes what Virilio sees as a kind of 'pathological fixedness' (Virilio, 2004: 135). It threatens both our sense of history and our confidence in the future. Virilio's analysis of the dynamics of instantaneity is, in the end, apocalyptic. In his idiosyncratic style (with the dangers in CAPITALS) he sets out the disastrous consequences of overvaluing speed and undervaluing delay: financial crashes are inevitable; our technological alienation from ourselves will be 'computerized terror'; the seductive 'reality effect' of real-time technology will make people abandon physical reality; political action will become impossible and climate change will accelerate. It is possible to see echoes of this kind of feared dystopia in *The Book of Strange New Things*, as Bea's letters describe climatic disasters on an exhausted earth and the collapse of the rule of law, while the alienated and temporally displaced colonists on Oasis assess the future in terms of technology rather than mutual relationships.

The art critic and cultural analyst Jonathan Crary expresses a similarly pessimistic view in his polemical book 24/7, which considers connections between technology and the human rhythm of sleep (Crary, 2014). For him, the term '24/7' describes a world of consumption made possible by technology, an environment of non-stop commerce that is hostile to the idea of sleep. When we sleep our temporal awareness is suspended; it is a pause or a time out from consciousness. Because sleep involves a suspension of activity too, it has become 'one of the greatest affronts to the voraciousness of contemporary capitalism,' Crary (2014: 10) argues. This analysis characterizes sleep almost as a form of active resistance to relentless commercialism: while businesses sell us thousands of products to satisfy other human needs, including thirst, hunger, friendship and sex, sleep stubbornly remains a part of our basic human experience that cannot be commodified. Crary's characterization of our '24/7' world is based, like Virilio's analysis, on an understanding of a natural, human time that is distinct from technological time. '24/7' means a 'time without time,' he suggests; 'a time extracted from any material or identifiable demarcations, a time without sequence or recurrence.' This is a hallucination 'of an unalterable permanence composed of incessant, frictionless operations. It belongs to the aftermath of a common life made into the object of technics' (Crary, 2014: 29). Like Virilio, Crary draws a contrast here between human life as 'the object of technics' and human life shaped by nature, in which our relation to time retains a sense of repetition and a sense of resistance. Without these senses we are experiencing, in fact, a kind of time with no sense of delay. Global digital communications, always on, have erased the rhythms that shaped our relationship with time: night and day, sleeping and waking. We are left, Crary argues, with an 'impossible temporality' that is 'always a reprimand and a deprecation of the weakness and inadequacy of human time, with its blurred, meandering textures' (Crary, 2014: 29). Our contemporary, technically-produced experience of time does not accommodate pauses, and waiting has become something intolerable. 'When there are delays or breaks of empty time, they are rarely openings for the drift of consciousness,' he writes, and '[t]here is a profound incompatibility of anything resembling reverie with the priorities of efficiency, functionality and speed' (Crary, 2014: 88). The experience of delay is intimately linked here with human thought: if we lose our temporal rhythms we risk, too, the loss of creative possibility.

The philosopher Bernard Stiegler has also explored our contemporary experience of time, a concern that I am suggesting is significant in multiple ways for *The Book of Strange New Things*. Like Virilio and Crary, Stiegler also sees 'countless problems' with technology, citing its effects on education, the over-exploitation of natural resources, fertility technologies and genetic modifications (Stiegler, 1998: 86-7). However, he rejects any basic opposition between a 'natural' human time and a technical or 'technics' time.[3] His argument takes a different route, but he too diagnoses a kind of time-sickness that is connected to the elimination of delay. Stiegler argues that humans are and always have been fundamentally technical beings. We use tools and are shaped by them in return, in a process of mutual invention that he calls a 'transductive relationship', adopting the term from the philosopher Gilbert Simondon. In *Technics and Time* (1998) – a dense, closely-argued work that combines anthropological, cultural and philosophical analyses – Stiegler aims to reconsider the relationship between humans and technology, specifically in the context of the dizzying speed of contemporary technological developments. An 'ends and means' understanding of technology, on which we have relied since the Industrial Revolution, is no longer adequate, he suggests; we need to rethink the connections between technical, economic and social systems as they develop. We need to look again at the fundamental relationship between humans and technology and look at it as a question of temporality; that is, our relationship with time (Stiegler, 1998: 29–43). Part of his argument is that humans and technology have developed together, with humans leaving a kind of exterior memory embedded in tools for future generations to use. Our capacity to think in temporal terms – to anticipate and to think back – is itself produced by our relationship with technology: all our relations to time are, essentially, rooted in technology. Stiegler explores this idea in both anthropological and philosophical terms (Stiegler, 1998: 134–79, 185–203).

In Stiegler's analysis the source of today's 'countless problems' is not so much the sheer speed at which technology operates, but rather the relative speeds of technical and cultural development. Technical development produces an inevitable succession of obsolescent technologies, he explains, and the social worlds that these technologies enabled must therefore change too. They must adapt or disappear, and this progression shakes the sense and self-awareness that we have of our own being. 'It is as if a divorce could now be pronounced between, on the one hand, the technosciences and, on the other, the culture that claimed to have produced them,' Stiegler suggests (Stiegler, 1998: 14). The grounds for this 'divorce' are to do with time: the timings of cultural evolution and technical evolution are now misaligned because technics is evolving more quickly than culture. There is an analogy here with the concept of the 'sound barrier':

> A supersonic device, quicker than its own sound, provokes at the breaking of the barrier a violent sonic boom, a sound shock. What would be the breaking of a time barrier if this meant going faster than time? What *shock* would be provoked by a device going quicker than its "own time"? (Stiegler, 1998: 15, emphasis in original)

Stiegler is suggesting the kinds of 'shock' produced by particular effects of technical development. These are the effects that we call 'real time' in computing or 'live' in the media, and they distort the way in which events take place, both in time and in space. These distortions are linked to speed and to the 'industrialization of memory', that is, the storage of large quantities of data in electronic media. We are encountering new problems as a result of changes in data storage, data handling and the speed of data transmission, including 'the delegation of decision-making procedures to machines.' Such machines 'are on the one hand necessary,' Stiegler (1998: 86) concedes, 'since humanity is not fast enough to control the processes of informational change […] but on the other hand [they are] also frightening'. In the second volume of *Technics and Time* Stiegler develops his analysis of the effects of technologies of memory. '*Today* is thus another time,' he argues; it is becoming defined by 'mnemo-technics' (Stiegler, 2009: 61). The phenomenon of real time is frightening and non-human too, because it collapses or displaces delay: it creates a situation in which deferrals of meaning or re-interpretations become impossible.

'What we today call 'real time' is industrial time,' Stiegler (2009: 63) asserts, 'the industrial production of time by the programming industries whose products suspend all traditional programs. [...] Thus so-called real time is not time; it is perhaps even the de-temporalization of time, or at least its occultation'. These 'traditional programs' are the temporal structures of delay, transmission and anticipation that we understand. Real time instead collapses, into one and the same moment, an event, the reporting of it, the transmission of the report and its reception. We are living in a new type of time that appears to admit no delay, processing of uncertainty, or reflection.

Virilio, Crary and Stiegler articulate, from their particular perspectives, a powerful sense of connectedness between questions of technology, delay and human temporality. If we continue to edge out delay and our appreciation of its value from contemporary life, they foresee profound consequences: losses of creativity, failures of responsibility, the collapse of accountable governance and the exhaustion of our planet. We need, they suggest, to understand the relationships between technology and the rhythms of time that structure our human experience. According to the logic of these accounts, Oasis and Earth in *The Book of Strange New Things* may represent two parallel possible outcomes of late capitalist technological development, differently dystopian. But these fictional worlds are also a backdrop against which to explore experiences of technology and communication, which the form of Peter's and Bea's letters links with the experience of delay. I suggest next how the idea of delay matters in reading the novel and finally, how the novel in turn offers a space in which to value delay.

The importance of delay

When Peter begins to live alongside the Oasans, he starts to feel the planet's tropical and enervating climate changing him. 'Just as the atmosphere penetrated his clothes and seemed to pass through his skin, something unfamiliar was permeating his head, soaking into his mind,' he senses (Faber, 2014: 297). As he spends more time in the

Oasan settlement, this unfamiliarity becomes more explicitly a sense of temporal loosening.

> The longer he spent among the Oasans, the less point he could see in clinging to ways of telling time that were, frankly, irrelevant. A day for him had ceased to feel like twenty-four hours and it certainly didn't consist of 1,440 minutes. A day was a span of daylight, divided from the next by a spell of darkness. While the sun shone, he would stay awake for twenty, maybe twenty-five hours at a stretch. (Faber, 2014: 318)

As earth time becomes irrelevant, Peter's wakefulness becomes a kind of manic ecstasy, possible because on Oasis the days and nights each last over seventy earth hours. His experience recalls other literary suspensions of time: the formless days of Tennyson's 'The Lotos-Eaters', for example, in 'a land/ In which it seemed always afternoon,' where the stranded mariners' former lives seem alien and distant (Tennyson, 1995: 35). The humans on Oasis subsist largely on a native plant they have called 'whiteflower', in fact; its name is a suggestion of the lotus plant. There are echoes here too of Marlow's journey along the Congo River in Joseph Conrad's *Heart of Darkness*, and its sense of temporal as well as geographical disorientation. 'You lost your way on that river as you would in a desert,' Marlow says, 'till you thought yourself bewitched and cut off for ever from everything you had known once – somewhere – far away – in another existence perhaps' (Conrad, 2008: 317). Peter, in this contemporary colonial outpost, feels increasingly cut off from his past life, and also from a narrative of events on Oasis itself. No matter how insistently he probes, he cannot establish a sequence of events to explain what happened to his predecessor Kurtzberg – whose name, echoing 'Mr Kurz', nods again in the direction of Marlow's journey. The Oasans cannot say, as their own construction of time is imprecise about both the past and the future. Their sense of time is strongly orientated towards the present, and this makes it difficult for Peter to translate any concepts, sacred or secular, that entail anticipation. The meaning of the Oasans' word for 'faith', he notes, 'was not what you'd call precise. Faith, hope, intention, objective, desire, plan, wish, the future, the road ahead ... these were all the same thing, apparently' (Faber, 2014: 439, ellipsis in original). Oasans struggle to locate past events in measured time because they do not reflect on them: 'Why should it matter exactly how many days, weeks, months or years ago a relative had died? A person was either living amongst them or in the ground' (Faber, 2014: 439). Without a structure of anticipation and retrospection, time on Oasis lacks a familiar human rhythm. It is curiously frictionless, rather like the colonists themselves, who live in a state of emotional disconnection. They have no obvious conflicts and do not chafe at their present situation and its strangeness; they have in fact been selected for the job because of their lack of emotional ties to earth (Faber, 2014: 373, 394).

As Peter starts to lose his grip on the life he shared with Bea, her letters give him a residual purchase on it. In the soupy temporality of Oasis, Bea's letters remind Peter of other understandings of time, which structure the experiences from which he has become loosened. Between the exchanges of their correspondence – in the 'time lags' that Altman identifies – the novel's main narrative is focalized through Peter. Its changing pace follows his experience of time, slowing down for his five-day visits to the Oasans, extending over thirty pages, even fifty pages. But the letters disrupt this. 'Unexpectedly,' when Peter returns from his first visit, 'Beatrice's messages loaded in at once. Their sudden arrival was a potent presence in the room, forcing him to sit down' (Faber, 2014: 233). The messages are potent because they challenge Peter's feelings about time.

> To his wife, these messages were already History. To him, they were a frozen Present, yet to be experienced. His head buzzed with the urgent need to open them all [...] and buzzed also with the knowledge that he could only take them in one at a time. (Faber, 2014: 232)

Peter struggles to reconcile his own temporal relation to these messages with Bea's, unable to answer the distress she expresses in the first two. '[H]ow could he, when she'd written nine more messages to him, in hours and days that were already gone from her, but of which he knew nothing?' (Faber, 2014: 237) The sense of temporal dislocation disempowers him. Bea's letters, as they arrive, set a crisper narrative tempo, relating her experiences of cataclysmic climate change and civil disorder. These events, though they are the result of years of decline, create an urgency that gives Bea's life an increasingly different temporal shape from Peter's. In particular, she finds his lack of response to her developing pregnancy – an experience that is defined by time, by the anticipation of its end – almost unforgivable. Both the narrative and temporal properties of letters are significant: in the strangely formless world of Oasis, the letters' nostalgic form and their structure of gaps and hiatuses focus the novel's explorations of time. The letters point, too, towards other forms of delay that are connected with the act of reading itself.

The epistolary form is 'unique among the first-person forms in its aptitude for portraying the experience of reading,' Altman states; we see the process of writing and we see intended and unintended recipients in the acts of reading and interpreting (Altman, 1982: 88). Letters make readers visible as well as writers, calling attention in turn to our own reading of both the letters and the novel in which we read them. *The Book of Strange New Things* shows Peter composing at the Shoot, and his thoughts interrupt the text of his letters as he gropes for phrases, distracted by his surroundings, only to produce, for example, '793 inadequate words' (Faber, 2014: 129–32). I wish you were here, he tells Bea later, '[n]ot because it would save me the trouble of trying to describe it (although I must admit my lack of skill in that department is becoming ever more obvious!) but because I miss you' (Faber, 2014: 159). It is true that Peter's writing style is at times halting and clumsy, as even the ever-supportive Bea acknowledges. 'You're more of a speaker than a writer, I know that,' she tells him (Faber, 2014: 235). Altman's study of epistolary form was published in 1982 and predates the widespread use of digital communication technologies. But her argument, that letters draw attention to the process of reading, finds a new relevance in the temporality of communication in this novel. Peter's and Bea's exchanges, which combine the futuristic technology of the Shoot's virtual messages with the anachronistic time constraints of paper letters, draw attention specifically to the experience of delay as part of the uncertainties and efforts of written communication.

A concern with the efforts of reading and interpretation surfaces in other ways, too, in the novel. *The Book of Strange New Things* introduces unfamiliar typographical symbols to represent the Oasans' pronunciation, of specific consonants at first and subsequently of whole words. 'I have no idea what he's saying to them or what they're saying to him,' Faber has said about Peter's conversations with the Oasans later in the novel, which are presented entirely in the invented alien script (Aslanyan, 2015). The typography actively resists any easy interpretation, but the first two symbols we encounter each have a clearly equivalent sound, which creates an expectation that it should be possible to decode the Oasan script. As more of these alien language symbols appear in the English narrative, we have to decide whether to spend time matching symbol to sound, or whether to allow ourselves to slide over the symbols as we read, avoiding the effort and delay of interpretation. Peter's new version of the Bible for the Oasans raises further questions about interpretation and textual resistance. He begins this rewriting project partly because the Bible's temporal and cultural metaphors are impenetrable to the Oasans and partly because Oasans cannot pronounce the English sounds 'ch', 't' and 's'. His radically simplified version of the twenty-third psalm largely avoids the letter 's' and therefore avoids the present tense, and without temporal precision it sounds infantile.

> The Lord be he who care for me. [...] He bid me in green land lie down. He lead me by river where no one can drown. He make my soul like new again. He lead me in the path of Good. He do all this, for he be God. (Faber, 2014: 487)

The colony's former translator Tartaglione (whose name means 'stammer' or 'stutter' in Italian) is both admiring and scathing about the new version.[4]

> 'You're a pro, what can I say, sheer class! *The Lord is my shepherd* without a fucking shepherd in sight! [...] You wrote that for the [symbols for Oasans], right? Like, Open up for Jesus, this won't hurt. A banquet with all the bones taken out, a meal in a milkshake, thesaurus semolina. *Bravo!*' (Faber, 2014: 488)

Tartaglione mockingly praises the text's simplicity, equating its lack of resistance with a lack of authenticity, and his question about the lack of effort involved perhaps begins to point towards us as readers of the Oasan script. Authentic reading, the pointing suggests, has to deal with 'the bones'. It encounters resistance, it demands effort and it takes time.

I have argued that different experiences of delay, Peter's and our own as readers, are connected in *The Book of Strange New Things*. These connected experiences suggest an answer to my opening questions about the persistence of letters in contemporary novels: letters offer ways to reflect on the temporality of communication, on instantaneity and on delay. The novel form itself, like letters, depends on structures of delay: there is always a temporal gap between the time of writing and our (later) time of reading, and as we read we negotiate the temporal gaps between a narrative's present, past and future moments. While this is true of any novel, the structure of *The Book of Strange New Things* seems to insist on making this clearly visible. Each chapter title is also the chapter's last phrase, a tantalizing prolepsis or flash forward that again draws attention to experiences of time. Like Peter's and Bea's letters, the chapter titles acknowledge the anticipation that is part of reading and they mark, in the narrative structure, the novel's awareness of its own dependence on delay. Peter's experiences are shared with us through these chapters, as the story is told from his point of view, but as readers we do not have to wait with him. Unlike Peter, we can decide to look ahead to see how the chapter ends, just as we can flick forward to find his next letter from Bea. For us, the end of the story is already there and our experience of delay is a choice: we decide whether to 'cheat' and look ahead, or whether to play along and sustain the reading experience – for nearly six hundred pages. This novel asserts and reasserts that patience is part of the experience: it presents us with an imagined technology of delayed written communication, the alien Oasan script that interrupts and slows down our reading, and recurring glimpses of a narrative 'future' we have yet to read. We may be living in a twenty-first century 'culture of CONNECTION and EVERYTHING, NOW', to use Paul Virilio's words, but here is an affirmation that waiting matters to us, even in an age of digital instantaneity. With its strange new story, its use of letters' particular time structure, and its connected explorations of temporality, Faber's novel quietly presses us to seek out and value experiences of delay.

Notes

1 Faber describes these works in his keynote speech at the conference *Michel Faber: Defying Genre*, Inverness, 21 July 2016.
2 These infinitesimal time intervals between the placing of an order and its receipt are hugely significant in financial terms. For example, Michael Lewis recounts that one group of businesses spent $300m on a cable that reduced the time taken to send a signal from Chicago to New York and back from 17 milliseconds to 13. Traders then paid $14m a year to use it, because those four milliseconds were so valuable (*The Economist*, 2014).
3 Stiegler's translators explain his terminology: 'technics' refers to 'the technical domain or to technical practice as a whole' and 'technology' refers to 'the specific amalgamation of technics and the sciences in the modern period' (Stiegler, 1998: 280–1).
4 Faber has said he was in fact unaware of the name's ironically appropriate meaning when he wrote the novel: he was thinking of the comic artist John Tartaglione. Conversation at the conference *Michel Faber: Defying Genre*, Inverness, 22 July 2016.

Works Cited

Altman, Janet Gurkin (1977) 'The "Triple Register": Introduction to Temporal Complexity in the Letter-Novel', *Esprit Créateur* 17(4): 302–10.
Altman, Janet Gurkin (1982) *Epistolarity: Approaches to a Form*. Columbus: Ohio State University Press.
Aslanyan, Anna (2015) 'Interview with Michel Faber', *The White Review* (13), URL (consulted 9 June 2020): http://www.thewhitereview.org/interviews/interview-with-michel-faber-3/
Conrad, Joseph (2008) *Heart of Darkness and Other Tales*. Oxford: Oxford University Press.
Crary, Jonathan (2014) *24/7: Late Capitalism and the Ends of Sleep*. London and New York: Verso.
Economist, The (2014) 'Fast Times', 5 April, URL (consulted 9 June 2020): http://www.economist.com/news/books-and-arts/21600090-author-liars-poker-uncovers-more-shenanigans-wall-street-fast-times

Faber, Michel (2006) *The Fahrenheit Twins*. Edinburgh: Canongate Books.

Faber, Michel (2009) *The Fire Gospel*. Edinburgh: Canongate Books.

Faber, Michel (2010) *The Hundred and Ninety-Nine Steps and The Courage Consort*. Edinburgh: Canongate Books.

Faber, Michel (2014) *The Book of Strange New Things*. Edinburgh: Canongate Books.

Stiegler, Bernard (1998) *Technics and Time 1: The Fault of Epimetheus*, trans. Richard Beardsworth and George Collins. Stanford CA: Stanford University Press.

Stiegler, Bernard (2009) *Technics and Time 2: Disorientation*, trans. Stephen Barker. Stanford CA: Stanford University Press.

Tennyson, Alfred (1995) *Alfred, Lord Tennyson: Selected Poetry*. London: Routledge.

Virilio, Paul (2004) *The Paul Virilio Reader*, ed. Steve Redhead. Edinburgh: Edinburgh University Press.

Virilio, Paul (2012) *The Great Accelerator*, trans. Julie Rose. Cambridge: Polity.

Chapter 6

Echoes of Poe
Absence and the Uncanny in 'The Fahrenheit Twins' and *The Courage Consort*

Nicholas Prescott

I want to begin with an anecdote that sets a context for this paper's particular reading of Michel Faber's works. My first contact with Faber's writing came through having been told by my partner that *The Crimson Petal and the White*, which she'd recently read in an 'un-put-downable' way, was the most remarkable thing she'd encountered for many months. Fascinated, and excited at the prospect of discovering a new author to follow, I decided to begin with the novella *The Courage Consort*, and was quite instantly transfixed by the exquisite, crystalline prose, and by the elegance and intelligence of the larger voice wielding it.

My first connection to Faber's work, then, was personal; the person I love loved his work; the second was aesthetic – the sheer beauty and precision of the language seduced me utterly. A third connection became manifest when I learned that Faber was working with that intellectual and artistic giant, Brian Eno, on a recorded reading of 'The Fahrenheit Twins' that was to be underscored by Eno's music. If a deeply trusted reader thought him remarkable, if he wrote prose that was so extraordinarily good, and if Eno had invited him into his studio to put music to his words, Faber must, I thought, by any definition, be quite the writer.

So, for a number of reasons, entering into a reading of Faber's work for me was to enter a state of what Nabokov might have called 'aesthetic bliss'. Yet, as I reached the point in 'The Courage Consort' where Catherine first hears the mysterious not-quite-human, not-quite-animal cry issuing from the depths of the forest, I became equally driven by that other great engine of literary engagement: the viscera. As I moved through the story it became clear that I was in the company of a writer who possessed that rare ability to 'elegantly unsettle' the reader, to engage with the mechanics of suspense and the orchestration of fear while sculpting with rarefied language; and, further, to wield a Lynchian bravery with regard to ambiguity and selective resolution. The more I read of Faber's work, the more examples I found showcasing the subtlety and sophistication of his use of the devices of suspense and the creation of a very particular, and strangely beautiful, kind of dread.

With the phrase 'Lynchian bravery' I mean to invoke an approach to creative art that demonstrates both a lack of fear on behalf of the artist (with regard to the supposed 'requirements' of genre, for example), and a willingness to evoke in the audience a very palpable sense of unease, a kind of psychological horror that exists alongside the aesthetic beauty of the piece. For this writer, one of the most important examples of a contemporary artist – working in whatever form – who is able to consistently conjure a palpable sense of uncanny dread, to create works as chilling and dark as they are beautiful, and to both satisfy and subvert readerly expectations regarding mystery and suspense, is painter/sculptor/musician/filmmaker David Lynch.

Blue Velvet (1986), the work that initially brought Lynch to the centre of critical attention, contains very particular archetypes of detective fiction, but remains a text that is as puzzling as it is cathartic; ultimately it is as ambiguous as it is ingeniously structured. Furthermore, it remains a text that is exquisitely beautiful in every visual and aural sense, and this remarkable stylistic sheen functions in a bizarre, ironic, decidedly unnerving way. This description fits much of the rest of Lynch's work, and – I would argue – strongly illuminates our experience of Faber's oeuvre.

Thus, with Lynch invoked as a touchstone, this paper will now reach backwards in time in order to consider certain connections that link Faber's work (or elements of his writerly technique, at least) to the work of that much earlier artist and legendary scribe of the macabre, Edgar Allan Poe. While not necessarily arguing any direct or overt influence wielded by Poe over Faber's works, it is clear that the two writers share certain elements of technique, certain interests in – and uses of – mythology, and a fascination with aspects of the macabre.

What I am most interested in doing here is using our sense of what characterizes Poe's work to define the unusual *affect* produced by reading certain of Faber's fictions, and to describe the curious and compelling kind of dread that I see operating centrally in both of the Faber stories I'll be examining. One of my tethering points, then, in trying to elucidate this rather subjective series of feelings and responses to fiction, feelings of unease and dread and not-quite-articulated horror, is the *experience* of reading Poe – an experience that entails precisely the kind of 'pleasure-in-the-uncanny', precisely the kind of fascinating cognitive dissonance we feel when drawn to fictions that are both alluring and unsettling, that are cathartic even in their lack of an entirely comfortable (or perhaps *comforting*) resolution.[1] This pleasure-in-the-uncanny is one of the most striking affects one encounters when reading Michel Faber's stories.

In introducing a collection of Poe's works, William Allan Nielsen, writing in 1917, claimed:

> His poetry is marked by an extraordinary and highly individual quality of melody, and by a power of rendering with great effectiveness moods of strange and mysterious subtlety. [...] In 'The Fall of the House of Usher' we have an example of his creation of an unreal but vividly imagined situation, wrought out with almost unparalleled richness of suggestive detail, and making its appeal not so much to our senses as to our nerves. 'Eleanora' is more akin to his poetry, and is one of those pieces in which he may be supposed to have started

with personal experience and to have idealised and heightened it till it produces almost the effect of pure fantasy. (Nielsen, 1917: 5)

The parallels between the effects described by Nielsen for a reader of Poe and those we experience when reading any of Faber's short stories are indeed uncanny, a word which will become a crucial term for this paper.

The longer *Oxford English Dictionary* tells us simply that something uncanny is something 'Partaking of a supernatural character; mysterious, weird, uncomfortably strange or unfamiliar', (Simpson and Weiner, 1997), and while this is indeed a useful starting point, this paper will use a kind of adapted definition that has its source in Freud's famous essay *Das Unheimliche* (1919). Freud elucidates the meanings of both *Heimlich* (very loosely the 'homely', or the as it were 'canny'), and the *Unheimlich*, the unhomely, unfamiliar, uncanny. In an etymological sense, something *Heimlich* is something associated with the everyday: something comforting, reassuring; something that might be found in a domestic environment, in a peaceful household setting. The *unheimlich* is of course the opposite of that: it's something unfamiliar, eerie, untamed, discomforting, unnerving. There are large doses of all of these elements in the works of both Faber and Poe, yet while examining Faber's use of the uncanny stories under considerationh here, I also want to touch on another image that scholars including Freud frequently explore when looking at the uncanny: that of the doppelgänger. From Freud:

> The theme of the 'double' has been very thoroughly treated by Otto Rank [...]. He has gone into the connections which the 'double' has with reflections in mirrors, with shadows, with guardian spirits, with the belief in the soul and with the fear of death; but he also lets in a flood of light on the surprising evolution of the idea. For the 'double' was originally an insurance against the destruction of the ego, an 'energetic denial of the power of death', as Rank says; and probably the 'immortal' soul was the first 'double' of the body ... The same desire led the Ancient Egyptians to develop the art of making images of the dead in lasting materials. Such ideas, however, have sprung from the soil of unbounded selflove, from the primary narcissism which dominates the mind of the child and of primitive man. But when this stage

has been surmounted, the 'double' reverses its aspect. From having been an assurance of immortality, it becomes the uncanny harbinger of death. (Freud, 1919: 233–4)

While today's readers might find the notion of 'primitive man' somewhat problematic, Freud nonetheless establishes, in the passage above, the mercurial ways in which the idea of the double or doppelgänger can be seen to operate as an element of horror, fear, and the uncanny. The figure of the doppelgänger will become particularly relevant for this paper's analysis of 'The Fahrenheit Twins'.

To return to Poe, for a number of reasons, I think the most useful story through which to begin exploring these ideas of affect and the uncanny is 'The Murders in the Rue Morgue' (1841). The first of these reasons – and one might imagine this writer's tongue just slightly in his cheek at this point – is that even those readers who despise the work of Poe would probably be familiar with this one story; 'The Murders in the Rue Morgue' is arguably Poe's most widely-read text. Secondly, despite its fame, 'The Murders in the Rue Morgue' is one of those slightly unusual Poe tales in that it is essentially realist in style,[2] and is – in a fundamental way – 'resolved': which is to say, its action is given a rational explanation that is, for the most part, utterly unexpected by the reader, and which challenges the very notion of rationality while providing a blueprint for what would become one of the key archetypes of detective fiction – the ratiocinative investigator: the exerciser of pure, cold logic. Thirdly, with the idea of resolutions in mind, 'The Murders in the Rue Morgue' is a foundational piece of genre fiction – it is recognized by many scholars as the first entry in what would become the great tradition of the detective story.[3]

'The Murders in the Rue Morgue''s conclusion reveals that an animal's attempt at a kind of self-anthropomorphization has led to an explosion of horrific violence. The premise, which readers of crime fiction will instantly recognize, entails the seemingly insoluble murders of two women, an investigation by a character possessed of a remarkable intellect, and a resolution that is as surprising and near-outrageous as it is exquisitely logical and brilliantly constructed.

Elements of the uncanny and the improbable haunt the story. When the bodies of Madame L'Espanaye and her daughter are discovered, the older woman's body is found having been thrust up a chimney with such force that it would seem impossible for any human to be responsible; further, in a trope that has become central to the crime and Detective genres, the apartment in which the murders occurred appears to have been firmly locked from the inside. The perpetrator of the crime is of course absent; the second body – horribly mutilated – is discovered outside, and numerous items of significant value have been left at the scene, thus ruling out burglary as a motive.

As alluded to above, the solution to this violent mystery involves a non-human perpetrator. Our ratiocinative investigator, C. Auguste Dupin, meticulously explains both the means and motive behind the grisly crimes, and demonstrates conclusively that the guilty party is an escaped orangutan – or, from the story itself, an 'Ourang-Outang of the East Indian Islands' (Poe, 1841: 94).

The very fact that the perpetrator of the crimes is an animal, albeit one that is genetically near-identical to a human, is the primary uncanny element of the story. The orangutan is not human, yet seemingly desires to be seen as such, and the schism this causes initiates the creature's murderous behaviour. Again, we can see this as a kind of cognitive dissonance, although in reverse; the orangutan's inability to reconcile his animal nature with his desired human self is the inciting incident of this tale. This is all immaculately explained by Dupin, and ingeniously orchestrated by Poe. There are further haunting narrative peculiarities that the author also manages to explain exquisitely; as the crime takes place, the neighbours of the victims hear, 'a voice foreign in tone to the ears of men of many nations, and devoid of all distinct or intelligible syllabification' (Poe, 1841: 93). This non-human voice is ultimately understood to comprise the shrieks of the Ourang-Outang as it carries out its butchery. Improbable and nightmarish though much of the story is, Poe manages to provide the reader with a crystalline explanation for its ghoulish central dilemma.

So, despite all its near-fantastical elements, 'The Murders in the Rue Morgue' is both perfectly, rationally resolved and deeply unsettling, in that its resolution manages to retain a number of deeply uncanny elements. Yet beyond both its horror and its narrative peculiarity, for this reader the experience of reading the 'The Murders in the Rue Morgue' is overwhelmingly one of pleasure. The text is ingenious, evocative, surprising, and convincing, and a vivid sense of dread lingers with the reader, tantalizingly, after the resolution has been provided. In a way that is different from Poe tales like 'The Black Cat' or 'The Tell-Tale Heart' or even 'The Facts in the Case of M. Valdemar', where characters we know logically to be dead seem to come back from the dead, or behave as if alive, or beckon to the culprits of their deaths from beyond the grave, 'Murders in the Rue Morgue' seems to have its uncanny cake and eat it, too, in that, as I have said, it is ingeniously resolved in the sense of strict deductive procedure, while remaining deeply unsettling and near-fantastical in the process; its action is driven both by an unassailable internal logic and a deeply transgressive worldview. The frisson this near-contradiction creates remains palpable long after one has finished reading the story.

I would argue that this pleasure-in-the-uncanny is the kind of experience we have when we read *The Courage Consort* and particularly 'The Fahrenheit Twins'; and, indeed, when we read much of Faber's other work. Further, I want to consider the importance that the notion of *absence* plays in the short stories I'm examining, and to suggest that this idea resonates again with Poe but also with the notion of the uncanny in a wider sense; much of the unease we feel when confronted by any of the tropes of the uncanny is, I would argue, caused by *absence*: absence of resolution, absence of logic, absence of information, the absence of comforting or quotidian explanations.

Both of the worlds presented in 'The Fahrenheit Twins' and *The Courage Consort* are particularly uncanny places; they are comprehensible, perfectly envisaged worlds, but they are crucially dislocated from anything quite everyday or familiar. 'The Fahrenheit Twins' has its central characters living on the Arctic island of Ostrov Providenya, in an 'almost perpetual arctic twilight' (Faber, 2005: 231); while *The Courage Consort*'s action largely takes place in an exquisite, rather hyper-real château situated – and isolated – within a 'surreally pretty' forest (Faber, 2002a: 11). The Château is initially referred to as 'the wicked witch's gingerbread house' (Faber, 2002a: 13); just one of many gestures in both stories to fairytale, myth, and folklore, all of which are made to carry unnerving undertones.

The Fahrenheit twins themselves are both adorable and simultaneously faintly nightmarish in appearance, and are thus deeply uncanny. Faber describes them as follows:

> Their hair was naturally black, hanging long over their ivory-white faces. Each pair of cheeks was sprinkled with cinnamon freckles, as well as a smattering of tiny puckered scars from a mysterious disease that had thankfully run its course without needing medical attention. Their brown eyes were large, with something of the seal about them; all dark iris and no whites, or so it seemed. […] (Faber, 2005: 233)

These are indeed *unheimlich* children. Their unsettling and, crucially, *physical* characteristics (that is to say, their objective character-description, undeniably present within the diegesis of the story) function alluringly, as do many elements of Poe's works and of *The Courage Consort*, and tease the reader with central story elements that are utterly uncanny, almost fantastical, fairy-tale-like, in narratives that are ostensibly realist in nature. In 'The Fahrenheit Twins', this co-existing of the realist and the uncanny also manifests in the twins' uses of ritual; as the children of scientists, they nonetheless believe that a kind of self-made pagan magic might be able to halt the passage of time; the twins also wholeheartedly feel that 'the universe' will direct them and acknowledge their behaviour through the provision of complicated signs and omens.

As characters, the twins possess many other heightened or alluringly unusual characteristics: at the opening of the story, we learn that they have 'uncannily keen vision' (Faber, 2005: 232), we are also given the odd sense of some kind of immaculate – or at least miraculous – conception: '[Una] was fifty-nine years old, and had produced her children well past the age where such things were considered feasible' (Faber, 2005: 232). Faber also explains that the twins resemble neither of their parents, and that 'They conversed with the huskies as equals' (Faber, 2005: 233). As the story progresses and we see just how bizarre the twins' behaviour turns out to be, we realize that these uncanny creatures, isolated as they have been since birth in the Arctic

Circle, have come to resemble not other recognizable, socially-nurtured human children, but simply one another. They are, in a crucial way, doppelgängers.

Yet liberal dashes of the uncanny are not the only elements Faber has chosen to place within his characters. The characters of the twins have also been constructed to encompass frequent references, both explicit and implicit, to religion, folklore, and myth. This too, I would argue, renders the twins uncanny; this weaving of mythic significance into the characters renders them decidedly *unheimlich*: they are far from 'everyday' or 'homely'; they are tantalizingly abnormal and other – surrounded by magic and an air of the sinister.

In their freedom and privilege to roam literally to the horizon and to play together forever, they are likened to a prince and princess. Their mother describes their environs as a 'little paradise' (Faber, 2005: 232), and their names, of course, Tainto'lilith and Marko'cain, directly evoke Judeo-Christian myth and folklore. The complicated mythological figure of Lilith was, according to Robert Graves and Raphael Patai's useful distillation of Hebrew myth, a woman created by God from filth and sediment, the mother of Demon children: 'an unclean animal', a monster, a demon; a night-creature or a 'screech-owl'. (see Graves and Patai, 1964: 65–9). Once cast out of Heaven, Lilith was tainted with a physical mark or colour that symbolized both the shame she bore and her relationship to animals. Lilith and other Lamiae, who seduced and mutilated sleeping men, were also known as, or likened to, 'frightening wolves' (Graves and Patai, 1964: 69). (This too adds a particular resonance when we consider the roles played by foxes and huskies in 'The Fahrenheit Twins'.) Cain's story is – arguably – far more widely known than Lilith's; the narrative describing the crime that the biblical character commits – the murder of his brother – and the curse (and mark) that God puts upon him as a result can be found in Genesis.[4]

The fact that both of the twins bear the mysterious markings, the aforementioned 'smattering of tiny puckered scars from a mysterious disease,' (Faber, 2005: 233) renders even stronger Faber's evocation of the Judaeo-Christian stories he is referencing; both children are literally marked, and the mystery surrounding the disease that caused their disfiguration fits perfectly with the sense of unease that pervades the story.

Perhaps completing the circle of Judaeo-Christian reference is the way Faber deals with the death of the twins' mother. When Una is taken ill, the children 'put aside all childish things in order to nurse their mother'. After Una's death, Marko'cain briefly considers whether Angels will arrive to take her body away to some kind of heaven. Much later in the story, the blades of a helicopter form a crucifix upon which the children consider placing their mother; and lastly, in a lovely pun, Faber has Marko'cain affirm certain ideas about their journey and treatment of their mother's body by yelling 'I feel it in my testaments!' (Faber, 2005: 264).

To return to that other important narrative element that I have argued helps render Faber's stories uncanny – absence – there is, perhaps ironically, an abundance of it in 'The Fahrenheit Twins'. The story's setting emphasizes notions of isolation and the absence of any broader, normalizing society from the very beginning: the absence of comfortably delineated seasons is a reality of the narrative's Arctic setting, where instead of night and day there is the aforementioned perpetual twilight; the twins, it seems, despite periodic attention lavished upon them by their mother, have more or less raised themselves, and have thus remained absent from any conventional parenting; other children are also entirely absent from the lives of the two central characters, and while the huskies in many ways are stand-ins for the kind of companionship that playmates would provide, they are of course animals rather than human beings, and this absence of humanity is both literal and figurative in the story. (The gruesome ritual involving the trapping of a fox and the stabbing out of its eyes at the appearance of the summer sun speaks of the twins' lack of any conventional sense of empathy or kindness, another absence, and something that normalizing companions or attentive parenting would have corrected.)

The story's central narrative turn – the death of the twins' mother – directly reinforces the very notion of absence, and forces Tainto'lilith and Marko'cain to undertake an open-ended journey in order to try and understand what they must do with the body of their dead parent. Now that their mother is to be forever absent, and given the significant lack of guidance or emotional support provided by their father, the twins journey out into the void that is their physical environment, with vague notions of making some kind of contact with the Guhiynui – the indigenous tribe their parents had been studying but whom the twins have crucially never seen – in order to learn from them the proper ritual governing the disposal of a loved one's body. Both in its imagery and its narrative significance, the journey undertaken by the twins utterly reinforces just how alone they are, and just how significant the very idea of absence has been in their lives.

When the twins finally locate the Guhiynui dwelling and its remarkable contents, they are immediately struck by another uncanny fact: 'The whole interior seemed to glow much brighter than the single ray of sunlight through the entrance slit could explain, and the air, for all its chill, seemed aromatic with intimacy' (Faber, 2005: 266–7). These contradictions pass without explanation, yet the twins are used to things remaining unexplained; their decision to leave their mother's body in the seemingly abandoned yurt is also something they simply understand that they need to do.

The 'shape' of Faber's story is fittingly circular: the twins, having dealt with their mother's body, having noted the evidence of Una's previous visits to the yurt, and – crucially – having run out of food, decide that the only logical thing to do is to take the dogs and return to what their father still calls 'home'. Yet, when they arrive, the fact that all is not well comes as no surprise to the reader: the twins will never again be comfortable living with their father (nor he with them); the inevitable and unnerving spectre of puberty still lies before them; and as they watch their clothes spin in the washing machine, they realize that they soon will have to leave their sanctum for places unknown. Faber's story is indeed open-ended, and positive in its way, though – like the twins – we realize that the action we have witnessed will have dire emotional consequences. The narrative voice has it thus: 'It was their insides that would never be the same. Something had happened to them, out there in the wilderness' (Faber, 2005: 273).

A very different kind of wilderness is the setting for *The Courage Consort*, the other Faber story central to this chapter. As noted at the beginning of this piece, the predominant setting for the story is an exquisitely-maintained Château (the 'Château de Luth').[5] (Faber, 2002a: 14) set within the environs of an extraordinarily beautiful forest near Martinekerke, Belgium. We follow the titular Courage Consort as they spend two isolated weeks in the Château, rehearsing the avant-garde a-capella piece they will soon be performing at a festival.

The setting of the story, like the setting of 'The Fahrenheit Twins', again features a very particular kind of absence, and – given the ways in which it is described – a striking dose of the uncanny. For what was a domestic dwelling, the building exudes idiosyncratic and seemingly inexplicable characteristics. Things at the Château simply don't make sense; what's more, our central character, Catherine, discovers early in the group's time at the Château that something decidedly unusual and uncanny seems to be lurking in the forest that surrounds them.

On entering into the Chậteau for the first time, Catherine 'began to feel a polite unease finding a purchase on her shoulders' (Faber, 2002a: 17). Absence again forms a crucial part of the action; wandering through the eighteenth-century building, Catherine notes 'the superb smell, or maybe it was an absence of smell: oxygen-rich air untainted by industry or human congestion' (Faber, 2002a: 18). The most significant absence, however, is an absence of sound: the forest surrounding the Château seems – initially, at least – to be unnaturally bereft of noise; Catherine notices this on the first night, and Julian agrees: 'as soon as Catherine mentioned the silence, he said he'd noticed it too, and that it wasn't natural. He'd lain awake all night because of it.' (Faber, 2002a: 27)

Faber is thus carefully evoking elements of the *unheimlich* once again; the Château, though previously lived in by a normal family, seems improbably, impossibly clean, and its surrounds, which would logically be filled with birds and other animals, appears to be unnaturally, deathly silent. Thus, the comforting and homely location that Catherine expects is instead unnerving and inexplicable.

Catherine herself, as the character at the centre of the story, is the perfect locus, as it were, for a story that is largely about fear. In the opening lines of the story Catherine is toying with suicide, sitting with her legs hanging over a window frame in the London apartment she shares with her husband, watching children play on the street below and wondering quite blankly how they might react to seeing her body land on the pavement next to them. Subtly-delivered images of death and the sinister are also made to revolve around the character; we are told that Catherine 'always slept like a corpse on planes and trains' (Faber, 2002a: 9), and, on learning of her tendency to hide half-finished food, we read that 'liquefying black bananas would lie like corpses inside the coffins of her shoes' (Faber, 2002a: 43).

The anxieties suffered by the character are in part explained when we later learn that Catherine's mother committed suicide when she, Catherine, was twelve. The mother took sleeping pills and put a plastic bag over her head in order to suffocate herself. When the subject of her mother's death awkwardly arises, Catherine explains to Julian that '... the polythene bag wasn't a plain one. It was a UNICEF one, with pictures of smiling children all over it. I always wondered about that.' (Faber, 2002a: 33)

Thus, we come to understand that Catherine's consideration of suicide is in some way a direct echo of her mother's; further, given that Faber establishes very early in the story that Catherine has a near-paralysing aversion to the sexual intimacy her husband so desires, images of children, birth, infancy and motherhood – all of which are peppered liberally throughout the story – acquire a significantly ominous tone. (The eerie image of the instrument of Catherine's mother's suicide being decorated with pictures of smiling children is perhaps the zenith of this seemingly very deliberate mixture of the everyday and the horrifying.)

Throughout *The Courage Consort*, notions of absence and the uncanny are directly connected. During the singers' initial period at the Château, Catherine becomes obsessed with the deathly silent forest and attempts to confront her fear by walking through the wood during the day. Her attempt, however, is unsuccessful:

> Catherine was aghast to find herself becoming afraid: afraid of all the millions of silent birds, infesting the trees, waiting. And, knowing how irrational this fear was, she despised herself. Surely she was too crazy to live, surely it was high time she cleaned herself off the face of

the planet, if she had sunk to feeling anxiety even at the thought of birds sitting contentedly in a forest. It was as if the frayed and tangled wiring of her soul, submitted to God for repairs, had been entrusted to incompetent juniors instead, and now she was programmed to see danger in every little sparrow, dire warning in music, deadly threat from the love of her own husband. (Faber, 2002a: 25–6)

Yet the absence of sound at the Château quickly transforms into something far more chilling: on the third or fourth night of sleeping in the building, Catherine, having had another difficult conversation with her husband, is crying herself to sleep when:

> Suddenly, she heard a short, high-pitched cry from somewhere quite far away. It wasn't Axel, she didn't think; that boy slept like an angel all night through and, during the day, hardly uttered a sound unless you set fire to a slab of Belgian bread right near his nose.
> Catherine's skin prickled electrically as the cry came again. It didn't sound human, or if it was, it was halfway toward something else. (Faber, 2002a: 30)

Thus, the unnatural silence of the forest is replaced by an equally unnatural sound, a sound indicating distress, what's more, a cry. (One might note the parallel here to 'The Murders in the Rue Morgue' and the cries that seem impossible to identify as issuing from a human mouth or from something else's.) Initially Catherine cannot understand why she is the only member of the Consort who is able to hear the sound, and begins to doubt her own sanity. She seeks reassurance from her colleague Julian, asking whether he also heard the strange cries, but his response is puzzlement. Catherine, however, is adamant: 'I definitely heard them, said Catherine. 'Human. But terribly forlorn and strange. Just cries, no words.' (Faber, 2002a: 40)

As the story progresses, Catherine seems less troubled by the sound, but, ominously, it is later described as emanating from '[a] creature', thus: 'No sooner had the piercing, plaintive cry of the creature in the forest woken her up than she was drifting off again' (Faber, 2002a: 65). Again, as with both the Poe story and 'The Fahrenheit Twins', *The Courage Consort* is deep realist in style while containing a single bizarre, almost supernatural element.

Further, Faber turns this unnerving, seemingly inexplicable story element on its head, in that the initial eerie absence of sound is turned into a very particular and disturbing sound that only Catherine seems to be able to hear. The cry, human or inhuman, provides a point of unification for all of Catherine's fears and anxieties. Later in the story she again ventures into the forest, this time for reasons that seem to elude even her. It is daytime, and for the first time since arriving at the Château she seems comfortable to wander into the forest by herself. For the first part of her of her walk she feels quite safe – yet without any warning, anxiety assails her again:

> *What would she do if she heard the cry?*
> The thought came suddenly, like an arrow shot into her brain. She was alone in the forest of Martinekerke with whatever had wailed out to her during the night. Its eyes were probably on her right now, glowing through the trees. It was waiting for the right moment to utter that cry again, waiting until she had blundered so close that it could scream right into her ear, into the nape of her neck, sending her crashing to her knees in panic. Catherine ran, whimpering anxiously. She would be a good girl from now on, if only Roger would come and rescue her.
> Breathless, half-blind, she broke into the clearing. For all the intensity of her dread, she'd only taken a couple of minutes to put the forest behind her; she hadn't strayed very far from home at all. The Château was right there across the road, and the little white Peugeot parked outside spoke of the impossibility of supernatural cries. (Faber, 2002a: 51–2)

Ultimately, in ways that echo the resolution of the Poe story, the 'explanation' for these deeply strange events is articulated as historical fact that has somehow come to life in the present. Faber has placed at the heart of *The Courage Consort* a chilling – and, in narrative terms, chillingly *unresolved* – folk tale that relates to the cry Catherine hears emanating from the forest.

We learn that the cry is part of a legend that has circulated about the area, and which has its roots in real events that occurred toward the end of the Second World War. Jan, the director of the festival at which the consort is to perform, has visited the singers at the

Château. Catherine has asked him about the cries in the forest, and he responds:

> 'This is a story I have heard before, yes,' he said. 'In fact, it is a kind of legend about the forest here.' […] 'It began, I think, at the end of the war. […] A mental defective mother ran away from Martinekerke with her baby, when the Army, the liberating army, was coming. She didn't understand these soldiers were not going to kill her. So she ran away, and nobody could find her. For all the years since that time, there are reports that a baby is crying in the forest, or a … a spirit, yes?' (Faber, 2002a: 75)

Thus, as an audience, we are given both explanation and delicious ambiguity. The real-life tragedy of the woman and her baby again speaks to the story's fascination with motherhood and children, and the fact that a 'legend' sprang from this story is quite convincing. The fact that Catherine herself seems to have been privy to some sort of real-life echo of this event and legend is not, however, explained to us in rational terms – it may be that Catherine's mental state has played tricks upon her; it may be that a distressed animal was the source of the cries; the reader is never allowed to know.

Yet despite its ambiguity, the 'explanation' that Jan provides somehow allows Catherine to heal internally. The novella's larger narrative concludes as the weather abruptly changes; the crushing heat that the singers have been suffering through breaks, metaphorically, with the sudden death of Ben, one of the singers; earlier that evening, Catherine overcomes her aversion to sex and she and Roger make love; after Ben's death, the performance is cancelled and Catherine sings the consort home (or toward the airport at least) in the minicab.

Thus, much is left unresolved in this 'resolution'. The novella concludes, of course – in the sense that there is a last page and we stop reading – but many narrative threads are left to float enticingly without conventional explanation or logical resolution. To return to 'The Fahrenheit Twins': once our central characters discover the Guhiynui's mural-like paean to their now-dead mother, they leave her body resting comfortably in that mysterious, deserted yurt, and they allow the huskies to lead them home. They decide *not* to kill their father and Miss Kristensen, and ultimately content themselves with the fact that 'they had much to look forward to in the big wide world ...' (Faber, 2005: 276.)

These conclusions, these end-points, are closures of sorts; they mark the endings of their respective narratives, but they are not, I would argue, comprehensive or comfortable *resolutions*. This stylistic choice on behalf of the writer – this choice of absence (absence of traditional resolution), is both a reinforcement of the uncanny and an underlining of the particular aesthetic beauty of these most affecting texts.

Notes

1 This, again, is a response viewers frequently have to the works of David Lynch. The one thing that the many and varied reactions to *Twin Peaks – the Return* (Showtime, 2017) shared was a kind of striking cognitive dissonance: an inability to articulate what Lynch had been trying to do, but a strange sense of pleasure at having experienced the extraordinary dread and suspense that the series comprised.

2 One could argue at length about what comprises Poe's style, of course; yet the vividly nightmarish and hallucinogenic style that characterizes stories like, for example, 'Berenice' and 'The Tell-Tale Heart' differs importantly from the largely matter-of-fact style Poe employs in 'The Murders in the Rue Morgue'.

3 See, for example, the introduction to Dennis Porter (1981) *The Pursuit of Crime – Art and Ideology in Crime Fiction*.

4 Extensive work on both the Christian and Hebrew versions of the story can be found in John Byron, (2011) Cain and Abel in text and tradition: Jewish and Christian interpretations of the first sibling rivalry. Leiden: Brill Publishers.

5 This would roughly translate as 'The Château of the Lute', reinforcing the tropes of music and performance the fill the story's action.

Works Cited

Blue Velvet (1986), dir. David Lynch. [Film]

Byron, John (2011) *Cain and Abel in Text and Tradition: Jewish and Christian interpretations of the first sibling rivalry*. Leiden: Brill Publishers.

Faber, Michel (2002a) *The Courage Consort*. Edinburgh: Canongate.

Faber, Michel (2002b) *The Crimson Petal and the White*. Edinburgh: Canongate.

Faber, Michel (2005) *The Fahrenheit Twins*. Edinburgh: Canongate.

Freud, Sigmund (1919) *Das Unheimliche*. Leipzig: Internationaler Psychoanalytischer Verlag.

Graves, R. and Patai, R. (1964) *Hebrew Myths. The Book of Genesis*. London: Cassell.

Nielsen, William Allen (1917) 'Introduction', in Edgar Allan Poe, *Eleonora, The Fall of the House of Usher* and *The Purloined Letter*. Vol. X, Part 3. Harvard Classics Shelf of Fiction. New York: P.F. Collier & Son.

Poe, Edgar Allan (1841) 'Murders in the Rue Morgue', *Graham's Magazine*.

Porter, Dennis (1981) *The Pursuit of Crime – Art and Ideology in Crime Fiction*. New York: Yale University Press.

Simpson, John and Weiner, Edmund (eds) (1997) *The Oxford English Dictionary*. Oxford: Oxford University Press.

Twin Peaks – the Return (2017) dir. David Lynch. [TV show]

Chapter 7

'In Separate Time' after *The Book of Strange New Things*

Rodge Glass

+4hrs

Dear Claire,

I'm writing to you from Heathrow's Terminal 5, just outside the Multi-Faith Prayer Room on the first floor of the Departure Lounge. Yes, that one. There's still the same sign-in book by the door, I checked. Psalm 34:18, large and clear on page one: 'The Lord is near to the broken-hearted and saves the crushed in spirit'. (How typical of you to write something designed to give *others* solace.) Wi-Fi has been down for a while, but I'll send this once I get a signal.

    For now, I'm sitting here on the cold tiles, a million light years away, or what feels like it, tapping with my two index fingers, pretending you can read my thoughts. My love, I hope you're warm, and well, and not too wobbly. As Corinthians reminds us, 'Love bears all things, believes all things, hopes all things, endures all things'. Or roughly translated, 'Distance is a real killer, isn't it?' Of course, the two photographs in my wallet haven't changed the whole time we've been apart. One of Boo as a puppy, on the bed, licking his paw like it's an ice cream. And one of you, smiling outside the base. Just before you went in for intensive training and I flew home. The longer this all goes on, the harder it is to look at either of them.

My flight has been delayed for some time. Well, when I say 'some time', I mean, 'perhaps forever'. I'm sure it'll all be fine but what I'm discovering is, round here they pretty much leave you to stew. I've been circling the Departure Lounge for a while now – stretching to fill the next minute, then the next one, wondering what on earth our Maker's plan is. Every so often I find myself back at this spot, listening to the incantations of the faithful inside, hoping that just sitting here will somehow make a difference. But God refuses to magic me to you just yet, and you refuse to appear.

Inside the Multi-Faith Room, right now, there's a man singing in Arabic. At first, I assume he's a Muslim, but then I hear your voice in my head: 'presumption is prejudice, and prejudice is presumption'. And yes, for all I know he could be praying to a nearby radiator, or the cooling system, or nobody at all. He could be entering his allocated worry period. But either way, the man's voice is a trumpet being played softly, sonorous and slow, always searching out the minor notes. The sound of his song makes me think about what you and I might talk about when we're finally reunited. Whether maybe we just won't talk at all. I wonder if the trumpet man will write in the sign-in book, and if so what he'll write. Who or what he's singing for.

I know.

But I can't help it. Thinking of all those messages that we read, fingers interlocked, the last time we were in Heathrow, on the way to the first round of interviews. After all, they're still there. Exposed, like cuts, to the eyes of every visitor. There are now hundreds more names than there were then, the pages are filling up fast – and they say we live in a secular world! – but I keep coming back to the first page. Yuko Oyama from Hyoyo, Japan, praying to find a good partner; Pat and Ray Murchiston from Langton, Kent, praying for their son Dave, killed in a car crash yesterday; the anonymous mother praying for reconciliation with the family who can't accept her remarriage. It's not the words themselves, Claire. It's what's hiding between them. Without you here to keep me closed, my mind is all flung-open windows. The draft is a storm. I think about how Yuko Oyama is doing, and whether she's still alone. I worry about her burying herself in work. Neglecting family and friends. Reducing her chances of ever meeting the partner she hopes to find. I pray for Pat and Ray Murchiston too. I'm their cheerleader, waving my believer's pom-poms, willing them to tough out the future, to find a way to hold their family together through Jesus, though a Dave-sized hole has turned them into doughnuts, and who among us could really survive that? Only an hour or two ago, sitting right here, I was bawling. Who knows why? If Pat and Ray Murchiston walked past me right now, I wouldn't recognize them, would I? Or perhaps they'd be all too obvious. Pacing the Terminal like zombies. That look on their faces, both desperate for distraction.

Anyway, more soon. From the other side!

Your loving husband,

Simon

+9hrs

Dear Claire,

We were so sensible. We factored in all that spare time to ensure we'd see each other at the base, before your take-off into the great beyond. A *whole day*, just for us. And now, who knows? The presents in my bag are moaning. They can't bear the tension either. Initially my flight was just put back by a couple of hours, reason unspecified by the Departures Board. Then it was four. Then a message on the tannoy said there would be more information 'as soon as possible'. Which wasn't very soon at all. It was then that I headed for the Multi-Faith Prayer Room. Five hours ago, that filled some minutes up. But time, or possible time, was yawning out in front of me. After writing you that first message, I tried to think of something positive to do. Or something safe.

A map explained the layout of Terminal 5's restaurants, shops and cafés. I scanned it then found the Japanese place on the 1st Floor and asked for a seat with a view; the waitress showed me to the bar-like row of lone diners lined up at the side of the space, dangling over the precipice. That side of the restaurant hangs partially over the runway and partially onto the people waiting their turn at the departure gates: perfect. I soon recharged on warm Japanese vegetable broth with thick noodles, and I took my time too, not thinking about the price. I laughed at myself because really, I'd been starving, hadn't I? But was just too anxious to notice. My body was thankful. I was confident that a full stomach would give me strength for the long trip ahead.

I watched everyone below as I completed my meal – the families and singletons, the business suits and travellers' rucksacks, the grandmothers and small boys, the Africans and Asians and Europeans and North Americans – all those shades of colour and gait, all those perspectives, histories, all those cultural references beyond my ken, all those myths and marvellous legends, the myriad physical and mental ailments and talents all held tight in God's glorious big airport palm. I slurped at the last of my broth and thought about how so many kinds of person can exist, in unknowing harmony, in one Terminal. I thought about what sorts of sentient beings you'll be meeting on your travels, and for a moment was at peace. I thought about how lucky we used to be, and how lucky we are today. As you go beyond our life, into the great starry unknown, I hope you'll remember our luck, and not leave me too far behind. Though even as I type that, I realize how it must sound. And my stomach groans in response.

When the waitress asked if everything was okay, I was far away in my own thoughts and didn't twig she was talking about the meal. 'It's enough to give you hope,' I said to her, peering over the handrail to the hum and clattering below. 'Even now. Don't you think?' It was unlikely, given the context, and amount of customers she had to attend to, that an opportunity would arise to mention Christ. But you can't be sure, and it's important to be ever-ready. As Proverbs tells us, 'If you faint in the day of adversity, your strength is small.' But then, you know your Proverbs. What I should have said to the waitress was, 'My wife's an adventurer. She's a hero.' But I always think of the right thing too late. Besides, if I'd spoken those words out loud, I might have collapsed into my noodles. Which probably would have made her uncomfortable.

Anyway, more soon. And this time, hopefully from the other side!

Your loving husband,

Simon

+15hrs

Dear Claire,

The laptop is on low. Once I've finished this message, I'll turn it off until the Wi-Fi is fixed. If that ever happens.

Since I last wrote, I've tried to help time pass without doing too much damage, and without thinking too much about the flight. Drifting up a level to the toilet, then back down again. Revisiting the Multi-Faith Prayer Room to thumb the sign-in book and pray for your success in the world on the other side of the stars. (I also prayed for Pat, Ray and for Yuko Oyama.) Later, I scanned the not-very-wholesome magazines in the newsagents, trying to find something we'd approve of, even gazing at the displays in Cartier and Chanel, wondering what kind of person spends thousands on a handbag while waiting for a flight. Who has the money for that? We don't know anyone who has the money for that, do we? I mean, under what circumstances would we blow three thousand pounds on a handbag? I'm not sure what I was playing at, God forgive me, but after a few minutes obsessing over this sort of thing, then a few more back in the main Terminal – or perhaps more like an hour? – I just lashed out at the nearest target. Such things remind me that salvation is not a straight line, Claire. And even a keen convert can be knocked off course. But of course, you're wondering what my trigger was.

Nothing much. There was a man sitting in a place called The Caviar House, a mock-fine-dining restaurant plopped, like a swear word, right in the middle of the ground floor. It was something in the way he was eating, maybe, while scrolling through his phone. Or something about his haircut. Or something in my perception of it. Anyway, I was wound tight. I walked over, tapped him on the shoulder and asked, 'Excuse me, but are you an ostrich? You do know there are 65 million human beings on earth with no home, right?' He held his fork in midair, poor man, and said nothing. It wasn't so much that he ignored me, Claire. It was more like he couldn't see me. He turned away, wiped his mouth with a napkin and went back to his caviar, and I wondered if I'd become invisible. Not just to this man, but you too.

If you'd been here, you'd have touched my arm. Done something. Quoted just the right line of scripture to help me see beyond myself. In terms of my Heathrow prison sentence the ostrich incident was perhaps after only ten hours – that seems days ago now. But the truth is I'd had enough, even then. Time was passing both too quickly *and* too slowly for this weary passenger. It was turning in on itself then, and continues to do so now. No news from the boards. The minutes piling upon minutes. And with every minute, every quarter hour, my chances of seeing you receding. Now I'm trying to accept this turn of events. If this is what the Lord wills, then so be it. But talk about mysterious ways! What if you doubt me? Think I just haven't bothered to make the effort to come and say goodbye? What if you spin off into space and never come back, and die thinking I'm having some sleazy affair with the woman behind the counter at Chanel? Perhaps this list of questions gives you a flavour of what preoccupies me in this place. And explains why I cannot sleep.

What followed after the ostrich incident was an age going back and forth, back and forth in the Terminal, trying not to crack. I listened to ambient music on my headphones. I listened to a Relaxation Podcast with my eyes closed. The sun set. Night fell. (Was it early morning when I arrived here?) Eventually I collapsed, feet tight in my shoes, one headphone dangling, into a pew at the bottom of the escalator between Gates 8 and 9. I tried to doze off. But you know what the seats are like in these places, Claire. Designed to keep you prickly. A reminder of how temporary this all is. And yet, the good citizens of the Republic of Heathrow love them! So many of my fellow travellers are, as I write this, stretched out, snoring away as if they were at home, in the warmth, with the lights off and loved ones close, like these cold, hard spots in the middle of nowhere are really soft mattresses in heaven. (Yes, I did persevere. Used my rucksack as a pillow. And yes, after a while I gave up.) Half-asleep, I wandered among the sleepers. Like the Jews in the desert! Like I used to in my darkest days. I've not been having flashbacks, exactly. More like, *vivid moments*. From the past, and future too. It's all very well having a designated worry period, but what if all time suddenly becomes a blob, one single period indivisible from the next, or the last?

I know.

The time dragged on. Every time I noticed one new sleeper settling down for a rest close to me, several more seemed to appear around them, like shadows, or mirrors. It was night, after all. I needed to escape, but before moving away I just stood in front of one of these sleepers for a while, watching, up close. He was an unusually tall specimen, Scandinavian perhaps, lips fluttering in the midst of a shock of blonde hair. I was holding my bag. Thinking about how jealousy is a sin. And judging others is a sin. And envy is a sin. And alcohol is a short cut to nearly every sin you can think of. As is being in possession of 'feet that be swift in running to mischief' – which, until I met you, were the kinds of feet I was very much in possession of! But I should tackle one sin at a time. And anyway, I'm doing what the counsellor calls 'grasshoppering'. Jump, jump, into the possible horrors of the future, spoiling any chance of peace in the present. That's something else you do – keep me in the now. It sounds corny, but as you say yourself, some of the truest things in Creation are corny as corny can be. I wish I could un-set the sun and go back in time to my arrival at Departures. At first, on entering the main Departure Lounge, post-scanner, post-pat-down, I thought it wouldn't be long. Soon this place would be in the past, and I really felt quite sunny about all this. Or at least, I think so. I can't really remember.

The timings are getting fuzzy here, I've been up so long. But by the time my flight was, I think, fourteen or fifteen hours late, I'd done countless laps of the circuit, checked the departures screen eighty or a hundred times and harassed the poor workers at the information desk to within an inch of their plastered-smile wits. No conspiracy, I don't think. They said nothing because they knew nothing. And though yes, technically, I was entitled to compensation and a hotel for the night, I really could receive news on my flight at any moment! – so they advised I just wait here. No, sorry, they couldn't confirm how far away 'any moment' might be. Still, safety is gainful, accident is painful and all that, eh sir? They were sure there was a perfectly good reason for this delay, there always is, and they recommended I come back in short while, keeping a look-out for Departures board news in the meantime. Perhaps a coffee, to keep your energy levels up? Or a nice meal? Claire, I tried not to betray what was within me. I asked, how could *nobody know where my plane was*? Had it *folded into itself*? Had it been *plucked from the sky*? I glanced around, thinking about my fellow passengers. How they were coping with the silence. Where they were hiding. Whether they were used to this kind of thing. Or didn't want to go home anyway. Perhaps they were quite happy going back to Wagamama's for another helping of noodles.

I hope this is my last message to you from the airport. If not, I won't be seeing you at all. And anyway, there's still no Wi-Fi. So basically I'm just a madman, talking to himself.

Your tired but loving husband,

Simon

+*21hrs*

Dear Claire,

Finally found a free charger!
It's probably too late now, but I can't help hoping that the Lord has seen fit to also delay you in your great mission to spread His word on other planets. Just long enough, perhaps, for us to appreciate each other one more time. I recognize that hope is a mirage. Which means you're already in mid-air, the rocket already launched. You're probably already lost to me. I think about Peter and Bea, that lovely couple who also made it to the final round of interviews, both stuck here on earth – but *together*. In the last few hours, I've been thinking about

them a lot. Bea at home, as Peter zipped up his bags. Peter, looking at her one last time, here in Heathrow. Making promises. Imagining the unimaginable. Then waving weakly and leaving for another corner of the galaxy. It never happened, because you happened instead. I wonder if they're lying in bed right now, arms clamped around each other, thanking God for being rejected at the last. Sure, they don't get to convert anyone on Oasis. They won't make *The History of the 21st Century*. But they do get to have breakfast in bed every single Sunday morning, touching toes. What, I ask you, am I going to do now? I don't even have Boo to distract me. The thought of going to church without you makes me want to set up camp in Heathrow for good. And to hell with the sleeping conditions.

You've probably worked out that since the last time I wrote, I've been losing my mind. The sign 'information pending' – flashing, flashing, like a nervous tic – has continued appearing and disappearing, for so many hours now it's quite unreal. The thing is, you get in the habit of checking and rechecking. Making sure, just once more, that you haven't read the message wrong. Aren't reading the wrong line. Haven't somehow missed your flight. You find yourself running a hundred yards further down the terminal, to another board, to see if that one by the charging ports says the same thing. Suddenly it seems likely that the boards might keep secrets from each other. Tell lies. What you imagine is, watching the damn thing take off without you. That gut-punch as the wheels tuck under the body of the plane and it slips into the pocket of a cloud. How could I ever explain it? That missing you was unnecessary? The longer this cursed between-time went on, the more it seemed likely. That my seat would skip off into the sky, and I wouldn't be in it. That somehow this would be my fault. Eventually, after I-don't-know-how-long, I started to get the shakes.

By the seventeenth or eighteenth hour of my wait I'd given in to the facts. Clearly I'd be here for hours longer, maybe days, and though I didn't know what to label the meal – second dinner? supper? breakfast? – it was probably time for more food. So I decamped to a colourful ground floor spot called the Giraffe Stop, apparently a 'funky, child-friendly chain serving international favourites'. My love, it seemed like a decent choice, right up to the moment it was too late to leave. I looked around, suddenly so tired, unable to even see properly. I sensed harassed parents as I scrubbed at my reddened eyes. I heard bored toddlers. Businessmen shouting into their phones. I let my eyes close and I heard two teenage girls calling each other names. Clearly, Giraffe Stop was a magnet for everyone in Heathrow Airport who didn't want to be there. The vibe was what my Relaxation Podcast would call 'an unproductive setting for contemplation'. The time, officially, was 'Breakfast Menu Time'. Though the sun wasn't up yet, at least not in this part of the world.

On this occasion, I didn't bother to engage the waitress in conversation and couldn't help but clock the prices. I ordered a veggie breakfast, which I wanted to un-order as soon as the sad little thing arrived. Still, I ate it, and too fast. Half way through I realized that my stomach was confused. Hadn't I just eaten broth? Or was that twelve hours ago? Before I finished, the waitress left a bill on the table and I understood that, unless I wanted to get up, I'd need to order something else. Otherwise it'd be out of the comfy chairs and back onto the cheap seats. I then spent the next half hour pecking at a decaf I didn't need, biting my nails and fingering my 'Postpone Your Worry' help-sheet, now creased and double-folded, wearing at the edges.

The list makes it seem simple –

a) Create a Worry Period

b) Postpone Your Worry

c) Come Back to Your Worries at the Designated Worry Period

That's all very well, as far as it goes. The idea that, by filing tension away, you limit it. Box it. Teach yourself to get on with living and forget for a while. It even makes sense that somehow this worry period, when it finally arrives, will be somehow liberating. But what happens when your flight is delayed by an indeterminate amount of time? What happens when your wife is due to leave for another planet, you're not going to catch her before she has to leave, you're already sweating, scratching, overheating, pawing at your red watering eyes, desperate for a shower and busy imagining untold grasshoppers – and that's all before you realize that you've forgotten you ever agreed to do a) on the worry sheet, never mind that you forgot to do b), or feared you'd not live to see c)?

 And where, might I ask, is God in all this?

 I didn't think I'd ever be here. In this kind of situation. With these kinds of choices.

 The menu was back on the table and the description of the Superfood Scrambled Eggs seemed to blink at me, like the sleep I never had. The menu, it suddenly occurred to me, was in direct competition with the help sheet. This seemed an important revelation. So I folded up the sheet and put it in my back pocket. Help sheets don't help if you expect them to provide all the answers. You have to use your agency. And in this circumstance, I could be pretty sure that whenever my designated worry period was supposed to be, it certainly wasn't now. Watching the twitch of the Departures Board. Thinking about how each passing second was loosening my hold on the one person who knew how to talk me down. So I counted to ten, ordered the Banana and Strawberry Porridge with Honey and Toasted Seeds (yes, you read that right – porridge soon after a full breakfast, even though I just said I wasn't hungry), tried to tune out the sounds of the parents and toddlers around me, and focused on God's London sunset. Which – if you're also able to tune out to every horror, every natural and human-made disaster, every broken heart, every couple separated, every love lost and war fought and faith abandoned and every piece of nonsense being spewed simultaneously in the universe while the sun dips behind the horizon, suddenly leaving light a memory – is really quite...*uplifting*. Even in Terminal 5 of Heathrow Airport.

 What next, for your loving husband, Simon?

+?

Dear Claire,

'For I know what plans I have for you', declares the Lord. (Jeremiah 29:11). Well excuse my English, but I certainly bloody hope so! Even as I write, our world is shifting, bubbling. What I recently believed was concrete is now sand, what was sand now seems more like the sea. There's STILL NO WI-FI HERE, and maybe there never will be, but if I don't use try to write to you, then all I'm left with is a feint whoosh, the sound of what's being swiftly and silently removed from below my shoes. Even our Lord and Redeemer can seem disappeared when I am isolated from those who see Him with me. I try to push down those thoughts, and remember that once you are on Oasis, I will be able to send you all of these messages, and they will draw you into me once again.

After what seemed an age, I asked for the bill at Giraffe Stop, the porridge untouched. The Terminal was now cloaked in a strange mixture of the brightness of inside and the darkness of outside which somehow flooded in, eating up the artificial light. All those windows, perhaps. They have a wearing effect. Meanwhile, the parents at the table next to me wheeled their children off to their on-time Lanzarote flight and, as a clutch of other flights also seemed to depart in a flash, suddenly the Terminal began to feel too big for the amount of people it was holding. I looked around and could only see spaces, empty cups and sandwich wrappers. I thought, what if God plans to leave me here, as a test? Or a punishment? What if the whole building collapses, or I'm lifted from this place and abandoned in the middle of the desert to die? What if all other passengers get called, every last one of them, leaving only me and two-hundred staff and all that caviar? 'If only my wife was here!' I wanted to cry out. 'She's the one who stops me coming out with this sort of claptrap!' Claire, I don't think I've ever loved or needed you more than I did while sitting in fucking Giraffe Stop, holding the money in my hand, wondering whether it really could be that expensive for porridge.

Perhaps I'm confusing 'loving' and 'needing' there. Thinking about the difference between those two things, I get a headache. Thinking about *time*, I get a headache. Perhaps there's no difference between 'loving' and 'needing' at all. Perhaps time is a joke God is playing on us. Still, it's not all darkness. God is with us always, that's what you'd tell me if you were here. And despite our distance, we are with each other in spirit. Also, the sun has come back up now, and I must force myself to remember that the Oasans are going to love you. I keep hallucinating, in drifting half-sleep, that I'll make it to the USIC base after all, in time to wave you off. But each time I process that thought, I remember it's already too late. Unless everything I thought I knew was wrong, it's too late. Claire, by the time my flight was a full day late, I couldn't take it anymore. I thought about going to the enquiries desk, one more time. I was Yuko Oyama. I was Pat and Ray Murchiston, in mourning. Darling, you've probably guessed what's coming here.

In the few minutes it took me to walk across the grey, neutral landscape towards its cheerful bright green entry point, I tried to concentrate on nothing at all: 'Wetherspoon Express' said the big sign, which I could see shining brightly from the other side of the Terminal. Nothingness, I thought, would protect me from changing my mind, from considering what I was planning on doing in Wetherspoon Express. I was right. Nothingness was a delicious warm blanket which covered me until I approached the bar. Even in these uncommon circumstances, surrounded by these strange energies and even stranger smells, it all felt exquisitely familiar. The order burst from my mouth, like I'd been holding it in for months and was only just ready to exhale. 'Dear God Almighty give me a drink!'

As I reached down for my wallet, I didn't think of you. As I handed the money over, I didn't think of you. When the drink was placed in front of me, I just supped deep and long, feeling the liquid slip down my dead dry throat, the bubbles worming their way into my thirst. And how thirsty I'd been! It was only after swallowing the first sip that you re-entered my head. Where is she now, I thought? Time had closed around me, or split into two roads, with you on one fork, foot hard on an accelerator, and I trapped on the other, frozen still. The presents in my suitcase would never be given, never received. So, in fact, what was the point in remaining sober? All this gave me a feeling of seasickness. Terminal 5 seemed like a tiny cabin on a vast ocean liner, helpless in the storms, and I, the only bloodless passenger, weak and needy, was being thrust from wall to wall, just blindly hoping everything I ever thought I knew was a lie. I thought about you, in your own departure lounge, taking a deep breath as the rockets fired up. Putting on your helmet. Facing the unknown. I wanted to throw up.

Airports and addicts, Claire. How many people do you think have been unable to resist? It's one thing to stay home, out of temptation's way. Keep the house on lockdown. It's quite another to be forced to spend a whole day and night, running out of ways to pass the time, in a place fully stocked with poison. I gulped at the pint like a man who knows it's too late. As I drained the last of the glass, I was already grasshoppering. Thinking about the last time we saw each other, how you said there was no badness in me, how I was the kindest man in the solar system, and how nothing on earth or the sky could change that. 'There's seventy-four days down the drain, then,' I said to the boy behind the bar, slapping the empty glass back down, my insides sinking and flying. I don't think he understood. Or he did, and had just seen it all before. 'It's okay mate,' he said, eyes drifting to the departures board. 'Tomorrow's another day'.

Soon, I knew, I would return to the Multi-Faith Room. Wrap myself in the sounds of all those different beliefs and confess this to you and to God. Start again once more. I'd be at seventy-four days again in no time. Perhaps, in seventy-four days, this Terminal would feel like home. But before the confessions, another drink. If the toxins are already doing their thing, I thought, if the executioner is on his way, axe swinging from his fist, and your head is already on the block, then you might as well get comfortable and keep drinking.

Chapter 8

A Compassionate Fictional Universe
Michel Faber's *The Book of Strange New Things* and the Art of the Creative Response

Rodge Glass

'In Separate Time' is a creative response to *The Book of Strange New Things*, a novel by Michel Faber about a man, Peter, selected to be a Christian missionary on the planet Oasis, leaving his beloved wife Bea behind on earth. Any carefully composed novel is multifarious, containing many untold stories, multiple potential interpretations, with lots of possible points of departure, and Faber's novel is bursting with possibilities. So, what exactly is my story a response to, and how do the mechanics of it work? The following commentary is in two parts. First, a look at Michel Faber's engagement with the art of the creative response, using case studies from his oeuvre. Second, an interrogation of my own creative process.

Faber and the Creative Response: Three Short Case Studies

At a reading hosted by Edge Hill University (7th February 2017), I asked Michel Faber a question about form. Over the last fifteen years he had hopped between the novel and the short story, also across various genres and forms, often working in hybrid forms. Recently, his first collection of poems had been published. I asked him, for each project, which came first – the form or the story itself? He answered, 'You have to listen to the story, and give it what it needs.' This is exactly the sort of corny statement of faith in the unknown that frustrates those who prefer to think of writing as a process in which the writer's intentions, influences, designs and actions can be broken down into concrete elements. It may be frustrating, but this is something Faber has been unashamed about exploring throughout his writing life. As Peter states in *The Book of Strange New Things*, 'most true things are kind of corny don't you think?' (Faber, 2014)

I am not sure whether I entirely agree with Peter about that – but I certainly agree that experiments, both artistic and scientific, are a far-from-precise mixture of exploring the known and the unknown. And, in terms of writing, I know from my own experience that the process of creating imagined worlds is primarily about the interplay between what writers know and what they intuit. So this is not unique to Michel Faber. But, based on the evidence of his literary output, it is an idea that applies to his work in particular. This is not vague abstract theory, but something evidenced clearly by Faber's various works, ranging through projects as dissimilar as *The Crimson Petal and the White*, *The Fire Gospel* and *Undying: A Love Story*.

In the first of these, Faber responds to the familiar patterns and concerns of the Victorian novel by rendering his own attempt in the present tense, in all its 'foul language and sadism' (Fox, 2011). He has described himself as 'open-eyed about what poverty does to people', and this compassionate consciousness about the distance, the tension, between the canonical Victorian novel and the nineteenth-century London he wished to portray. This explains the creative approach taken in *The Crimson Petal and the White* (Faber, 2002). He strips readers of the ability to read in comfort, instead engaging fully with the visceral trauma, dirt and downright jeopardy of the period, his protagonist Sugar leading readers by the hand, making promises, drawing attention to the extremities of experience. Or, as Professor Kathryn Hughes, biographer and Victorian history specialist wrote at the time of publication:

Michel Faber has produced the novel that Dickens might have written had he been allowed to speak freely. All the familiar tropes of high-Victorian fiction are here - the mad wife, the cut-above prostitute, the almost-artist, the opaque governess - but they are presented to us by a narrator with the mind and mouth of the 21st century. Where once the Victorian novel was lace-like with decorous gaps and tactful silences, now it is packed hard with crude fact and dirty detail. (Hughes, 2002)

What interests me about this quote is the suggestion that Faber sought to refresh the Victorian novel by using its tropes as triggers for his own story. Without knowledge of the Victorian canon, the reader's experience is undoubtedly diminished. Without the author's intimate knowledge of that canon, the novel could not have been written. But once completed, Faber's novel is designed to, as Hughes has it, 'skip free of its literary borrowings', as any good creative response should. Faber's next novel, *The Fire Gospel* (Faber, 2008) was a very different kind of response. But there are notable commonalities.

The Canongate Myth series (2005–13) was a hugely ambitious multi-national, multi-lingual publishing project conceived by Jamie Byng, the MD of Canongate, Michel Faber's only publisher since his debut collection of stories, *Some Rain Must Fall*, in 1998. Byng commissioned major writers to pen novella-length creative responses to world myths, and featured writers as diverse as Russia's Victor Pelevin (*The Helmet of Horror*, 2005) responding to Theseus and the Minotaur, China's Su Tong (*Binu and the Great Wall*, 2006) responding to the myth of a mourning woman's tears at the Great Wall of China, and the Brazilian Milton Hatoum (*Orphans of Eldorado*, 2008) responding to the myth of Eldorado and the Enchanted City of the Amazon. In Faber's case, he already had the idea for a next book, but his idea fitted Byng's model.

His eventual contribution was, on the surface, the contemporary story of Theo Griepenkerl, an academic who, in a looted museum in Iraq, stumbles upon a fifth Gospel written by an eye-witness of Jesus Christ's last days. Griepenkerl publishes the Gospel, and the reception unleashes the fire of the novel's title. But *The Fire Gospel* was also a creative response to the story of Prometheus, the enduring Greek myth remade countless times through the ages. This rich tradition stretches right across the arts, but in literature it reaches, in just the last three centuries, from Goethe's eighteenth-century eponymous poem, to Mary Shelley's *Frankenstein* in the nineteenth, to Alasdair Gray's playful twentieth-century hybrid novel *Poor Things*. Each of these perceived the myth differently, focused on differing elements, and each tackled Prometheus afresh. In *The Fire Gospel*, alongside Prometheus, Faber also slipped in responses to Dan Brown's *The Da Vinci Code*, a novel ubiquitous at the time of writing, as well as a few notable swipes at the workings of the publishing industry, on which this novel was a satire. The work, then, was not just one but multiple responses, to multiple texts, multiple realities, all housed in one new work you could read perfectly well without having the slightest clue who Prometheus is. (That word, 'Prometheus', is only used once in the whole of Faber's novella.)

Despite being a creative response to an established work, what struck me on first reading *The Fire Gospel* was that, despite being thematically different from his previous works, it is immediately recognizable as the writing of Michel Faber. It contains his own mark, what Raymond Carver famously called 'the author's particular and unmistakable signature' (Carver, 1997). But what was that signature? Another question I asked at the Edge Hill reading was about what he felt he carried throughout his oeuvre. Did all these disparate works of his have anything in common? 'Compassion,' was his one-word answer. The schools of critical thought that consider the author's intentions and considerations irrelevant are well documented. Perhaps, as a writer, I am bound to reject any definition that entirely sidelines an author's intention. As discussed, there are mysterious elements in the process, but surely not *all* elements are mysterious? With Faber, I wish to assert there is a conscious attempt by the author to suffuse all his major literary works with compassion, a factor which, as evidenced in *The Book of Strange New Things*, is a key driving factor not just in the narrative arc but in the creative process itself. Though I could not label it at the time, it was the compassion in the work which first drew me to Faber's early short stories. It is also what I sought to respond to with my short story, 'In Separate Time'.

The first two examples used so far, *The Crimson Petal and the White* and *The Fire Gospel*, give a sense of just how common it is for contemporary literary writing to be triggered by an existing work. Also, they show the kinds of fictional worlds Faber has engaged with when working over an unusually varied writing life, and how he has experimented with various triggers. But the most potent example of Michel Faber as a 'creative responder' is the most recent example.

As described in his eventual Foreword, Faber was sitting in Room 212 of Parkside Hospital in London by his wife Eva's side in June 2014, while she was sleeping, when he composed two poems. These became the first in what became a series eventually published in 2016 as *Undying: A Love Story*, the book which would document Eva's death and Faber's raw grieving process. This is how Faber describes the key event:

> On Eva's laptop, on the bottom of an untitled Word document I'd been using for all sorts of purposes including a final copy edit of my last novel and drafts of emails to well-wishers, I suddenly wrote two poems, 'Cowboys' and 'Nipples'. Both were alarmingly grim but were imbued with whatever it is that poems must have in order to go deeper than the words.
>
> I wrote only those two poems, and then it was time for Eva's cancer to kill her.
>
> Afterwards, as I tried to cope in a world that did not have my dearest friend in it, I wrote more. Sometimes none for several weeks, sometimes five in a day. I have never known such need for poetry before. I wish I'd lived into my nineties, with Eva by my side, and never written these things. (Faber, 2016)

This was both an emotional response to a critical situation, and a creative lashing out. Those moments by Eva's bed, typing onto that unnamed document, are a clear and concrete example of the author 'giving the story what it needs'. In this case, what the story needed was to exist in a different form, specifically one which, spare and unforgiving, fragmentary and concentrated, seemed suited to the situation at hand. Prose, that had served the author in all contexts for over twenty years, seemed suddenly inappropriate. Or perhaps, seemed to be the wrong language for this new horror. But it wasn't only that. When explaining the chronological events of the start of this project borne in traumatic circumstances, Faber alludes, even here, to an element of mystery, saying he noticed the new work contained 'whatever poems must have in order to go deeper than the words'. As if there is no way he, as the mere author, could know.

I recognize something in this corny, vaguely spiritual view of the creative process. Yes, creativity can be broken down into some constituent parts. You can plan, revise, read widely, research thoroughly. When writing novels, writers make conscious decisions about key elements in prose in terms of character, plot, prose quality, tone and delivery. Also, I believe writers are always creatively responding to *something* in the world around them. (With *Undying*, it was cancer, or the grim prospect of its end.) But, as the great Spanish writer Enrique Vila-Matas writes in *There Is Never any End to Paris* (Vila-Matas, 2014), a novel almost entirely a discussion of the creative process, many literary lifetimes are spent 'seeking the mirage of a future beyond reach'. Not only is there no shame in this, in admitting to an element of mystery in writing – but, on the contrary, I think it is a crucial element, necessary to embrace, though it is a ghost you cannot really embrace at all.

The following commentary explores the process of writing 'In Separate Time'. As the writer, that process will always be partly a mystery to me. Though other parts of it seem, on reflection, to be clear, identifiable, traceable.

A Response in Time

What I wanted to do at the outset of this experiment was take one part of *The Book of Strange New Things* which had spoken to me as a reader, and respond to it as a writer, giving that story what it needed. That is, to lift some representative or symbolic element and make it new, 'skipping free' of literary borrowings, in a way that spoke to the original but also lived independent of it.

I could have chosen one of many possible ways in. I did consider trying to write my way into Peter and Bea's existing narrative. Before Peter's departure for Oasis, perhaps. Or after he tries to return to earth. Or zooming in on a moment of drama Faber had skipped over. I also considered exploring something that nearly happened, but did not happen, like Peter's potential affair that never was, a kind of alternative history hidden inside the novel. But these options seemed obtrusive to my mind. Creepy, by being too close. After all, the director Jonathan Glazer had permission to recast Isserley, Faber's protagonist, in his own creative response, the critically-acclaimed film adaptation of Faber's novel *Under the Skin*. I had no such thing. So, instead of stepping on the original I chose to only lift several marginal details instead – ones most readers of the novel might not even notice, but to me contained something of the spirit, the mystery and crucially, the compassion of *The Book of Strange New Things*.

In my alternative fictional world, Faber's Peter did apply for the missionary job on Oasis with Bea, as he does in the original. Also, he did make it down to the last two candidates interviewed by USIC for the mission, but in my story world he simply fell at the last hurdle. Instead, another couple – also devoutly religious, also devoted to each other – get close to succeeding together. I imagined these two new characters, Simon and Claire, might have spent time with Peter and Bea in and around the interview rooms. Noticed them as kindred spirits. Empathized. Talked about their cats. In my reading of *The Book of Strange New Things*, USIC, the company hiring missionaries for interplanetary travel, seemed to have an unusually clear idea of the kind of candidate they were looking for. It therefore was not too outlandish to imagine the shortlisted applicants might have plenty in common. This gave me the excuse to make the interviewees similar, but not the same.

I imagined my story would take place several weeks after my character Claire accepted the job. Since then Claire has been busy in training at the base, her husband Simon (like Bea, rejected at the last) at home. The story opens as he is back in Terminal 5 of Heathrow, returning to her one last time to say goodbye before she leaves earth. He has presents in his bag. He is delayed. And he is trapped for the duration of the story, surrounded by temptation, powerless to escape his own otherworldly surroundings. This allowed me a stable setting in which to explore Faber's ideas in the novel, without simply repeating them. The fact that I myself happened to be delayed, waiting for a flight in Heathrow Airport Terminal 5 on my way back from Belgrade on July 2nd 2016, when I was working on an early draft of this story, was also certainly a factor in my decision-making. The Japanese noodle restaurant that features in 'In Separate Time' was the one I ate in that day, the perspective looking onto the travellers below the same as the one described by Simon. The entire geography of the story's setting is exactly as I experienced it in those moments of frustration in London, checking the board for news of my connecting flight to Manchester that refused to come. Though Heathrow was a part of the opening of Faber's story in *The Book of Strange New Things*, it was passed through quickly. In mine, that landscape comes to feel as alien, then as familiar, to Simon as Oasis does to Peter, or earth does to Isserley in *Under the Skin*. As in Faber's original, my Simon uses technology to communicate with his wife, writing heartfelt letters. Though in this case, technology refuses to co-operate. Soon, his resolve is tested.

Once the rest of the first draft of 'In Separate Time' had been written, and after inserting those initial minor details, I hardly thought about Faber's novel at all. A new story cannot aim to speak only to those who are familiar with the text from which the story's epitaph is lifted. Bearing that in mind, at a certain point I was happy to forget the original for a while, set myself free from the text I was responding too, and concentrate on making my own characters believable, their world too. Only in later line-to-line editing did I return to my copy of *The Book of Strange New Things*, making decisions over what to include or exclude based on the author's world. I tried to give the story doubt, and anxiety, and separate time, also the draining effect of distance, a quiet danger which seems to hover darkly over the original. I gave my story belief, shaken. These ideas seemed to contain the spirit of Faber's novel – or at least the spirit *as I experienced it*. Of course, the story also needed compassion. And plenty of it.

Compassion Editorial

It was compassion specifically that drove me, in a second draft, to include the other seemingly minor details that directly link my story with the original text it is responding to. Faber's novel starts with Peter and Bea's difficult lovemaking, then painful parting at Heathrow. In my story, Simon is the one left behind (the alternative, unincluded narrative of life back on earth was a key driver in Faber's original), and he stumbles across the very same sign-in book in the Multi-Faith Prayer Room referenced in *The Book of Strange New Things*.

In my story, I've used a few lines of that imagined text, lifting a few walk-on characters from the sign-in book which features in Faber's Chapter One. Pat and Ray Murchiston, whose son has recently died in a car crash. Yuko Oyama, who is looking for someone to love (Faber, 2014: 19). These are characters who never appear in person, and only appear once in Faber's novel. We readers experience them as Peter does in *The Book of Strange New Things*. Fleetingly, as part of a list containing others; wondering for a moment about the lives hiding behind the messages. As my boarding card from Heathrow reminds me (Faber's novel was in my hand luggage the day I was working on that early draft, the boarding card since kept inside it as a bookmark), I also used several other short quotations which were triggers of a kind, or seemed to suggest who my own characters might be.

In the time between that day in Heathrow and when I returned to 'In Separate Time' to complete it some months later, I forgot about the

Figure 1. Boarding Card, Dr R. Glass, Belgrade to London Heathrow, 2 July 2016. Later scribbled on, while awaiting news of connecting flight to Manchester.

existence of this bookmark, much less its contents. Looking back at this now, some of the intentions behind my scribblings are a mystery to me, but I can connect up how certain notes ended up influencing the final story. For example, I notice that one quote in particular was key. I've written on the boarding card, 'p12 – She was the one who stopped him coming out with claptrap'. Turning to my same copy of Faber's novel again now, I see I underlined the following:

> He sighed, squeezed her hand. What was he going to do without her, out in the field? How would he cope, not being able to discuss his perceptions? She was the one who stopped him coming out with claptrap, curbed his tendency to construct grand theories that encompassed everything. (Faber, 2014: 12)

I had forgotten this was the case, but this quote explains the personality I eventually gave my own protagonist: his dependence, his inevitable unravelling, also his over-thinking, his hyper-perceptiveness, his inner life. In examining this now, I notice I had even subconsciously stolen 'claptrap', which seems to be the kind of word only a certain kind of repressed, self-contained person would use. Certainly 'claptrap' is not a word that any characters from my novels or other short stories have spoken before. Even this part of my protagonist's make-up was directly impacted upon by Faber's original.

For me, the above examples from *The Book of Strange New Things* represented possible alternative narratives for my own tale, even possible appropriate language, as we have seen. But they were also examples of Faber's ability to sketch characters compassionately in just a few words. This was what made me want to respond to his work in the first place. Crucially, I noticed on rereading *The Book of Strange New Things* that what defines Peter as a character is just how desperate he is to reach out. Through missionary work. Through contact with the woman he loves. In every scene, he is seeking connections with others. Maybe it's because I am oversensitive myself, but I felt I could feel that sensitivity in every line of the novel, underpinning the linguistic choices and narrative twists and turns. Carver's unmistakable author's signature.

From that point of departure, that desperate need to reach out, it seemed a natural (though mysterious) next step to imagine my own protagonist Simon, in tears, on the floor of the airport outside the Multi-Faith Prayer Room, crying for Pat and Ray Murchiston from Langton, Kent, two people he has never met and knows virtually nothing about. And only another small step to show him collapsing under the pressure of distance from his wife, utterly incapable of coping without her. After all, at least for this reader of *The Book of Strange New Things*, here is the implied threat hovering over the entire narrative. That distance is a real killer.

Works Cited

Faber, Michel (2000) *Under the Skin*. Edinburgh: Canongate.
Faber, Michel (2002) *The Crimson Petal and the White*. Edinburgh: Canongate.
Faber, Michel (2008) *The Fire Gospel*. Edinburgh: Canongate.
Faber, Michel (2014) *The Book of Strange New Things*. Edinburgh: Canongate.
Faber, Michel (2016) *Undying: A Love Story*: Edinburgh: Canongate.
Fox, Genevieve (2011) 'Interview with Michel Faber', *The Daily Telegraph*, 1 April, URL (consulted March 2017): http://www.telegraph.co.uk/culture/books/bookreviews/8418821/Week-One-Interview-with-Michel-Faber.html
Hatoum, Milton (2008) *Orphans of Eldorado*. Edinburgh: Canongate.
Hughes, Kathryn (2002) 'The Crimson Petal and the White – review', *The Guardian*, 28 September, URL (consulted February 2017): https://www.theguardian.com/books/2002/sep/28/fiction
Pelevin, Victor (2005) *The Helmet of Horror*. Edinburgh: Canongate.
Tong, Su (2006) *Binu and the Great Wall*. Edinburgh: Canongate.
Vila-Matas, Enrique (2014) *Never Any End to Paris*, trans. Anne McLean. London: Harvill Secker.

Chapter 9

Double Vision
Adapting Michel Faber's *The Crimson Petal and the White*

Natalie O'Keeffe

It is no secret that film and television have always had a fondness for novels. By 1915, just fifteen years after the inception of narrative cinema as we now know it, there were already three adaptations of *Alice in Wonderland*, five incarnations of *Sherlock Holmes*, and five retellings of *A Christmas Carol*. And, as cinema developed further, both in scale and technical ability, adaptations of contemporary fiction and the ever-enduring classics remained a vital part of the filmmaker's repertoire (Duguid, 2014).

This literary legacy is still visible today throughout all strands of film and television – drama, comedy, horror, romance, thriller and so on. Certainly, there can be little doubt that the adaptation business continues to grow stronger and stronger, year on year – despite the often-aired adage that the best books usually make the worst adaptations. And television, particularly, has strived to maintain its long-standing relationship with literature. With small screen adaptations and appropriations including *War & Peace, And Then There Were None, Poldark, Dickensian,* and *Death and Nightingales*. These titles are not only a veritable testament to both on-going reader/viewer interest and the strength of the published novel as source material, but a demonstration of how Michel Faber's novel, *The Crimson Petal and The White* (2014), set in Victorian England, fits into the BBC's larger creative vision. A vision in which adaptations, particularly period pieces, continue to prosper.

(In)fidelity

One of the most remarkable facets of the adaptation industry is the love/hate relationship that many readers and viewers have with the adaptation process itself. Of course, many viewers enjoy and experience adaptations without issue but for others it can be an incredibly emotive and divisive experience. In relation to this second group of spectators, to those members of the audience who find adaptations to be consistently problematic, several thought-provoking questions can be raised and should be addressed. For instance, why do some audience members feel the need to judge page-to-screen adaptations so strongly? Why, as readers and viewers, do some of us yearn for on-screen authenticity and correctness? And why must the indefinable 'spirit' of the novel be present if adaptive success is to be achieved? The answer to each of these questions is the same. The answer is our obsession, as readers and viewers, with the concept of fidelity, defined here as: 'faithfulness [...] demonstrated by continuing loyalty and support' or 'the degree of exactness with which something is copied or reproduced' (Oxford Dictionary, 2017a).

This is nothing new and adaptation academics have historically fixated on the perception that a coherently recognizable sameness is the principal benchmark for adaptive success, a legacy which progresses from Bluestone's 1957 consideration of expectation and the fundamentals of medium to Harold's 2018 study of thematic fidelity and the role of aesthetics. After all, to adapt is to take something pre-existing and make it fit within new circumstances. As Edwards suggests, it is a process of introducing one thing into another, while also making the adapted entity 'suitable for a new use or purpose' (Edwards, 2007; Oxford Dictionary, 2017b).

This now outdated obsession with fidelity, with decipherable semblance – which appears to stem from a 'hierarchical literary culture' (Rizzo, 2008: 300), self-perpetuated by the belief that film will always be 'secondary' to the 'reality' of the text (Semenza, 2013: 143) – has started to give way. This change could not have come soon enough for many academics and critics who have described the fidelity model of adaptation studies as being 'stagnant' (Leitch, 2003) and 'frustrating' (De Zwann, 2016), both for its inability to form any strong conclusions and for its persistently underwhelming repetition of an 'unilluminating' debate regarding successes and failures (Murray, 2008). Indeed, this 'dead end' line of enquiry (Ray, 2000: 39), which so often found itself 'hamstrung by the inadequacy trope' (Murray, 2008), had initially stunted the growth of adaptation criticism and, more importantly, it had largely ignored the complex relationship between adaptation and audience.

A deliberate shift away from a textual studies approach, which consistently prioritized the verbal over the visual and the literary over the cinematic (Rizzo, 2008: 300), also moves us towards a more rigorous engagement with the 'economic, cultural, political, [and] commercial' contexts of film production (Aragay, 2004: 24). Refocusing adaptation studies away from what has been described as prudish and tedious 'literary elitism', recent deeper social and cultural examinations have considered the nature of filmmaking and the role of the audience more thoroughly (Raitt, 2010). In keeping with this progression, this chapter will remain fundamentally uninterested in determining the successes and failures of the BBC's interpretation of *The Crimson Petal and the White*; rather it seeks to explore more complex considerations, such as the roles and responses of audiences and creators, and the ways in which visual techniques are often used to convey unspoken, but vital, narrative information.

Nevertheless, it is inappropriate to remove fidelity from the conversation entirely; despite the criticisms regarding the enduring use of fidelity as a determining concept, the approach continues to prevail. In fact, the fidelity complex remains 'rampant' throughout published media and fan culture and, accordingly, this is reflected in almost all of the reviews written regarding the BBC's version of *The Crimson Petal and the White* (De Zwann, 2016).

As we may expect, audience opinion varies widely; with the pendulum of judgement swaying back and forth across a colourful spectrum of diverse outlooks. From those who considered the adaptation to be an incredibly successful piece of television to those who seemed almost offended that the BBC had even attempted to make real the world and characters that they had envisioned so clearly with nothing but Faber's words to guide them.

Those who praised the adaptation called it a 'fantastic production' of a 'wonderful book' (Kate, 2012), drew attention to the 'magnificent visuals' (Veronika), 2013, and commended the 'good performances amid a dark and grimy backdrop' (Chatterforth, 2011). With one reviewer disclosing – almost gleefully – that they had enjoyed the BBC's adaptation of Faber's tale more than anything else they had seen on screen in 'a long time' (Jones, 2011).

At the other end of the spectrum, there were those who found themselves unsatisfied by the mini-series; with one reviewer declaring that 'the drama is excellent, but the book is better' (Chowney, 2001), and another suggesting that the adaptation fails to do the book 'any justice' at all, which they go on to describe as 'unfortunate' (Brandt, 2015). The standout comment was made by an impassioned viewer who stated, in no uncertain terms, that '*obviously* the book is better, no question, and as a literature nut I highly recommend you read it…' (Beanie Luck, 2011).

This last comment explicitly highlights the importance of a viewer's previous experiences and preconceived expectations of the text, whilst also drawing upon that sense of literary elitism, conscious or otherwise, that so often gets in the way of spectators enjoying a literary adaptation. From this, we come to understand that a pre-existing awareness of Faber's novel often makes the source material a 'priority' and this, in turn, 'overrides' the existential experience and overall judgement of the television series as a piece of art in its own right (De Zwaan, 2016). There is certainly clear evidence of prioritization amongst online reviewers, where a significant amount of pre-viewing scepticism is on display. For instance, one reader felt that she was 'too attached to the book' to be able to 'let go' of the mental picture she had created (Kirsty D, 2008). Whilst others found that although they were 'pleasantly surprised' by the mini-series they had been 'prepared for disappointment' and had been 'concerned' that the show would succumb to the 'usual book-to-series disease' (Snow, 2013; Kindle Customer, 2013).

Of course, as we have already touched upon, adaptation, as a method, embodies the processes of creation and reception; fundamentally depending on its knowing audience, like those above, who not only recognize the BBC's *The Crimson Petal and the White* but can appreciate it as an adaptation, therefore allowing it to achieve its 'full effect' (Edwards, 2007: 120). Again, there is evidence for this theory amongst the reviewers. Indeed, a noteworthy number of those who reviewed the BBC's adaptation had found themselves feeling a little out of the loop, or a little left behind, compared to those who had read the book. This unknowing audience sometimes felt like they were missing out on something, or that they were lacking vital interpretative information – 'I haven't read the book and I regret it now' one viewer wrote before confiding that they felt 'some things were not explained' and that this had left them 'not understanding' the narrative arc (Veronika, 2013). Another viewer, in a similar state of mind, described how they 'wish[ed]' they had read the book first so they could understand 'more clearly what was going on' (Ramsey-Hardy, 2012). In fact, those who had read Faber's book before viewing the mini-series seemed to largely feel the same way and there was the prevailing connotation that if you had not read the text then you were 'seriously missing out' (Sheppard, 2011). Moreover, it was suggested that the unknowing viewer might be left feeling 'slightly disappointed at the lack of detail' transfused into the adaptation (Kate, 2012). A third reviewer also drew attention to the fact that Faber's sizable novel contained 'much more in the way of historical detail', although they conceded that so much information could not be 'easily conveyed on screen' (Luddite Writer, 2014).

It is important that we remember that an audience member can become a part of the knowing audience after the fact; indeed, many reviewers of the BBC's adaptation saw the television programme first and then went on to read the book. These 'curious' viewers then entered a new community and held a new perspective (Edwards, 2007: 120). Would a second viewing change their perceptions and judgements about the quality of the adaptation as an adaptation? Or would they then, perhaps, be in danger of falling into the (in)fidelity trap, restricted by determining successes and failures while lamenting what has been left behind?

There can be little doubt that *The Crimson Petal and the White* was an effective piece of television: The *Independent on Sunday* declared it their joint 'drama of the year', praising it as a 'thrilling, visceral portrait of Victorian mores'; while multiple award nominations and wins demonstrate its strengths in terms of narrative ambition and technical craft (Montgomery, 2011a: 60). So, then, we are left with a difficult and largely unanswerable question. If adaptations can be so divisive and so troublesome for their knowing viewers, regardless of production quality, is it in fact preferable for the viewer to be a member of the unknowing audience, even if that position could potentially leave them feeling a little left behind? Does the lack of a previous relationship with the text free those who struggle with adaptations from watching an adaptation as a sceptic, waiting to be convinced by the efforts and choices of an outside creator or creators?

(Sub)versions

At its heart, Faber's book is a deconstruction of Victorian literature or, to put it another way, it is an unpacking and examination of the classic Victorian novel and all of its constructs – the likes of which could have been implemented by George Eliot, Anthony Trollope, or Wilkie Collins. Indeed, Faber's storytelling is as epic in scope as that of Charles Dickens or Thomas Hardy and yet, as one critic writes, it is somehow 'more enlightening' than the greats because it fuses the author's 'modern sensibilities' with a familiar literary past (Russell cited in Faber, 2014). Consequently, the book reads like a Victorian novel written about the Victorian novel – like a contemporary adaptation of a nineteenth-century classic – and as such it is 'teeming with the ghosts of literature past' (Anderson, 2002). Faber fills in the genre's 'polite gaps' until there is 'literally nothing left unsaid' (Hughes, 2002). And it is this subversive backbone, supporting both the text and the modern reader's understanding of it, that the adapters of Faber's book actively adopted and sought to advance.

Director Marc Munden indicated that his principal 'challenge' was to create a 'credibly Victorian' London that was not only distinguishable but 'unrecognisable' from the 'cosy historical world' that had been realized on-screen before (Munden, 2011). Just as Faber had positioned himself against Victorian literature, 'borrowing' all of its clichés before destabilizing his reader's expectations, the director aimed to 'set [himself] up similarly against the TV period drama' (Munden, 2011). This was achieved, in part, by giving the viewer uncensored access to the realms that costume dramas usually ignore completely – such as the bedroom and the bathroom – just as Faber had. This included, for example, dealing openly with the uncomfortable nature of prostitution. For instance, in his novel, Faber has Sugar using a 'tureen of contraceptive' and a spongy 'plunger' to remove her customer's semen from her body – we are told that this is a 'ceremony' she has performed hundreds of times, with the novel's protagonist taking a moment to wonder exactly how many 'sponges and swabs' she has 'worn away' and how often she has prepared her 'witches' brew' with a sense of 'mindless precision' (Faber, 2014: 123). This is just one isolated example of the unflinching realism found within Faber's text but it is memorable. Thus, it seems appropriate that the adaptation would seek to carry such a unique perspective across media. This was an important decision made by the creative team but the only one that could be made if they intended to earnestly embrace and visualize Faber's text – a text that thrust us into Sugar's uncompromising world, from the dirt up, with little reprieve in sight.

Ultimately, television period dramas are popular, and maintain their popularity, because they rely so heavily on reusing the same tropes and themes – rags, riches, love, betrayal, denial, discovery etc. – at a safe, well-mannered distance. Or, as one critic playfully put it, period dramas have developed a winning formula that draws in an audience time and time again and it can be summarized thusly: 'blushing ingénues, handsomely lit drawing rooms, and Judi Dench in a bonnet' (Romney, 2011: 60). Such dramas are usually cosy and warm affairs – even if their stories are not – because of how familiar yet distant they seem to the modern viewer. The stories may be original but they are rarely demanding of their audience. However, the BBC's adaptation of *The Crimson Petal and the White* is demanding, in fact, its use of camera and content are unusual enough that they render the whole thing slightly uncanny, like an examination of the period drama and all of its anticipations. The adaptation manages to 'shake the good manners of costume drama'; it is a grim, explicit, and provocative affair because it subverts viewers' understandings of what a period piece should look, feel, and sound like (Williams, 2001: 64). This unusual approach left the audience with mixed feelings; indeed, a rather bewildered and disappointed Maureen Lipman, while appearing on the BBC's *The Review Show*, described the adaptation as being just like 'Downton Abbey with fellatio, really' (Lipman, 2011). While *The New York Times* reviewer, Mike Hale, expands on this sentiment by succinctly summarizing precisely what it is that sets the mini-series apart from other period pieces:

> Chamber pots, and the rear ends of those using them, figure prominently, as do blood, vomit, foul odours and the fully naked bodies of men and women who have not been to the gym in a long time, if ever. (Hale, 2012)

As with the novel, the televisual adaptation of *The Crimson Petal and the White* is decidedly visceral and uncensored and, because of this, it is difficult for the viewer to find those threads of sentimentality, or to encounter those enticing waves of warm nostalgia for a time gone by, and what we are left with is an image of the past without any pleasantries or, indeed, pleasantness. This approach captures the essence of Faber's novel perfectly, where even the ending of the book abstains from the usual 'satisfactions' that readers have come to anticipate from those beloved Victorian classics – Sugar and William do not marry, indeed the lack of clarity surrounding their final circumstances prevents the reader from even entertaining the prospects of an 'unhappy ever after' (Hughes, 2002).

This sense of expectation, found in those viewers who frequently watch and enjoy costume dramas, mimics the dilemma found amongst knowing book audiences who watch adaptations of familiar texts – there are expectations, visions, and very particular ways of being. As one academic has outlined:

> Indeed, the one thing that perhaps most defines [period drama] productions is an impressive, active knowledge of both how the same scene or moment is played out across different films or series and also how key generic tropes or conventions are presented in varied ways. (Louttit, 2013: 180)

However, such repetitions can become barriers or challenges for readers/viewers when their ideals/ideas of what something is – whether that be a book or an entire television genre – are adapted or redefined in some unexpected way. And, from this alone, we can see once more how complicated and multifaceted audience responses can be.

When cementing their thematic vision, the adapters of Faber's novel had a multitude of themes to bring to the fore: ambition, sexual politics, prostitution, personal struggle, confinement, and even adaptation. From all of these options, scriptwriter Lucinda Coxon decided to make parenting the 'prism' of her view – 'I think it's a story full of people looking for mothers' (Williams, 2011: 64). This is a pertinent and thoughtful selection of a key theme. Indeed, mothers and mothering are referenced throughout the novel – Sugar is arguably damaged by her mother, Mrs Castaway, who introduced Sugar to her world, the world of prostitution, when she was just thirteen years old (Faber, 2014: 285). Emmeline Fox becomes a kind of surrogate mother to the 'fallen' women she comes across on her rounds with the Rescue Society; furthermore, she feels she has developed a familial relationship with one of the women, her maid-of-all-work, Sarah, for whom she has made it her 'policy' to help 'as much as a can', and they are described as being 'more like aunt and niece than mistress and servant' (Faber, 2014: 208). While William Rackham's daughter is eradicated entirely from his early narrative, and Agnes' by proximity – in fact, we don't even realize Sophie exists until we are halfway into the narrative, something that appears to frustrate and irritate Sugar – 'come on, give it to me [...] speak the name of your own daughter, why can't you?' (Faber, 2014: 456). This elucidation of theme is perhaps what might be referred to as an attempt to capture the elusive 'spirit' of the piece, the emotional vision. The actress who plays Sugar, Romola Garai, was particularly pleased with Coxon's decisions – '[the] themes were discussed honestly and accurately, which is not always the case' (Garai, 2011).

In terms of visual narrative editing, the creative team took the decision to vary the range and style of their camerawork - creating a sometimes jarring and unfamiliar worldview, very like that found within the text, especially in those early dizzying pages, but conveyed in a dramatically different way. One critic recalls those early scenes:

> As we tumble in and out of doors, up and down stairs, a cavalcade of squalor – dead-eyed urchins, bloodied horses, the Lucian Freud-esque spectacle of a morbidly obese wench splayed naked across a bed - is made queasier by camerabatics. (Montgomery, 2011b: 64)

The camera is also used to capture unflinching close-up shots of Sugar's face, as she has sex with William, which resemble appropriated fragments of a gritty, observational documentary. The overall tone is decidedly 'sweaty and dehumanised' and so instead of being sexy the adaptation's sex is 'played for revulsion' (Montgomery, 2011b: 64). From the very beginning, viewers are left with a more 'sinister pitch' than they are used to and this is further exacerbated by the 'subtly off-kilter framing and hazily-shifting focus' employed by Munden (Montgomery, 2011b: 64). This was a deliberate choice that scriptwriter Coxon made, intending to highlight that fact that Sugar is not as compliant as her clients believe her to be, and to intensify the tension between her ambitious brain and her social position. Indeed, Faber makes sure his readers are aware of Sugar's unhappiness, with written close-ups rather than physical ones. In one instance, 'half dead with exhaustion', Sugar confesses that although she has been paid very well by William she could have 'happily have done without getting fucked in the end'; her physical reflection showing an 'angry young woman' who is ready to 'murder anyone or anything' as she tiredly attempts to remove all evidence of sex from her bed (Faber, 2014: 124). This abrasive and unflinching textual imagery is replicated on-screen most effectively by maintaining a sense of jarring, physical closeness between the actors and the camera, mimicking the intimacy of the written word.

The Fireside, a tavern filled with active bodies, in various states of dress, made-up, and accompanied by song, reads visually like the setting for a rambunctious music video; while more classic or 'proper' sequences, readily associated with period drama, consistently underpin the story, giving the viewer a false sense of security and familiarity. Consequently, the camera's lens, the eye through which we see the actuality of Faber's world onscreen, offers the familiar and the unfamiliar at a sometimes-destabilizing pace; and the viewer is left to wonder if this vision of Victorian London is, in fact, a *truer* portrait of Victorian London. To quote from Faber's text, we are left with a distinct feeling that '[we] have not been here before. [We] may imagine, from other stories [we've] read, that [we] know it well, but those stories flattered [us]; indeed, [we] are alien[s] from another time and place altogether' (Faber, 2014: 3).

With a novel as lengthy as Faber's, or indeed any novel, an adaptation cannot be expected to deliver a word for word, page by page, account – change must take place, alterations must be made, details must be cut, new bridges must be built, and a new viewpoint must be constructed. For, ultimately, while the team behind the adaptation of *The Crimson Petal and the White* are generally 'unconstricted' and able to create as they wish (Deacon, 2011) – they are nowhere near as free, both in terms of vision and execution, as Faber was when he originally constructed his novel. Indeed, in comparison, television is a medium 'rather more demure' than the literary text and, in many ways, constructed television sets are incredibly narrow when compared to the sprawling possibilities of an imaginative mind (Deacon, 2011). Because of this, the adapters of any written source material must keep in mind that their objective is to discover 'uniquely cinematic equivalents of the literary trope(s)'; not to translate a text literally (Bluestone, 1957: 27). But what does this mean for the vision of the whole?

It can be argued that it is impossible to adapt a text without creating a new one – this resulting creative response does not replace, nor does it seek to replace, the original but instead becomes a kind of parallel, a new vision of the familiar. This opens the debate about authorship, or co-authorship; wherein an adaptation is not only a new product, but becomes a 'repository' of collected ideas that cooperatively aim to reach the 'truth', or offer the 'promise of truth' to an audience (Donaldson-McHugh and Moore, 2006: 232). It is a 'gathering together' of apparently dissimilar 'signs' into a harmonious creative vision, in which 'all the elements articulate the unity of an ideal configuration', even if the purpose of the vision is to demonstrate how achieving the ideal is impossible (Donaldson-McHugh and Moore 2006). Indeed, an ideal adaptation will only ever be an 'impression', an impression with features and facets that vary innumerably, from person to person; thus, making the ideal a 'spectre' incapable of corporeality that looms hauntingly over the process and its authors (Donaldson-McHugh and Moore, 2006: 232).

Authors play an interesting role in adaptations. It can be argued that books are the product of a single, isolated author, while television is a collaborative and industrialized process. Indeed, a successful novel, like Faber's, is supported by a dedicated literary audience, produced by an individual, and is free from censorship; while film is supported by a larger audience, produced collaboratively under industrial conditions, and is heavily restricted by broadcast codes and guidance. There are, of course, problems with this generalization – it assumes an imbalance in reader/viewer audiences, it suggests that producers and directors are fundamentally egalitarian in their approach, and it fails to acknowledge that author's do not write in sacrosanct isolation, rather they are consistent influenced by their own social, cultural, and political experiences.

(Corpo)reality

Beyond the emotional and metaphysical, there is the physical processes of adaptation to consider – that is, the process by which adaptations are born into tangible reality. How can the collaborative vision of a large creative team replicate and make real Faber's world in a satisfactory way? Particularly when the pre-established visuals, produced in the heads of each individual reader, will naturally express any number of infinite variations.

The first step is to ensure that the adaptation's creative team have a synchronized vision, a task requiring the flexibility and receptibility of those expected to adhere to the overall creative vision. There must be an understanding of what is desired, a unity of perception and interpretation. Series director Marc Munden (2011) has described himself as being 'a bit like a conductor of an orchestra', or the possessor of a 'clear and vivid dream' who needs to inspire others with the same 'vision'. For *The Crimson Petal and The White*, praised universally for its 'distinctive visual idiom', art played a vital role in creating the unified look and feel of the series – acting as another set of outside influences which were then applied to the original text by all of those involved (Wilson, 2011). This is vital because, despite the obvious limitations of televisual adaptations – restricted length, fewer details, limited sets, fixed camera angles etc. – they can do something that novels are incapable of   generate a stylized aesthetic or 'look' (Wilson, 2011). The BBC's adaptation has a very distinctive visual style; and it appears precisely as Sutcliffe suggests it does in his review of the series – it is 'as if a *Vogue* art director had decided that Victorian underbelly was going to be this season's big thing' (Sutcliffe, 2011: 22).

For the adaptation of Faber's novel, the mini-series's distinctive visuals were primarily inspired by artists, with Max Ernst, Otto Dix, and Gustav Doré cited as the major influences alongside obscure Polish pornography (Montgomery, 2012). However, it is Doré's presence that is vividly seen as we are introduced to Sugar's London on-screen for the first time – it is a place where the daylight barely filters down to the shadowy streets and the darkness seems to entrap and encase the players. Anyone familiar with Doré's depictions of London – for example, *Houndsditch* or *Wentworth Street Whitechapel*, both created in 1872 – will recognize this dark, dirty, crowded depiction of Victorian London – while anyone who has read Faber's tale will consider the artist to be perfectly compatible with novel's atmosphere. After all, Sugar has told us that 'the city is a filthy place' before drawing attention to the 'muck' on the streets, the 'muck' in the water, and the 'muck' in the air'; even sharing that a 'layer of black grime' would often settle on her skin (Faber, 2014: 248).

Colour, and its very particular use, also plays a vital role in generating the look of the series, not only in terms of creating the adaptation's physical vision but as a vehicle for Sugar's emotional journey. The mini-series opens with a visceral but earthy palette of deep reds and muddy browns. Before long, the colours begin to shift, the frames becoming whiter and brighter in scale – here, whiteness is used as a metaphor, utilized when the audience is falsely led to believe that Sugar is escaping and/or rising up through the ranks of society. These sets were referred to by production designer Montgomery as 'safety sets' (Montgomery, 2012). In the adaptation, Sugar's room at Mrs Castaway's, where she writes and ponders her dreams, has four pale, near-white walls – inviting us consider the notion that Sugar's aspirations are also capable of confining her. While her bed, draped in vibrant red fabric, conjures familiar emotions and positions entwined with the colour – love, hate, anger, passion, fire, danger.

Then, there is the subtler, liver-red of the Rackham house to consider. Montgomery suggests, it is peppered with references to Italian filmmaker Dario Argento's work, particularly his 1977 horror film *Suspiria* – which explores a sinister ballet school where all is not what it seems. This choice of inspiration may appear unusual for a costume drama but it is very fitting, in relation to the Rackham house – a house with a dark history; where William's wife Agnes is semi-imprisoned by her doctor. In terms of technique, Argento is famous for his atmospheric use of colour, particularly shades of red, for his use of dramatic lighting, and for employing camera angles to generate the unnerving, nightmarish settings of his films. It is these 'unconventional' reference points, and the process of placing them within something as highly conventional as a period piece, that exacerbate feelings of instability and give the production an air of 'daring' (Montgomery, 2012).

As the series moves along its narrative track, Sugar's world flickers with white a few more times, but in one significant and damning shot, Sugar is set against a large red wall, its colour visually overwhelming her, shrouding her in a rich and unforgiving crimson, and we come to understand that she is perhaps more trapped than she has ever been.

In terms of spatial use, amidst dark and dreary London, we find a muddy sewer that almost splits the screen in two, like a battle trench in the heart of the city. This was inspired by a Flanders' battlefield, and it became a metaphor for Sugar's emotional journey, for her personal war, for her desire to leave the world she finds herself in and all of its dirt far behind (Montgomery, 2012). This social grime metaphor is teased again, the set that acts as William's perfume factory is, in reality, a sewage factory (Montgomery, 2012).

Throughout the adaptation process, emphasis was also placed on creating a Sugar that not only looked the part, but carried aspects of her character and personality on her clothing and through her posture. Throughout the early scene at The Fireside, Sugar's back is straight, her head is held high, her eyes sparkle with control; while her standout red hair, her height, and her flaking lips, all make her seem otherworldly (Williams, 2011: 64). This is especially true if we compare Sugar directly to the other sex-workers in the tavern who, as one critic wrote rather bluntly, 'look like squat toads' by association – they are, after all, familiar Victorian prostitutes, complete with 'too much bosom bulging from their too-tight bodices', too much hair 'spilling' around their faces, and too much face powder covering their 'over-bright' cheeks (Williams, 2011: 64). This observation mimics one that Faber makes in his novel as he describes a 'trio of unattached women' who approach William with 'too much of everything' - 'too many teeth', 'too much hair', 'too-elaborate bonnets', 'too much powder', and 'too many bows' (Faber, 2014: 94). Echoing the way in which Faber set Sugar apart from her co-workers – by creating a world where most of the other women in the narrative are somehow 'less beautiful' than her and seem 'sour-faced, commonplace, and surplus to requirements'; as if Sugar is the only woman in her world worthy of acquainting yourself with (Faber, 2014: 104).

Make-up and hair designer Jacqueline Fowler (2012) stressed her desire to capture the true spirit of Faber's Sugar – 'I wanted her to stand out […] I broke a lot of rules [regarding a leading lady]', expressing her intentions to 'play' on the flaws that her job usually insists she covers up; Fowler achieved this by limiting Sugar's make-up and including her skin condition, which was something they had to fight for. In addition to this, Sugar is also the only character with her trademark red hair and Fowler (2012) made sure that it was 'just [Sugar's]' colour; drawing directly upon Faber's text, in which he vividly describes her distinctive 'flame-red' hair, to find the perfect shade and make her unique within her world (Faber, 2014: 98). There can be little doubt that Sugar is a distinctive character – both onscreen and in print – and, as Faber (2014: 98) suggested when he introduced Sugar to William for the first time, there is a prevailing feeling that she brings with her a 'whiff of fresh air'.

Apart from being used as an individualizing technique, Sugar's hair is also employed as an externalizing tool – much like the production's use of colour – and it develops alongside her character and the story's narrative advancements. Initially, her hair is dressed in a more 'innocent' style which shows an awareness of fashion but also a desire to be individual and playful (Fowler, 2012). Then, as Sugar begins to mix with the upper-classes she is given ringlets, with her hair parted over to the side – like her hair, she is becoming 'more decadent' both socially and emotionally (Fowler, 2012). Before, finally, Sugar becomes a governess and cuts her hair into a professional-looking fringe – this is the concluding look which then starts to 'breakdown' as time goes on and her inner weariness grows (Fowler, 2012).

Fowler (2012), like her colleagues, also cites art as an influence on her designs for the series – particularly highlighting the 'grotesque' aspects of Otto Dix's paintings as something she tried to infuse into 'Victorian life'. She did this, in part, by playing with the images of various prostitutes who can be seen loitering in the background with smeared lipstick, heavy makeup, and prominent beauty spots and by recreating the Mrs Castaway of Faber's novel. In the text, William

Rackham notes that Mrs Castaway is 'decked out entirely' in scarlet, save from a 'dissenting' veil of dusty pink, her red lipstick 'tainting' the 'hundred tiny wrinkles' that frame her mouth to transform her lips into 'furry red caterpillars' – this leads William to consider the sanity of the woman who would seem like a 'mad old witch' were it not for her obvious self-possession (Faber, 2014: 110). Fowler captures her perfectly and these visually grotesque characters' recall paintings such as *Brothel Mother, Lady with Mink and Veil, Salon,* and *Leonie* – all by Otto Dix.

Make-up and hair are just two of the many examples that demonstrate the complexity of the relationship between internal vision and interpersonal visuals – wherein the feeling behind Faber's words are translated into a series of visual cues and codes. For example, visual coding was also employed by the costume department and, as clothes are an important part of Sugar's trade, it is especially appropriate that they should be fundamental in underpinning her character in the series. Again, to set her apart as distinctive within her realm, Sugar is given an 'extraordinary', 'vibrant' silhouette; and the motif of Sugar as an angel – a reference to Agnes mistaking her for an angel – is literally stitched onto her clothing: the wings can be seen on the back of her jacket throughout both the opening and closing scenes, while the wings on the buttons, while not seen by the viewer, demonstrate the thoughtfulness and consideration behind the idea (Garai, 2011). And so, we come to understand that, as with make-up and hair, costume is used extensively to reinforce Sugar's psychological state; this includes the weariness she feels by the end of her story. To achieve this, the costume department decided to convey Sugar's disillusioned emotions and feelings of confinement by employing a high collar and a sizable bow – this gives the impression that Sugar's own clothes are strangling her. This is both a powerful metaphor and a subtle visualization of a vital development that Faber's character experiences. It ultimately demonstrates how the creators of the BBC's adaptation could convey details that, while nowhere near as numerate as those found within the novel, gave viewers the visual information they needed to understand and appreciate the journey that Faber sent his readers on.

Hence, revealing how the novel's adapters managed to capture the ever-elusive 'spirit' of Faber's work.

Finally, in terms of physicality or corporeality, while an adaptation may make Faber's world seem more 'real', the process of adaptation can also have the opposite effect – if art 'draws from life', then art adapting art must be one step further away from what is 'real'; after all, any adapted piece is a representation of a representation (Elliot, 2003: 162).

Conclusion

From all of this, we not only come to understand how Faber's original vision has been developed by a host of creative collaborators into a tangible, real-life vision; we understand that an adaptation is far from being a simple transposition of a novel. Instead, it draws upon a range of pretexts and outside influences that interact unpredictably throughout the creative process to form a representation of the novel. While we acknowledge that the novel is the source, it is not necessarily the primary or ultimate custodian of found meaning, making the fidelity argument futile. Although such examinations should not be rashly or thoughtlessly dismissed, not when a notable proportion of viewing audiences still find adaptations so difficult and/or divisive. Due to time and structuring constraints, editing and the highlighting of specific themes and characteristics became a way for the adapters to ensure that their knowing viewers recognized a familiar source material. While visual coding – relating to space, camerawork, and colour – allowed the creative team to convey vital information in a subtle and unforced way. Ultimately, we are left with two versions of the same story, one textual and one visual; thus, we experience a form of double vision that transcends the boundaries of medium. We can see and interact with two forms of the same narrative, something which should not cause widespread division or concern; after all, both parts share a message and a set of key principles. In this way, Faber's text and the BBC's resulting adaptation are two sides of the same coin, and they should be treated as such.

Adaptation is a vital part of an ever-thriving industry and it shows no signs of giving way – therefore, as both knowing and unknowing audiences, we need to move past our hang-ups and embrace the creative double visions that they offer. Moreover, we should turn our critical attention more pointedly towards explorations of narrative strategy, the roles of creators, and the positive transference of creative energy from one medium to another. For it is there that we will discover more about our appetites for storytelling and the ways in which we tell, and retell, our greatest stories.

Works Cited

Anderson, Hephzibah (2002) 'Hold on to your bustles – *The Crimson Petal and the White*', *Guardian*, URL (consulted January 2017): https://www.theguardian.com/books/2002/sep/29/fiction

Aragay, Mireia (2005) *Books in Motion: Adaptation, Intertextuality, Authorship*. Amsterdam: Rodopi.

Beanie Luck (2011) 'Substantial Entertainment, but more suited to film adaptation', *Amazon.co.uk*, URL (consulted May 2016): https://www.amazon.co.uk/gp/customer-reviews/R3JW4QDGGSZ8F4/ref=cm_cr_arp_d_rvw_ttl?ie=UTF8&ASIN=B004P9MVG8

Bluestone, George (1957) *Novels into Film*. Baltimore, MD: John Hopkins University Press.

Brandt, F (2015) 'Two stars', *Amazon.co.uk*, URL (consulted May 2016): https://www.amazon.co.uk/gp/customer-reviews/R1GAQBG3R911IK/ref=cm_cr_getr_d_rvw_ttl?ie=UTF8&ASIN=B004P9MVG8

Chatterforth, Ralph (2011) 'Dark and Gripping', *Amazon.co.uk*, URL (consulted May 2016): https://www.amazon.co.uk/customer-reviews/R37NJA26FWD3EA/ref=cm_cr_getr_d_rvw_ttl?ie=UTF8&ASIN=B004P9MVG8

Chowney, D.J. (2011) 'Very good, but the book is better and fills in gaps!', *Amazon.co.uk*, URL (consulted May 2016): https://www.amazon.co.uk/gp/customer-reviews/R1AC9RNOOBDUOZ/ref=cm_cr_arp_d_rvw_ttl?ie=UTF8&ASIN=B004P9MVG8

De Zwaan, Victoria (2016) 'Experimental fiction, film adaptation, and the case of Midnight's Children: in defense of fidelity', *Literature-Film Quarterly* 43(4): 246–62.

Deacon, Michael (2011) 'The Crimson Petal and the White: a Victorian horror story too big for the small screen', *The Telegraph*, URL (consulted

July 2016): http://www.telegraph.co.uk/culture/tvandradio/8432885/The-Crimson-Petal-and-the-White-a-Victorian-horror-story-too-big-for-the-small-screen-review.html

Donaldson-McHugh, S. and Moore, D. (2006) 'Film Adaptation, Co-Authorship, and Hauntology: Gus Van Sant's Psycho (1998)', *Journal of Popular Culture*, 39(2): 225–33.

Duguid, Mark (2014) 'Literary Adaptation: British cinema's lifelong love affair with literature', *BFI Screen Online*, URL (consulted October 2016): http://www.screenonline.org.uk/film/id/444951/

Edwards, Paul (2007) 'Adaptation: Two Theories', *Text and Performance Quarterly* 27(4): 369–77.

Elliott, Kamilla (2003) *Rethinking the Novel/Film Debate*. Cambridge: Cambridge University Press.

Faber, Michel (2014) *The Crimson Petal and the White*. Edinburgh: Canongate Books.

Fowler, Jacqueline (2012) 'Jacqueline Fowler: Make-Up & Hair Design Mini Masterclass' *YouTube*, URL (consulted May 2016): https://youtu.be/wv8YlnkFNvk

Garai, Romola (2011) 'The Crimson Petal and the White: Romola Garai' *BBC Press Room*, URL (consulted May 2016): http://www.bbc.co.uk/pressoffice/pressreleases/stories/2011/03_march/14/crimson3.shtml

Hale, Mike (2012) 'Victorian London, Hypocrisy and Filth Included - The Crimson Petal and the White', *The New York Times*, 9 September, URL (consulted June 2016): http://www.nytimes.com/2012/09/10/arts/television/the-crimson-petal-and-the-white-encore-mini-series.html

Harold, James (2018) 'The Value of Fidelity in Adaptation', *The British Journal of Aesthetics*, 58(1): 89–100.

Hughes, Kathryn (2002) 'Whores, porn and lunatics: The Crimson Petal and the White', *Guardian*, 28 September, URL (consulted June 2016): https://www.theguardian.com/books/2002/sep/28/fiction

Jones, P.A. (2011) 'Wonderful', *Amazon.co.uk*, URL (consulted May 2016): https://www.amazon.co.uk/gp/customer-reviews/R2BG4KC9GMGOPU/ref=cm_cr_getr_d_rvw_ttl?ie=UTF8&ASIN=B004P9M-VG8

Kate (2012) 'Great if you haven't read the book!', *Amazon.co.uk*, URL (consulted May 2016): https://www.amazon.co.uk/gp/customer-reviews/R1UI8XB33VBWCH/ref=cm_cr_arp_d_rvw_ttl?ie=UTF8&ASIN=B-004P9MVG8

Kindle Customer (2013) 'Absolutely Superb', *Amazon.co.uk*, URL (consulted May 2016): https://www.amazon.co.uk/gp/customer-reviews/RO8C5N5MPUJ4B/ref=cm_cr_getr_d_rvw_ttl?ie=UTF8&ASIN=B-004P9MVG8

Leitch, Thomas (2003) 'Twelve Fallacies in Contemporary Adaptation Theory', *Criticism* 45(2): 149-71.

Lipman, Maureen (2011) 'The Review Show – 01/04/2011', *BBC Two*, URL (consulted May 2016): http://www.bbc.co.uk/programmes/b0101pt1

Louttit, C (2013) 'Remixing Period Drama: The Fan Video and the Classic Novel Adaptation', *Adaptation: The Journal of Literature On Screen Studies* 6(1): 172–86.

Luddite Writer (2014) 'A very good read', *Amazon.co.uk*, URL (consulted May 2016): https://www.amazon.co.uk/gp/customer-reviews/R384M6LP7HXDN8/ref=cm_cr_arp_d_rvw_ttl?ie=UTF8&ASIN=1782114416

Montgomery, G. (2012) 'Art-Inspired Set Design: A Talk by Grant Montgomery' *YouTube*, URL (consulted May 2016): https://youtu.be/IUIs_OglG40

Montgomery, Hugh (2011a) 'You've no idea how much we liked watching', *The Independent on Sunday*, 18 December, URL (consulted May 2016): https://www.independent.co.uk/arts-entertainment/tv/features/arts-review-of-2011-television-youve-no-idea-how-much-we-liked-watching-6278589.html

Montgomery, Hugh (2011b) 'Filth, Victorian sex, and a loser for a hero: bring it on!', *Independent on Sunday*, 10 April, URL (consulted March 2017): https://www.independent.co.uk/arts-entertainment/tv/reviews/the-crimson-petal-and-the-white-bbc2-wednesdaycampus-channel-4-tuesday-2265613.html

Munden, Marc (2011) *The Crimson Petal and the White*. Fremantle Home Entertainment.

Murray, Simone (2008) 'Materializing adaptation theory: the adaptation industry', *Literature-Film Quarterly* 36(1): 4–20.

Oxford Dictionary (2017a) 'fidelity', *Oxford Dictionaries*, URL (consulted May 2016): https://en.oxforddictionaries.com/definition/fidelity

Oxford Dictionary (2017b) 'adaptation', Oxford Dictionaries, URL (consulted August 2016): https://en.oxforddictionaries.com/definition/adaptation

Raitt, George (2010) 'Still Lusting After Fidelity?', *Literature Film Quarterly* 38(1): 47–58.

Ramsey-Hardy, S. (2012) 'What a shame', *Amazon.co.uk*, URL (consulted May 2016): https://www.amazon.co.uk/gp/customer-reviews/R2QVEXUG1PSTGV/ref=cm_cr_getr_d_rvw_ttl?ie=UTF8&ASIN=B004P9MVG8

Ray, Robert B (2000) 'The Field of 'Literature and Film', in James Naremore (ed.) *Film Adaptation*, pp. 38–53. London: Athlone.

Romney, Jonathan (2011) 'Never mind the bonnets - let's remix the classics', *The Independent on Sunday*, 13 November, URL (consulted March 2017): https://www.independent.co.uk/arts-entertainment/films/features/never-mind-the-bonnets-lets-remix-the-classics-6261267.html

Rizzo, S (2008) '(In)fidelity Criticism and the Sexual Politics of "Adaptation"', *Literature Film Quarterly* 36(4), URL (consulted May 2016): https://www.jstor.org/stable/43797495

Semenza, Greg Colon (2013) 'Radical reflexivity in cinematic adaptation: second thoughts on reality, originality, and authority', *Literature- Film Quarterly* 41(2) 143–53, URL (consulted May 2016): https://www.jstor.org/stable/43798943

Sheppard, Joanne (2011) 'Darkly brilliant Victoriana', *Amazon.co.uk*, URL (consulted May 2016): https://www.amazon.co.uk/gp/customer-reviews/R1N7TXTDO4DBSD/ref=cm_cr_getr_d_rvw_ttl?ie=UTF8&ASIN=1782114416

Snow (2013) 'Well done, Petal!', *Amazon.co.uk*, URL (consulted May 2016): https://www.amazon.co.uk/gp/customer-reviews/R38N7OA762PG6Y/ref=cm_cr_arp_d_rvw_ttl?ie=UTF8&ASIN=1782114416

Sutcliffe, Tom (2011) 'Last Night's TV: A thrilling trip to the underworld', *Independent*, 7 April, URL (consulted March 2017): https://www.independent.co.uk/arts-entertainment/tv/reviews/last-nights-tv-the-crimson-petal-and-the-whitebbc2vacation-vacation-vacationchannel-4-2264384.html

Taylor, G (2014) 'Empirical Middleton: Macbeth, Adaptation, and Microauthorship', Shakespeare Quarterly 65(3), URL (consulted May 2016): https://muse.jhu.edu

Veronika (2013) 'Amazing Acting', *Amazon.co.uk*, URL (consulted May 2016): https://www.amazon.co.uk/gp/customer-reviews/R3UZI1T92KHW6P/ref=cm_cr_arp_d_rvw_ttl?ie=UTF8&ASIN=B-004P9MVG8

Williams, Sally (2011) 'Sugar and Spice: the dark side of Victorian London', *Telegraph*, 7 March, URL (consulted January 2017): http://www.telegraph.co.uk/culture/tvandradio/8359166/Sugar-and-Spice-the-darkside-of-Victorian-London.html

Wilson, Benji (2011) 'The Crimson Petal and the White, final episode, review', *Telegraph*, URL (consulted May 2016): http://www.telegraph.co.uk/culture/tvandradio/8477652/The-Crimson-Petal-and-the-White-final-episode-review.html

CHAPTER 10

'BRANCHES OF GOTHIC COMPLICATION'
READING THE GOTHIC IN MICHEL FABER'S *THE CRIMSON PETAL AND THE WHITE*

Matt Foley

In the months before attending the 'Defying Genre' symposium at UHI, I taught two of Michel Faber's texts at University of Stirling. *The Crimson Petal and the White* (2002) was set on a Masters module on Stirling's MLitt in *The Gothic Imagination*; while *Under the Skin* (2000) had been critiqued in seminars by third-year undergraduate students.[1] In this chapter, I explore some of the questions raised by postgraduate students regarding the gothic credentials of *Crimson Petal*. These gothic elements, I argue, are often most visible in Faber's handling of space.[2] Somewhat provocatively, I asked postgraduate students in their spring 2016 seminar to consider if Faber's novel is 'quintessentially' gothic. As I had anticipated, their responses almost universally resisted the totality of perspective and intellectual ease implied by this statement.[3] Inspired by two years of teaching, in what follows I read *Crimson Petal*'s visceral gothic turns alongside its invocations of the terror gothic tradition to demonstrate that the 'branches of Gothic complication' (Faber, 2002/2011: 265) that intertwine throughout the novel form a gothic spectrum. One that encompasses a series of what I term resistance fantasies, gendered entrapments and systemic oppressions staged in the text. In so doing, my argument provides a sustained reading of *Crimson Petal*'s gothic iconography – which is yet to be undertaken by scholars – that finds its methodological novelty by drawing from classroom debate. My analysis takes on a tripartite structure. It begins by highlighting the teaching context and, more specifically, the ways in which student responses reworked existing scholarly criticism on Faber's novel. I then proceed with a close reading of the form and function of Sugar's gothic writings, one that culminates in my argument that Faber's handling of the gothic in *Crimson Petal* may be understood as forming a particular spectrum of representation. The urban decay, street hauntings, entombed domestic spaces, and grotesqueries that characterize the story's settings form the backdrop to its postmodern interrogations of both horror writing and the female gothic.

As Jacques Derrida has noted in his address 'The Law of Genre' (originally given in 1979, published in 1980), '[a]s soon as the word "genre" is sounded, as soon as it is heard, as soon as one attempts to conceive it, a limit is drawn' (Derrida, 1980: 56). Yet, such limitations are not absolute boundaries. In the gothic, for instance, inter-generic transgressions abound, even if Derrida himself resists employing a language of lawlessness in his conceptualization of genre:

> Every text participates in one or several genres, there is no genreless text; there is always a genre and genres, yet such participation never amounts to belonging. And not because of an abundant overflowing or a free, anarchic, and unclassifiable productivity, but because of the trait of participation itself. (Derrida, 1980: 65)

In other words, the demarcations arrived at through genre-analysis are always already traced by a resistance to classification – or 'belonging' – that the critic inevitably encounters, and hopefully registers, in any close reading of a literary text. At a fundamental level, any genre is a construct – an imperfect model – that both artists and scholars draw from and contribute to through appropriation (the artist) or detailed interrogation (the critic). At the end of his 'The Law of Genre', Derrida further argues that the space and place in which genre is being defined shapes both its parameters and the trajectories of the readings that are borne out of it: 'Elsewhere—in accordance with other subjects, other colloquia and lectures... other trajectories could have, and have, come to light' (Derrida, 1980: 80). As my understanding of the form and function of the gothic in *Crimson Petal* has arisen out of close study *and* teaching, the seminar room should not be an 'elsewhere' that is overlooked – or even hidden – in the course of making my argument.

The teaching context

The act of reading to which the title of this chapter refers, then, evolved from my teaching of Faber's novel. The students encountered *Crimson Petal* on a module entitled 'Twenty-First-Century Gothic', which was described to them in the 2017 module handbook as providing:

> an introduction to so-called 'Millennial Gothic', or the proliferation of Gothic forms, texts and modes in contemporary British, American, and Global culture since 2000. In seminars and written work, students will be expected to draw from the analytical skills that they have developed throughout the MLitt so far and bring fresh and decisive readings to these twenty-first-century texts. Discussions will be student-led.

Special care needs to be taken with the sense promoted by the module descriptor that students should provide 'fresh and decisive' readings of the primary texts under study. A 'fresh' reading is exactly the approach that Masters' students – particularly those in the final throes of the taught modules of an MLitt – should endeavour to undertake as they demonstrate how their arguments reshape established criticism. The particular connotations of 'decisive' are more slippery, however, than they may intuitively seem. *Crimson Petal*'s postmodern turns are clear in its open ending, the self-awareness of the narrative voice that guides the reader through the story's labyrinthine urban geographies, and, as I elaborate upon below, its parody of gothic narrative form: the female gothic in particular.[4] In other words, *Crimson Petal* is playful and often resistant to closed interpretations, to the extent that it draws attention to acts of misreading throughout its narrative. In this context, the injunction that students should write decisively about Faber's novel is always already traced by the need to acknowledge the text's ludic and complex attitude to artifice itself.

Suggestive of the complication of genre achieved by Faber's writing, in their Masters' seminars students were divided as to the merits of demarcating his novel as a gothic text – this is in spite of critical claims that the genre to which *Crimson Petal* could most clearly be ascribed, the neo-Victorian novel, is itself quintessentially gothic (Kohlke and Gutleben, 2012). Another critical reading of the novel has suggested that it 'draws' sincerely 'from the remarkable woman-powered gothic of the nineteenth century' (Snodgrass, 2011: 111). The critical reception of *Crimson Petal* is notable, then, for the ease with which scholars categorize it. After a broad-ranging discussion of neo-Victorian fiction, in our seminar I asked students to write short responses to the intentionally provocative question: is *Crimson Petal and the White* 'quintessentially' gothic? The students were sceptical. The written response of S1, for instance, reflects some of the paradoxical conclusions that we had earlier drawn from our discussion of *Crimson Petal*, a text, this student argues, which is not 'strictly gothic... but does have numerous gothic elements' (S1, seminar response). Another member of the cohort was equally torn over the fittingness of the appellation 'gothic' to describe the novel's over-arching genre: 'there is an argument in support of defining Faber's novel as gothic, but the question of it being "quintessentially" gothic is debatable' (S4, seminar response). As the title of this collection suggests, Faber's corpus often defies generic categorization – its textual forms throw into relief, from a Derridean perspective, the central paradoxes of genre. In this light, the students' detailed deliberations over *Crimson Petal*'s gothic credentials could be regarded as intuitive responses to the work of an artist who gains much of his originality of voice from creating fiction that seldom relies upon those patterning narratives that immediately distinguish genre fiction.

The novel's staging of recognizably gothic motifs or iconography, I argue, is more nuanced than has thus far been recognized by those scholars who conflate the neo-Victorian with the gothic, or who too easily pigeonhole *Crimson Petal* as a female gothic, or even gothic feminist, novel. One student response was also strongly opposed to such readings. The neo-Victorian re-imagining of the nineteenth century, they suggested, is 'no more inherently gothic than any other age'. *Crimson Petal* could even be accused of being 'pseudo-feminist without being at all radical or transgressive' and 'itself a bourgeoisie imagining of [the] Victorian tableaux' (S5, student response). If less provocative, other student responses, too, suggest the possibility of more complex explorations of the form and function of the gothic in Faber's novel than has hitherto been achieved. Our discussions drew attention, for instance, to an under-appreciated aesthetic of the 'grotesque' (S3, student response) in the novel's descriptions – in particular – of naked, male corporeality. With some input from my teaching notes, important intertexts for *Crimson Petal* were identified as Matthew Gregory Lewis' *The Monk* (1796),[5] Charlotte Brontë's *Jane Eyre* (1847) and Daphne Du Maurier's *Rebecca* (1938) (S3, student response).[6]

Inflecting some of our contributions to the 2016/7 seminar were conversations with a student – Ann Bradley – who graduated from the previous Gothic MLitt cohort (2015/16). Its initial premises emerging from seminar discussions, Bradley's essay for that year's iteration of 'Twenty-First-Century Gothic' was entitled 'Textuality and the Female Quixote in *The Crimson Petal and the White*' and its argument posited that Sugar – Faber's protagonist – was a darkly imagined Quixote.[7] An erudite reader of visceral or cautionary tales of violence against women, Sugar constructs her own imaginary world that is intimately tied to her reading habits. As I elaborate upon below, I agree that such dark fantasies, for Sugar, present a means of transcending her gendered entrapment, however briefly. Taking as her starting point Mark Llewellyn's reading of 'the slippage between' the texts that Sugar and Agnes Rackham, respectively, produce so that 'their exchangeability at this moment becomes symbolic of the futility of female writing' (Llewellyn, 2012: 195), Bradley's argument draws parallels between the quixotic tendencies of William's wife and his mistress. She argues that both characters, ultimately, are 'left to realize the deficit of fiction in conquering real problems' (Bradley, 2016:

8). Reading the act of writing in *Crimson Petal* as 'futile', as Llewellyn does, is perhaps an overstatement. Bradley's essay, I think, suggests an important nuance: if there is a deficit between art and social change in Faber's novel then, at least, art's worth for Sugar may still be calculable. Overall, student responses to the text had not only complicated existing critical work on *Crimson Petal* by adding several nuances that were teased out in discussions in class. As in Bradley's assignment, they had also presented fresh avenues of analysis that demonstrably enriched the relatively small body of critical writing on the text.

Sugar's revengeful resistance fantasies

In *Crimson Petal*, I would suggest that Sugar's novel – which she tentatively entitles *The Rise and Fall of Sugar* – can be read as a particularly gothic flight of fancy; albeit, one that fails to enact the kind of social change evident in her later flight from William with his daughter Sophie. Indeed, her visceral and pornographic stories seem to be sublimations of her traumatic experiences under the care of Mrs Castaway. Even amongst the most squalled and exploitative of conditions, her literary 'flights of Gothic cruelty' provide a medium through which Sugar may pleasurably imagine herself as a subject with absolute agency. Yet, as the deficit of fiction comes into focus, her appetite for penning revengeful writing becomes less voracious. At one point she even hesitates when deciding the fate of her protagonist's prey, as Faber's narrator recounts:

> A long succession of other men, earlier on in her manuscript, have inspired her to flights of Gothic cruelty; dispatching them to their grisly fate has always been sheer pleasure. Tonight, with this latest victim, she can't summon what's needed – that vicious spark – to set her prose alight. Faced with the challenge of spilling his blood, she hears an alien voice of temptation inside her: *Oh, for God's sakes, let the poor fool live.*
>
> *You're going soft*, she chides herself. *Come on, shove it in, deep into his throat, into his arse, into his guts, up to the hilt.* (Faber, 2011: 228, emphasis in original)

In the opening to this passage, Sugar recalls the many sadistic mutilations that she has penned, where each new baroque attack upon masculinity had, at least momentarily, strengthened her sense of self. Read from this perspective, Sugar's early imaginings in the novel are resistance fantasies: violent imaginings that help sustain her sense of self among the social deprivation and exploitation she faces.[8] These new hesitations, however, arise at a time at which Sugar, somewhat paradoxically, posits a certain futility to such literary rebellion:

> Her heroines takes revenge on the men she hates; yet the world remains in the hands of men, and such revenge cannot be tolerated. Her story's ending, therefore, is one of the few things Sugar has planned in advance, and it's death for the heroine. (Faber, 2002/2011: 229)

This anticipation of a death providing narrative closure – far removed from the sanitizing 'Romance' frames of the female gothic – is also symbolic of the end of Sugar's taste for literary juvenilia. Llewellyn argues, too, that,

> the 'dagger' represents both the seized penis and the seized pen, the tools of penetration and authorship combined in a supposed act of liberation for the female prostitute, except, of course, that it remains the case that Sugar's body is the one written upon. (Lleywellyn, 2012: 193)

There is a deficit, then, between the imagined agency of the protagonist of these stories and the restrictive and gendered socio-economic position that Sugar finds herself contained by. The gothic elements of Sugar's novel – her obscene fantasies of transgression – suggest, at the very least, that the patriarchal and systemic violence that marginalizes her finds its visual correlate in bloody fantasies of escape from it.

As both a reader and a writer of horrific fictions, her admiration for William Shakespeare's (and perhaps George Peele's) play of rape, mutilation and cannibalism *Titus Andronicus* is emblematic of the pleasure she takes in imagining pain.[9] Not a history, Shakespeare's early play is his goriest contribution to the genre of Elizabethan (later Jacobean) revenge tragedy. The ethics that guide the antagonists throughout the genre of the revenge tragedy are purely retributive:

'an eye for an eye and a tooth for a tooth' (5.38).[10] Faber's narrator notes, at first, that William and Sugar share a mutual interest in the Bard. At The Fireside Tavern 'they talk on and on, about Truth and Beauty, and the works of Shakespeare' (Faber, 2002/2011: 103). William is entirely ignorant of the play, which suggests, perhaps, that Sugar's sense of 'Truth and Beauty' is more brutally corporeal than her patron's who, at this stage in the narrative, disguises his identity under the moniker George W. Hunt. William, albeit condescendingly, praises Sugar's breadth of reading, if only for their tastes to evidently diverge once more when Sugar lavishes praise upon James Thomson's recently published *The City of Dreadful Night* (1874). After she recites some of Thomson's ghastly lines, which are infused with dread and awe, William comments: 'Grim poetry ... for such a beautiful young woman to have as a special favourite' (Faber, 2002/2011: 103). Importantly, it is the gothic novel of the late-eighteenth century that sets the pattern for these unrefined tastes. Later in the narrative, when she compares her upbringing with Sophie Rackham's, a memory provides a brief glimpse of the depravation in which young Sugar, at only six years-old, would sit 'next to her mother's skirts on a stool, her left foot bandaged after a rat bite, studying a ragged copy of a viciously gruesome Gothic novel called *The Monk*' (Faber, 2002/2011: 456-7). Horror gothic may be represented, here, as mere juvenilia but it is formative to Sugar's imagination.

Representing a change in register away from Faber's interrogation of horror towards a more parodic staging of the female gothic, Sugar's literary tastes have evidently changed when later, as a governess, she encounters Shakespeare's play in his collected works:

> She flips through the pages, searching for *Titus Andronicus*, which she used to think was unjustly underestimated – in fact, she recalls defending its gory frenzy for the benefit of a certain George W. Hunt when she first met him in The Fireside. Having found *Titus* now, she can't make head nor tail of it; she must have been mad. (Faber, 2002/2011: 695, emphasis in original)

This disavowal of *Titus* by Sugar suggests that her tastes have matured. Yet, *The Rise and Fall of Sugar* remains emblematic of her subjectivity from one important perspective. Upon finally discovering her writings after Sugar had fled from him with Sophie, William (mis)reads Sugar's identity as still inextricably tied to her pornographic and violent resistance fantasies. Sugar's writing is so abjectly sickening that his 'hairy belly churns in horror' until he can read no more. William soon recalls the hint Sugar gave to her transgressive tastes at The Fireside:

> Glowing in his mind is a vision of Sugar as she was when they first met, a gently smiling advocate of the bloodiest revenges. '*Titus Andronicus*, now *there's* a play,' she cooed to him across the table in The Fireside, and he failed to hear the warning bell. (Faber, 2002/2011: 819–20, emphasis in original)

This misreading of Sugar's writing by William is twofold in nature. Firstly, William erroneously ascribes her prose of another time and space as being a marker of Sugar's current identity – that she left her papers *behind* in fleeing him is unacknowledged.[11] Secondly, William's grandiose sense of self reimagines Sugar's pragmatic escape from patriarchy as a bloody and murderous violence against the sovereignty of his male dominance; one that is comparable to the sadistic murders that litter Sugar's novel. Even amidst its postmodern playfulness, the truth to which *Crimson Petal*'s sustained interrogation of reading and writing horror fiction points is once more the deficit between art and reality. The excesses of Sugar's novel are rendered in a purely phantasmatic register when compared to her mature and *pragmatic* escape from William with Sophie.[12] As a moneyed and male beneficiary of the systemic violence against women, however, William registers the claiming of agency by those whom he has marginalized as a form of bloody subjective violence against him. That is, he imagines that he is a victim of excessive violence rather than an example of privileged masculinity who has been dealt ethical justice.[13] Such horrors, in this guise, sustain systemic oppression through their baroque artifice as the lure of interpersonal conflict distracts from – rather than becomes exemplary of – the socio-political injustices that are elsewhere critiqued by Faber's novel. They are, though, not the only examples of the gothic narrative structures and iconography at play in *Crimson Petal*.

The gothic spectrum

As Fred Botting (2013: 12) has noted, 'since the eighteenth century the development of gothic fictions has involved similarly inter-generic patterns, adding a darker aspect to more acceptable literary forms'. In light of the above analysis, reading *Crimson Petal*'s staging of gothic iconography and concerns as part of an 'inter-generic' pollination is more convincing than straightforwardly fusing the neo-Victorian with the gothic. The latter is a position taken, as I mention above, by Kohlke and Gutleben (2012: 4, emphasis in original): '*neo-Victorianism is by nature quintessentially Gothic,*' they argue, 'resurrecting the ghost(s) of the past, searching out its dark and shameful mysteries, insisting obsessively on the lurid details of Victorian life, reliving the period's nightmares and traumas'. Forming part of its inter-generic borrowings, the historico-gothic novel accentuates and brings to the point of excess some of the quintessential elements of neo-Victorian fiction. As Silvana Colella has convincingly argued, one of the most powerful neo-Victorian techniques for rendering historical place is a sustained and often unsettling employment of olfactory metaphor. Reading *Crimson Petal*'s atmosphere of 'sour spirits and slowly dissolving dung' as exemplary of this grotesque, sensorial register (Faber, 2002/2011: 4), Colella argues that Faber 'addresses a contemporary readership immersed in an atmosphere of olfactory "silence"'. In light of Fredric Jameson's understanding of the 'image fixation' of postmodernism, Colella asks: 'does the odour fixation of Faber's narrative cut through the nostalgic patina of pseudo-historicism?' (Colella, 2010: 87).[14] Certainly, *Crimson Petal* resists nostalgia, but its postmodern turns also undercut any moral certainty. The narrative may show Sugar's escape and suggest her ascendency thereafter but its ending is, ultimately, an 'abrupt parting' that emphasizes pleasure over social change: 'I hope I satisfied all your desires,' the narrator teases, 'or at least showed you a good time' (Faber, 2002/2011: 835).

Indeed, reading *Crimson Petal* in this way encourages comparisons with another historio-gothic fiction that is preoccupied by scent: *Perfume* (1985) by Patrick Süskind. In Süskind's novel, the antagonist Grenouille's olfactory gift is compared to that of the musical prodigy or 'wunderkind', with the narrator emphasizing that 'the alphabet of odours' is 'incomparably larger and more nuanced' than any musical scale (Süskind, 1985/2015: 27–8). This metaphor of the (potentially sublime) olfactory spectrum bears an uncanny resemblance to a scene in *Crimson Petal* in which William tells his brother Henry Rackham that '[s]cents, like sounds … stroke our olfactory nerve in exquisite and exact degrees. There's an octave of odours like an octave in music' (Faber, 2002/2011: 189). In turn, William is implicitly aligned with one of the most malignant of the modern gothic's pantheon of deviants: Grenouille. The violence William represents, however, is systemic and it is conveyed more subtly through allusion to the female gothic. An emblem of their enterprise, the Rackhams's products and property are uniformly emblazoned with the letter 'R'. Intertextually, this signifier – which takes on the ominous surpluses of the matheme – recalls the insignia of the deceased Rebecca de Winter that so haunts the nameless narrator of Daphne Du Maurier's *Rebecca*. Thus, the visceral violence of Grenouille is substituted for a symbol of entrapment familiar to the female gothic, particularly the strand of the genre that relies upon Charles Perrault's *Blue Beard* (1697) as a patterning narrative.

Süskind's metaphor of a spectrum or scale is useful when conceptualizing the many notes to, or manifestations of, the gothic aesthetic as it is put to work throughout *Crimson Petal*. The parody of the gothic that Faber provides oscillates between sincerity and grotesque humour. With some sincerity, familiar gothic scenarios in the novel clearly foreshadow future oppressions. In the following section, William guides Sugar towards her new home as his mistress:

> At the end of the journey, [Sugar] is made to alight in a dark close, a very modern-looking terrace whose façades are all identical. Inadequate lamp-light is intercepted by a pair of massive stately trees, each with branches of Gothic complication. As the cab rattles away

into the distance, a cemetery quiet descends, and Sugar is led by the arm into the pitch-black porch of one of these strange new buildings.

William Rackham is at her side, an obscure figure in the darkness; she can hear his breathing and the rustle of her skirts as he brushes against them in his search for the key-hole... she sees William's face illuminated in the lucifer's flicker as he bends to unlock the door. His bewhiskered features are utterly unfamiliar to her. (Faber, 2002/2011: 265)

The 'branches of Gothic complication' that frame this route to Sugar's new abode foreshadow the – sometimes ironic – turning to the pantheon of the female gothic aesthetic that the novel moves on to undertake. The chiaroscuro lighting of the scene outside these 'strange new buildings', as William takes on an uncanny appearance with his face lit by the 'lucifer's flicker' of the keyhole, further indicates the danger of the pact that Sugar has made with him.[15] Thus, if an aesthetics of horror provides the novel's characters with a series of resistance fantasies that sustain their identity, then the terror gothic has a more formal and structural influence. The parodic, self-reflective nature of Faber's invocation of this well-worked genre is conveyed through the dramatic irony produced by Agnes Rackham's dismissal of *Jane Eyre* as low-brow literature, at a time at which William is fashioning her as his own Bertha Rochester. On seeing her maid Clara's copy of Brontë's novel, Agnes thinks that 'there's something very wicked about a lady's-maid savouring this horrid tale of a wife driven mad by illness and shut up in a tower by her husband while he attempts to marry another woman' (Faber, 2002/2011: 440).

As students on the MLitt in *The Gothic Imagination* noted, a sincere rendering of the grotesque situates itself alongside these female gothic patterning narratives. At times, Faber's characters themselves seem almost universally grotesque. Even if she comes to be regarded as an angel by Agnes Rackham, when Sugar is first introduced amongst the 'gloom' of London she is registered as a queer and unsettling figure: 'stick-thin, flat-chested and bony like a consumptive young man' (Faber, 2002/2011: 26). Male corporeality seems almost universally abject. A particularly grotesque aesthetic is evident in the body hairs of Henry Rackham that 'lie plastered around his abdomen and thighs like Gothic designs' as his 'penis hangs gross and distended, like a reptile head, and his testicles writhe irritably as he washes them; nothing could bear less resemblance to the compressed, seashell smooth pudenda of classical statuary' (Faber, 2002/2011: 314). This gothicized and grotesque corporeality is mirrored in the novel's visions of urban London. Henry records desperate social cruelty as he enters, to him, the Hell of urbanity. Not only is the parlour of Mrs Castaway's whore house, as described by William, a 'grotesquerie' decorated by 'half-naked, half-clothed versions' of Mary Magdalene (Faber, 2002/2011: 111), but urbanity itself provides a gothic setting from Henry's perspective:

> Already he has seen a severed dog's head rotting in the gutter, its protruding tongue swollen with lice; ... he has seen a host of spectres staring out of broken windows, their eyes hollow, their sex indeterminate, their flesh scarcely less grey than the rags that clothe them. (Faber, 2002/2011: 210)

In this cityscape, both of the gothic's central registers – that is, horror (bloodied corporeality) and terror (the spectralizing of the poor) – connote poverty and systemic marginalization. The sincerity of these imaginings seem unquestionable and, as with Colella's reading of the olfactory registers of *Crimson Petal*, their abject nature (emphasized particularly by the decomposing head) would surely disrupt any readerly tendency towards nostalgia for – or sentimentalization of – the Victorian city. Thus, the notes of the gothic spectrum that Faber hits upon here suspend the parodic or postmodern attitude of the novel and throw into relief the sobering effects of poverty and systemic oppression. As millennial gothic, then, *Crimson Petal*'s rendering of terror and horror oscillates between sincerity and postmodern play. In pedagogical terms, *Crimson Petal*'s spectrum of gothic concerns and images invites a series of conversations in the seminar room regarding neo-Victorian gothic, gothic as a form of juvenilia, urban gothic, and the postmodern gothic. Most notably, the flights of 'Gothic cruelty' that characterize Sugar's fictional writings act as resistance fantasies that allow her to experience, however fleetingly, absolute agency through artifice. Facing a different type of marginalization later in the novel as a mistress and a governess, she matures in mind and outlook; yet, for the privileged William, Sugar will always be defined by her violent fancy. If Sugar's horror writing once acted as a phantasmatic screen that allowed her to claim 'Reader, I murdered him' and, in turn, strengthened her resolve against urban deprivation, then the invocations of the female gothic in Faber's text foreshadow her new, sanitized entrapment as William's mistress: a prison house from which she ultimately flees.

Notes

1 In the undergraduate class on *Under the Skin*, I encouraged students to consider the novel's protagonist Isserley as an 'abhuman' figure: an alien who resembles the humanoid but whose appearance is estranging, off-human, or even queer. For a full definition of the abhuman as it is understood in relation to fin de siècle gothic, see Kelly Hurley's seminal *The Gothic Body: Sexuality, Materialism, and Degeneration at the Fin de Siècle* (1996).

2 The gothic, of course, began as a much more neatly definable body of writing in the late-eighteenth and early-nineteenth centuries. The genre of the British gothic romance began with the publication of Horace Walpole's *The Castle of Otranto* (1764; the second edition of 1765 was subtitled 'A Gothic Story') and ended with Charles Maturin's *Melmoth the Wanderer* (1820). With less clear parameters, the Victorian gothic is said to engage with a broad range of themes: monstrosity, secrecy, transgression, paranoia, barbarism, modernity, the urban, doubling, the New Woman, taboo, abjection, and degeneration. Certainly, by the fin de siècle, the gothic becomes more innately tied to representations of claustrophobia and urbanity and its textual forms undergo a revival.

3 Six Masters' students provided their written responses informally and anonymously at the end of our seminar on Faber's novel. After collecting their open-ended and qualitative answers to the broader question posed, I coded each of their answers S1-S6, where the 'S' is merely short for 'Student'. My sincere thanks go to the MLitt students in *The Gothic Imagination* cohort at Stirling (2016/17) who provided this data.

4 When the 2015/16 students on *The Gothic Imagination* approached reading *The Crimson Petal and the White* they had most immediately read and

discussed Mark Z. Danielewski's *House of Leaves* (2000). A labyrinthine novel itself, we had made much of the ludic possibilities presented by the postmodern gothic through reading Danielewski's text. The postmodern credentials of *The Crimson Petal and the White* are much more subtly rendered than in Danielewski's purgatorial metafiction, but the students immediately noted the self-reflexivity of Faber's narrator, whose invitation into the dens of Victorian iniquity from the very start of the novel signal that we are encountering artifice rather than a text with claims to realism.

5 A typically horrid scene in Lewis's novel occurs when Ambrosio – the titular character who falls from public reverence into sin and depravity – murders Elvira, the mother of the object of Ambrosio's lust Antonia: 'The Monk took off the pillow, and gazed upon her. Her face was covered with a frightful blackness: Her limbs moved no more; The blood was chilled in her veins; Her heart had forgotten to beat, and her hands were stiff and frozen. Ambrosio beheld before him that once noble and majestic form, now become a Corpse, cold, senseless and disgusting' (Lewis, 1796/2008: 304)

6 Suggesting a broader discussion of the gothic postmodern – and so placing Faber's text more explicitly within a spectrum of the postmodern turns of its contemporaries – two students advised undertaking secondary reading that could help better articulate and contextualize this discussion of genre: Mary Waldron's chapter on 'Historico-Gothic' in *The Handbook of the Gothic* (2009) (S2, student response) and Maria Beville's monograph *Gothic-Postmodernism* (2009) (S6, student response).

7 In Charlotte Lennox's *The Female Quixote* (1752) Romance usurps the place of the conduct book for the heroine Arabella who famously draws 'all her Notions and Expectations' from such tales, as Lennox's narrator puts it: 'supposing Romances were real Pictures of life ... she was taught to believe, that Love was the ruling Principle of the World; that every other Passion was subordinate to this; and that it caused all the Happiness and Miseries of Life' (Lennox, 1752/2008: 7).

8 Such a reading coheres with the Anglo-Irish gothic writer Elizabeth Bowen's suggestion in the 'Postscript' to her collection *The Demon Lover and Other Stories* (1945) that her stories act as 'resistance fantasies' for both author and reader. In an apostrophe to the readership of her WWII tales, Bowen writes that, '[y]ou may say that these resistance-fantasies are in themselves frightening. I can only say that one counteracts fear by fear, stress by stress' (Bowen, 1999: 97).

9 Jonathan Bate, in his introduction to the Arden edition, argues that *Titus Andronicus* was first performed in 1594 and written only shortly before that. Other estimates suggest that it was written as early as 1588 and co-authored by the playwright George Peele. The patterning narratives for Shakespeare's horrors are found in Ovid's *Metamorphoses*. As Jonathan Bate notes in his summation of Ovid's epic, it was in the '*Metamorphoses*, schoolroom reading for Shakespeare ... that the dramatist read of how the Thracian tyrant Tereus married Progne, but then burned with desire for her sister Philomel, raped her in a gloomy wood, [and] cut out her tongue ... the two sisters then took a terrible revenge by killing Itys, son of Tereus and Progne, and dishing him in a pie at his father's table' (Bate, 1995/2003: 91).

10 Drawn from St Matthew's version of Jesus' Sermon on the Mount in *The Bible*. Christ's sermon, of course, also contains a moral warning not heeded in revenge tragedy: 'For with what judgement ye judge, ye shall be judged, and with what measure you mete, it shall be measured to you again' (7.1–2).

11 As Sophie and Sugar run to catch the omnibus that will take them away from William, Sugar trips and both her and Agnes Rackham's writings spill out onto the streets, suggesting that artifice is being left behind in this flight from patriarchal oppression (Faber, 2002/2011: 810).

12 A. C. Hamilton (1995: 129) suggests of *Titus Andronicus* that '[o]ne word may some up the reasons for rejecting this play: excess ... This violence becomes only more horrific through the excessive artifice of language'.

13 My understanding of 'systemic' and 'subjective' violence is gleaned from Slavoj Žižek's *Violence: Six Sideways Reflections* (2008). In his treatise on violence, Žižek's urges us to 'learn to step back, to disentangle ourselves from the fascinating lure of this directly visible "subjective" violence, violence performed by a clearly identifiable agent. We need to perceive the contours of the background which generates such outbursts ... subjective violence is just the most visible portion of a triumvirate that also includes two objective kinds of violence. First, there is a "symbolic" violence embodied in language and its forms ... Second, there is what I call "systemic" violence, or the often catastrophic consequences of the smooth functioning of our economic and political systems' (Žižek, 2008: 1).

14 Works cited by Colella here: Corbin (2005) and Jameson (1991).

15 At the 'Defying Genre' symposium, Faber responded to this quotation with great enthusiasm, suggesting that the term 'lucifer' provided him

with the perfect metaphor for gesturing towards William's malignity (Conversations with the author).

Works cited

Bate, Jonathan (1995/2003) 'Introduction' in Jonathan Bate (ed.) *Titus Andronicus*, William Shakespeare, pp. 1–121. London: Arden Shakespeare.

Beville, Maria (2009) *Gothic-postmodernism: Voicing the Terrors of Postmodernity*. Amsterdam: Rodopi.

Botting, Fred (2013) *Gothic*, 2nd edn. Abingdon: Routledge.

Bowen, Elizabeth (1999) *The Mulberry Tree*, ed. by Hermione Lee. London: Vintage.

Bradley, Ann (2016) 'Textuality and the Female Quixote in *The Crimson Petal and the White*', submitted in partial fulfilment of the MLitt in *The Gothic Imagination*, University of Stirling, April.

Brontë, Charlotte (1847/2016) *Jane Eyre*. London: W.W. Norton & Company.

Colella, Silvana (2010) 'Olfactory Ghosts: Michel Faber's *The Crimson Petal and the White*', in Rosario Arias and Patricia Pulham (eds) *Haunting and Spectrality in Neo-Victorian Fiction: Possessing the Past*, pp. 85–110. Basingstoke: Palgrave Macmillan.

Corbin, A. (2005) *Storia sociale degli odori*. Milan: Mondadori

Derrida, Jacques (1980) 'The Law of Genre', *Critical Inquiry* 7(1): 55–81.

Du Maurier, Daphne (1938/2003) *Rebecca*. London: Virago.

Faber, Michel (2000/2014) *Under the Skin*. Edinburgh: Canongate.

Faber, Michel (2002/2011) *The Crimson Petal and the White*. Edinburgh: Canongate.

Hamilton, A.C. (1995) '*Titus Andronicus*: The Form of Shakespearian Tragedy', in Philip C. Kolin (ed.) *Titus Andronicus: Critical Essays*, pp. 129–43. New York: Garland Publishing.

Jameson, F. (1991) *Postmodernism or the Cultural Logic of Late Capitalism*. London: Verso.

Kohlke, Marie-Luise and Gutleben, Christian (eds) (2012) *Neo-Victorian Gothic: Horror, Violence and Degeneration in the Re-Imagined Nineteenth Century*. Amsterdam: Rodopi.

Lennox, Charlotte (1752/2008) *The Female Quixote; or, The Adventures of Arabella*. Oxford: Oxford University Press.

Lewis, Matthew Gregory (1796/2008) *The Monk*. Oxford: Oxford University Press.

Llewellyn, Mark (2012) 'Authenticity, Authority and the Author: The Sugared Voice of the neo-Victorian in *The Crimson Petal and the White*', in Claire Westall and Rina Kim (eds) *Cross-gendered Literary Voices: Appropriating, Resisting, Embracing*, pp. 185–203. Basingstoke: Palgrave Macmillan.

Snodgrass, Mary Ellen (2011) 'Michel Faber, Feminism, and the Neo-Gothic Novel: *The Crimson Petal and the White*', in Danel Olson (ed.) *21st-Century Gothic: Great Gothic Novels Since 2000*, pp. 111–23. Laham: Scarecrow Press.

Süskind, Patrick (1985/2015) *Perfume: The Story of a Murderer*, trans. John E. Woods. London: Penguin.

Waldron, Mary (2009) 'Historico-Gothic', in Marie Mulvey-Roberts (ed.) *The Handbook of the Gothic*, 2nd edn, p. 184. Basingstoke: Palgrave Macmillan.

Žižek, Slavoj (2008) *Violence: Six Sideways Reflections*. London: Profile Books.

Chapter 11

Under the Coats of Skins
'Flesh Remains Flesh' and *Under the Skin* as an Introduction to Gregory of Nazianzus' Anthropology

Oliver B. Langworthy

Instructors in the fields of Church History and Historical Theological often find themselves presented with diverse student audiences who have not necessarily been equipped to grapple with the complex intellectual world of late antiquity. Finding ready and contemporary examples to make immediate connections without sacrificing interpretative power represents a particular pedagogical challenge. This study presents a case-study in using modern literature, two works by Michel Faber, to provide a conceptual lens in order to introduce and interpret ideas in Christian late antiquity, in this case a difficult area of Gregory of Nazianzus' anthropology. A fourth-century Greek theologian, Gregory wrote that as a consequence of the Fall, Adam was adorned in a 'coat of skins' (δερμάτινος [...] χιτῶνας), 'like' (ἴσως) the 'thick flesh' (παχυτέραν σάρκα) or <heavy flesh> (σάρκα βαρεῖαν).[1] The language of the 'coats of skin' was used by a number of other figures in Christian intellectual history, having been drawn from Genesis, but it is especially difficult in Gregory. The 'coats of skins' can be read as a part of the fall of a pure soul into corruptible matter, or simply a metaphor for mortality, shame, or even a manner of gift, but for Gregory the coats of skins may be indicative of sin of fallen human nature in a more immediate way, as a thickening and change for and of another flesh. The issue, as proposed by D. A. Sykes, is that if Gregory's man was created as a confluence between the mind, soul and body, even his prelapsarian flesh, or garments of light, must have had something of this mixed nature about it (Sykes, 1994: 248). That is to say that an appreciation of Gregory's anthropology requires holding in mind a series of physical states whose delineation is both literal and in degrees, but without any ontological change.[2] This presents an ambiguity that must be resolved by any interlocutor. Such a resolution of the disparate language and images in Gregory's anthropology requires recourse to Origen, Aristotle, Plato, and more.[3] However, the relevant parts of these sources are not necessarily readily available, particularly to those approaching Gregory for the first time, and this presents a high bar for engagement. This paper contends that Michel Faber's *Under the Skin* and 'Flesh Remains Flesh' in *Fahrenheit Twins* provide a useful set of conceptual lenses for initial explorations of an ambiguity of Late Antique theology presented by Gregory's language surrounding the imagery of the 'coats of skins.' Both of these works by Faber are concerned with appetites and desires, though on different trajectories. 'Flesh Remains Flesh' dwells on the corruption, physical and mental, from a desire to capture the world as it is and remain rooted in it. *Under the Skin* is similarly vested with questions of appetite, but also with a desire to, having descended into the world, to escape from it. Each offers valuable conceptual handholds on Gregory's own anthropology, short-circuiting much of the background that would otherwise be necessary, especially for those encountering such thought in late antiquity for the first time. However, there exists a capacity for mutual interpretation in which Gregory's theological investments can help highlight elements of Faber's own work that would otherwise be missed.

While there is some risk of anachronism, the contention is not that these works map perfectly to Gregory's thought, or that Gregory's thought was influential on Faber. Rather, that they can create a conceptual space in which Gregory's thought can be more fully appreciated on its own merits, and in turn demonstrates the value of interdisciplinary dialogue between patristic and modern literature. A brief excursus into Faber's *Book of Strange New Things* is necessary to set the bounds of this sort of inquiry. While readily identified as in dialogue with the idea of faith, and described by one reviewer as a 'cauldron of theological inquiry,' it is more concerned to interrogate the notions of belief and communication that underpin any expression of faith (Morrison, 2015: 58-9). This entails theological reflection, the dialogue between modern and patristic literature, and Faber and Gregory, which is not predicated on the presence of reflection on the nature of God or God's relationship to man. Though the structure of Gregory's thought is inescapably theological in this sense, the ambiguity of the physical, rather than philosophical, implications 'coats of skin' concerns what it means to be a human, and how humanity understands itself: mortal, contradictory, and dying. The relevant passage is from Gregory's *Oration* (*Or.*) 38.12 expands on this:

> So he [Adam] was banished from the Tree of Life, from Paradise, and from God on account of his sin, and he put on *the coats of skins, like the thick flesh, mortal and rebellious*; and he first knows his own shame, and hides from God [emphasis mine].[4]

Broadly defined, Christian eschatology accepts a distinction between pre-lapsarian, that is, pre-Fall, humanity and a post-lapsarian humanity. Such a distinction can, depending on how the Genesis account is read, be populated metaphorically or literally. The relevant passage, from Genesis 3:21, reads, 'The Lord God made coats of skin for Adam and his wife, and clothed them.' While a superficially clear passage, Gregory's speculative introduction of the idea of a heavy flesh on a nude Adam and Eve is not limited to him or his context. Faber's works provide a valuable resource for those first approaching late antique anthropologies such as that of Gregory Nazianzen. This study will begin by identifying several trajectories in the popular interpretation of the physical consequences of the Fall in order to demonstrate the value of Faber over and against the visual arts in particular. Next, it will consider two of Faber's works, the short story 'Flesh Remains

Flesh', and his novel *Under the Skin*. In each case, the works will be considered against Gregory's own thought in an effort to get closer to an understanding of Gregory's ambivalence and ambiguity about the flesh we inhabit.

Trajectories of Popular Interpretation

While Faber's works represent a valuable conceptual handhold in modern literature for understanding the often obscure anthropologies of late antiquity, visual representations have often been called upon to serve in a similar role. Such a duality between a literal and an allegorical understanding of the 'coats of skins' is particularly apparent in the artistic tradition surrounding the expulsion of Adam and Eve from Paradise. In Curradi's *The Expulsion of Adam and Eve from Paradise* and West's *The Expulsion of Adam and Eve*, from the seventeenth and eighteenth centuries respectively, actual tunics adorn Adam and Eve. Despite stylistic differences between the two works, the appearance of animal skins is a clear and dynamic presence within each work. Without devoting too much to their history, the inclusion of literal clothing tends to suggest a disparity between displaying the sexualized shame of the banishment, or towards God's beneficence in offering Adam and Eve some protection in a newly fallen world. On the other hand, while not necessarily directly connected to a metaphorical interpretation of the coats, portrayals of a nude Adam and Eve in expulsion tend towards a more abstract thinking about shame, gender, and humanity in the same trajectory as Gregory. Without implying even shared philosophical influences, such a desire to emphasize the degree of change wrought by the Fall has occurred to a variety of interpreters. Masaccio's fifteenth-century *The Expulsion from the Garden of Eden* features no animal skins in the panel depicting the Adam and Eve leaving the garden. Instead, all motion is focused on Eve attempting to hide her nudity with her hands, and Adam attempting to cover his eyes. The most salient example of this focus on the human, rather than animal skin, is in a detail of Michelangelo's expulsion of Adam and Eve from the Garden in the Sistine Chapel. Most notably in Eve, there is a transition from a reclining, Classical form, to a thickened, twisted figure. This would be entirely consistent with the coarse or heavy flesh of Gregory's thinking. The diminishment of the divine in favour of the earthly is an interruption of an ideal balance, and opens the way to the unchecked experience of passions that can be seen contorting Eve's face in the panel. Other examples, nude and clothed, abound in paintings and mosaics.[5] While helpful, these illustrations do little on their own to help us conceive of the three, rather than simply two, states of humanity that Gregory's language and anthropology suggest. The first being the lighter, pre-lapsarian humanity of the Garden of Eden, the second the fallen, thickened humanity of the world, and the third being post-eschatological humanity, restored as the image of God.

'Flesh Remains Flesh'

However, the physicality of the change after the Fall, captured by Masaccio and Michelangelo, is of great significance in understanding the value of Faber's work in shedding light on this area of Gregory's anthropology, and their capacity for mutual interpretation. The very nature of humanity is altered by its sin, but only by degrees. As noted by Sykes, the elements of humanity's composition do not change, whether prelapsarian, postlapsarian, or post-eschatological – it is composed of earthly matter, and mind and soul (Sykes, 1997: 171-2).[6] The balance between them does change, and is, as per Gregory's own qualified reading of Genesis, reflected in their physical form. The destiny of humanity is not in a return to a prelapsarian state. Gregory regards this as largely impossible. Instead, the present humanity sits at a sort of crossroads, poised between elevating themselves through a purification that brings out that which is divine, or rejecting that divinity in favour of their animal, heavy flesh. Such a dichotomy is especially apparent in Gregory's poem *A Comparison of Lives, Carm.* 1.2.8.[7] In it, the worldly life and spiritual life dispute before a judge who ultimately decides that though the spiritual life is to be preferred, peace can only come in acceptance of both. Gregory's caricatures throughout are instructive, as when the worldly life says in line 6 that 'Being born of the world, I know and love the things of it,' and the spiritual life in line 8 that 'Being born of God, I know and worship God ... ' That these two must be resolved to each other, with preference towards the spiritual, is central to Gregory's anthropology and to the concern identified by Sykes. Towards this, Faber's 'Flesh Remains Flesh' helps provide a lens that clarifies an initial question: what is signified by Gregory having introduced ambiguity between animal skins and the heavy flesh into his exegesis of the 'coats of skins' in Gen 3:21, and what this has to say about the present state of humanity?

Ashton Alan Clark, the focus of 'Flesh Remains Flesh,' emblematizes the worldly life towards which Gregory pointed. At the same time, his description throughout accords with a caricature of fallen humanity. Most obviously, in a discussion of the 'coats of skins,' Clark himself is described as a 'small, meaty man,' whose appearance is subhuman, most resembling a 'grossly overgrown otter' (Faber, 2005: 91). Encompassing a literal and an allegorical reading of the coats of skin's Clark is not only thickened and of diminished humanity, but wears 'a black sable coat and doeskin trousers, and a top hat that was likewise furry (Faber, 2005: 91).' From the perspective of Gregory's reading of Gen 3:21, Clark is rendered inhuman through layers of heavy flesh. Whether these are added to his own form, destined for death, or formed from dead non-human animals only serves to emphasize his degenerate nature. This illustrates a strong possibility for why Gregory introduced ambiguity into the interpretation of Gen 3:21 at all: to be draped in the skins of the dead is equivalent, in Gregory's thought, to being attired in flesh that will die. Clark's death itself is an amplification of this, with his 'corpulent physique' bloating still further, resulting in his alteration into a thing utterly unrecognizable as human and finally 'irredeemably corrupted (Faber, 2005: 103).'

Gregory's caricature of worldly life in his *A Comparison of Lives* yields further evidence that Faber's thought has utility for understanding Gregory's own on the subject of the heavy flesh. The following exchange between the worldly life (W) and the spiritual life (S) concerns the benefits and perils of each in lines 91–95:

W) I can live in luxury. S) My luxury
is to have no luxury, with its bloatedness, its intestinal
swellings, its sickening with wealth's dyspepsia,
a smelling of treacly sludge outside the throat,
the mind diminishing as the mud grows thicker.

These lines have obvious thematic and conceptual connections to the first lines of 'Flesh Remains Flesh' and their description of Clark as 'the richest man in Altchester; he had money on his breath and a sticky ooze of luxury clogging up his ears' (Faber, 2000: 91). While excess is easily connected to physical corpulence, Faber and Gregory both point to the smell and internal decay brought about by excessive luxury and wealth. In each case suggested by smell, and in both a thickening sludge or ooze isolating the object from the world as it grows. 'Flesh Remains Flesh' helps to illuminate why Gregory introduced ambiguity into his reading of Gen 3:21, but also evinces parallels in thought concerning the degeneracy of heavy flesh between Gregory and Faber that illuminate Gregory's thought. Further towards this, *A Comparison of Lives* is far from a convenient or common text in Gregory's corpus. While it is one of a limited number of his poems translated into English and in circulation it is rarely considered at any length despite the its demonstrable significance for his anthropology. 'Flesh Remains Flesh' contains a resonant similarity to Gregory's ambivalence about the mortality of human flesh, and a capacity to illuminate the necessity of the ambiguity of Gregory's reading of the coats of skins – *Under the Skin* helps to explain the consequences of that ambiguity.

Under the Skin

Under the Skin naturally lends itself to thinking about different states of being, rather than only the fallen one evinced in 'Flesh Remains Flesh,' when approached from a perspective exposed to the ambiguity of Gregory's language. It is at this point that *Under the Skin*, with its own ambiguous language and imagery of humanity, becomes useful in coming to grips with the states of humanity in Gregory's thought.

Between Amlis Vess, Isserley, and the vodsels – all self-identifiably human – are three states of existence and degrees of heavy, or coarse, flesh all clothed in different coats of skin. This is a separation by degrees, however, not a material difference in constitution. In this way, despite the distance of Faber's novel from the problem, it helps to shed light on the contradiction in a humanity which must sit at the mixture of the divine mind and the immaterial soul and the material, animal world.

To avoid confusion, as far as possible, going forward 'human' and 'humanity' will refer to the humans of *Under the Skin*, which is to say as opposed to vodsels. And, while the humans of *Under the Skin* do not immediately come across as suitable mental models for un-fallen nature, it is not the moral character of Gregory's states of being that needs unpacked, but their physicality. In this sense, the lack of mercy – as Isserly notes, an untranslatable concept – is definitive. Through Isserley, who for our purposes represents the transitory, fallen, nature burdened with flesh, mercy is not without meaning. She recognizes it, thinks to attempt to ask for it, but like the heavy flesh this is an imitation of an even lower nature, the emulation of which is fruitless and even harmful (Faber, 2000: 113–14). This, combined with the essentially garrulous, professional, outgoing, or in the case of Amlis Vess, even innocent descriptions of the humans by Isserly render even those drawn from the Estates as purer, higher, and unburdened. They are all, to some limited extent, worthy of imitation.

Imitation is an important concept for Gregory, and the choice is open whether to ascend towards divinity or descend to animal excess through the choice of what to imitate. Such imitation is not directed towards something utterly alien. In Gregory's thought, the incarnate Christ is the chief object of imitation in pursuit of salvation (Hofer, 2013: 150). The difference between the incarnation of Christ and the mixed nature of humanity is such that Christ is perfected, and without sin. The imitation is of a lower form directed towards a higher. Postlapsarian humanity may also imitate that which is less admirable, and become less like Christ and more like the world. In each case this is a matter of extreme degree. The remaking of Isserly into a new, coarse flesh does not impact her essential humanity, but this physicality, this imitation, puts it at risk of further descent (Faber, 2000: 172). It is, in effect, a fall into a state reminiscent of postlapsarian humanity in Gregory's thought. While there are three clear states separated by degrees in Gregory's thinking around the coats of skins, the prelapsarian, the postlapsarian enclothed in flesh, and the deified, the second is dynamic, open to ascent in deification or descent towards an animal nature emblematized by a thicker, heavier flesh (Sykes, 1997: 247–8). Isserly's fear of identifying with the animals she now resembles sits easily with this. Although not a heavier or thickened in the same way as Gregory conceived, its inferiority is conceived of in terms of its similarity to what is described as 'meat' (Faber, 2000: 163, 165).

This gives a sense of two states, one adorned but unburdened by the coarse, rebellious flesh of mortality and meat, and capable of sin but innocent of this world. Such an ambiguity is highlighted in Amlis Vess's abortive harangue in which he charges that 'That meat you're eating [...] is the body of a creature that lived and breathed just like you and me' (Faber, 2000: 163). The other, burdened by a coat of skin and suspended between a descent into animal excess, of twisted muscle, or aspiring towards a higher nature that is – as Gregory would see it – unreachable without divine intervention. While the text offers useful conceptual handholds, it is the ascension towards the ultimate, third state of Gregory's thought, from this dynamic second state, that is most problematic both in the text of *Under the Skin* and in Gregory's works. While monthlings provide a sense of a truly fallen, thickened nature, *Under the Skin* provides an image of ascension in Isserly's self-destruction. What makes it a particularly useful lens for reading Gregory is that it encapsulates the paradoxical idea of metamorphosis without a change in nature. The following selection demonstrates this well:

> Instead of ending up buried in the ground, she would become part of the sky: that was the way to look at it. Her invisible remains would combine, over time, with all the wonders under the sun. When it snowed she would be part of it, falling softly to the earth, rising up again with the snow's evaporation. (Faber, 2000: 296)

This dissolution into nature, an unburdening of flesh that retains essentially physical character is, while not identical, closely related to Gregory's thought. Death and deification do not entail a loss of those earthly or physical parts of created nature, but a rebalancing of them with the divine. This deification, and Isserly's dissolution, are characterized elevation above a previous state that nevertheless retains an essential commonality with the world. It is a unification with the cycles of nature that renders her immortal, ineluctably part of the cycles of the world. This captures an essential, difficult, and often overlooked element of Gregory's thought. While his language of deification seems dramatic, and should not be denuded of its force, it does not involve abandonment of humanity's status as created, and composed in part of same material as the world. Despite Gregory's often negative tone about matter and fleshly bodies, particularly in his funeral orations, his concern was this current life represented a trial before an ultimate reward in the perfection of what was divine and material in humanity (Ruether, 1969: 135).[8] Isserley's dissolution shares close thematic parallels. In shedding a heavy, burdensome flesh she is not rendered into something alien from the world, as she was, but is instead manifest more fully within it. While the passage quoted above provides a valuable lens through which to consider Gregory's thought, the final scene of the film adaptation of *Under the Skin* makes such a translation literal, superimposing Isserley over a forest. Although powerful in the context of the film, this lessens the explanatory power for Gregory's work of the same events in the novel.

Glazer's 2013 adaptation of *Under the Skin* picks up on many of the same linguistic-visual cues on the significance of enclothing, disrobing and degloving as significant for the ascent and descent of natures by degrees. There are three principle scenes in this respect. First, Isserley's descent into the animal world is occasioned by putting on clothing taken from the dead. It is, in the same sense, a coat of skins, and a burdensome fall from light into the material world. In the next, we can see a vodsel descending into darkness, tempted to destruction. The next, an evocative image of degloving, in which all that remains of a fully degraded nature is its coat of skin, or its coarse flesh. Finally, Isserley's examination and shedding of a literal coat of skin before her immolation offers a useful image, but still falls short of the parallel in the original text when it comes to providing a lens for Gregory. Despite these superficial similarities this lack is down to their isolation in the novel to the character of Isserley, and the film's emphasis on Isserly as utterly alien. Ultimately, the novel is concerned with the same anthropological conundrum as Gregory: the tension between being and world, the impossibility of return, and the hope, however abstract, of elevation.

Conclusion

Between the two, there is a shared investment in the burdensome nature of flesh, the transitory nature of physicality. The passable nature of that heavy flesh, that mixture between divinity and animal nature is central to Gregory's thought on those states of human, or vodsel, as it were, nature. In a funeral oration for his brother, *Or.* 7.22, he writes:

> Are we not, even if we are somewhat grieved, to be on the contrary distressed at our lengthened sojourn, like holy David, who calls things here the tents of darkness, and the place of affliction, and the deep mire, and the shadow of death; because we linger in the tombs we bear about with us, because, though we are gods, we die like men the death of sin?[9]

While properly coming to grips with his thought will always require an understanding of Gregory's sources, theological investments, and philosophy, *Under the Skin* and 'Flesh Remains Flesh' offer a useful conceptual lens through which to start coming to grips with a late antique thinker who saw himself and others as a truly spiritual natures in potential trapped in bodily tombs, but whose essential nature was always inescapably of the world. At the same time, this discourse between patristic and modern literature finds Faber on the same trajectory as Gregory, Masaccio, and Michelangelo, reflecting on the place of humanity in the world concretely, clothed in heavy flesh.

Notes

1 See Or. 38.12 for παχυτέραν σάρκα and Carm. 1.1.7 for σάρκα βαρεῖαν. The inclusion of ἴσως in Or. 38.12 adds some further ambiguity. I have here split the difference between Browne and Swallow who render it as 'perhaps' and Gallay who provides 'ç'est-à-dire.' There are plausible arguments in favour of each, although the balance certainly favours Moreschini, with Browne and Swallow allowing for too much ambiguity on Gregory's part (see Browne and Swallow, 1894: 348; Gallay, 1990: 131).

2 This paper treats only with a very focused area of Gregory's anthropology, which is diverse and has been subject to extensive study elsewhere. The most significant recent works that touch on the subject are Beeley (2008: 116–28), Tollefsen (2006: 257–70) and Hofer (2013: 120). On interpretations of the coats of skins more generally in antiquity, Moreschini's recommendation of Beatrice (1985: 433–84) remains very good. For the purposes of this paper it is only necessary to keep in mind that the aim is not to provide the clearest possible illumination of Gregory's thought, but to demonstrate the capacity of a dialogue between modern and Patristic literature.

3 Gregory's education included time in Alexandria and Athens, training in rhetoric and philosophy, and so he had a demonstrated facility with the literature and critical methodology of his own period. For biographical details of Gregory, and for this period in particular, see McGuckin (2001: 1–83). On the history of Christian reception of Greco-Roman literary critical methods see Ayres (2004: 34–7).

4 Translations are my own except where specified.

5 The history of interpretation of such representations is even more extensive. Particularly relevant to a fuller discussion are Anderson (2001: 117ff.) and (Jensen, 2004: 25ff.) as representative of scholarship on the artistic representation of Adam and Eve.

6 Sykes rightly points to Or. 7.21 for an account of Gregory's view of a post-eschatological body. While it is sufficient for the purposes of this chapter to understand that humanity remains body and soul, Gregory's understanding of the cleansing, recombination, and dissolution of both is more complex than that.

7 Translations of this poem are taken from Gilbert (2001: 119–28).

8 Ruether captures this by noting that the Fall was not a 'total perversion of his nature.' Ruether likewise notes some of the philosophical antecedents

and implications of to the enclothing of the Fall which are not the focus of this chapter.

9 Translated by Browne and Swallow (1894: 237).

Works Cited

Anderson, Gary A. (2001) *The Genesis of Perfection: Adam and Eve in Jewish and Christian Imagination*. Louisville: Westminster John Knox Press.

Ayres, Lewis. (2004) *Nicaea and its Legacy: An Approach to Fourth-Century Trinitarian Theology*. Oxford: Oxford University Press.

Beatrice, P. F. (1985) 'Le tuniche di pelle – Antiche letture di *Gen.* 3, 21,' in Ugo Bianchi (ed.) *La Tradizione dell'enkrateia: motivazioni ontologiche e protologiche: atti del Colloquio Internazionale, Milano, 20–23 aprile 1982*, pp. 433–84. Rome: Edizioni dell'Ateneo.

Beeley, Christopher A. (2008) *Gregory of Nazianzus on the Trinity and the Knowledge of God: In Your Light We Shall See Light*. Oxford: Oxford University Press.

Browne, Charles and Swallow, Gordon, trans. (1894) *Nicene and Post Nicene Fathers, Second Edition*. Volume 7, ed. Philip Schaff and Henry Wace. Buffalo, NY: Christian Literature Publishing Co.

Faber, Michel (2000) *Under the Skin*. Edinburgh: Canongate.

Faber, Michel (2005) *The Fahreinheit Twins*. Edinburgh: Canongate.

Faber, Michel (2014) *The Book of Strange New Things*. London. Hogarth.

Gallay, Paul, trans. and Claudio Moreschini, introduced and ed. (1990) *Grégoire de Nazianze: Discours 38-41. Sources Chrétiennes 358*. Paris: Les Éditions du Cerf.

Gilbert, Peter, trans. and introduced (2001) *On God and Man: The Theological Poetry of Gregory of Nazianzus*. Crestwood: St Vladimir's Seminary Press.

Hofer, Andrew (2013) *Christ in the Life and Teaching of Gregory of Nazianzus*. Oxford: Oxford University Press.

Jensen, Robin (2004) 'The Fall and Rise of Adam and Eve,' in Heidi Hornik and Mikeal Parons (eds) *Interpreting Christian Art: Reflections on Christian Art*, pp. 23–52. Macon: Mercer University Press.

McGuckin, John (2001) *St Gregory of Nazianzus: An Intellectual Biography*. Crestwood: St Vladimir's Seminary Press.

Morrison, Michael (2015) '"The Book of Strange New Things" by Michel Faber,' *World Literature Today*, 58–9.

Ruether, Rosemary (1969) *Gregory of Nazianzus: Rhetor and Philosopher*. Oxford: Clarendon Press.

Sykes, D.A., trans. and introduced and Claudio Moreschini, ed. (1997) *St Gregory of Nazianzus: Poemata Arcana*. Oxford: Clarendon Press.

Tollefsen, Torstein (2006) 'Theosis according to Gregory,' in Jostein Børtnes and Tomas Hägg (eds) *Gregory of Nazianzus: Images and Reflections*, pp. 257–69. Copenhagen: Museum Tusculanum Press.

Notes on Contributors

Timothy C. Baker is Senior Lecturer in Scottish and Contemporary Literature at the University of Aberdeen. He is the author, most recently, of *Writing Animals: Language, Suffering, and Animality in Twenty-First-Century Fiction* (Palgrave, 2019) and *Contemporary Scottish Gothic: Mourning, Authenticity, and Tradition* (Palgrave, 2014).

Ian Blyth is a lecturer in Literature and Philosophy at Inverness College, University of the Highlands and Islands | Colaiste Inbhir Nis, Oilthigh na Gàidhealtachd agus nan Eilean. His research interests include the works of Tolkien, environmental philosophy, mediaeval eco-literature, and science fiction and fantasy in the anthropocene.

Tomasz Dobrogoszcz works as assistant professor at the Department of British Literature and Culture, University of Łódź, Poland, teaching courses and seminars in British literature and literary translation. His main fields of research include contemporary British and postcolonial literature, as well as poststructuralist and psychoanalytical literary theory. He is the author of *Family and Relationships in Ian McEwan's Fiction* (Lexington Press, 2018). He edited *Nobody Expects the Spanish Inquisition: Cultural Contexts in Monty Python*, a collection of essays on the British comic group (Rowman and Littlefield, 2014) and co-edited *Reading Graham Swift* (Lexington Press, 2019). He translated into Polish a seminal work in postcolonial theory, The Location of Culture by Homi K. Bhabha, as well as many other critical and literary texts, for instance by Hayden White or Dipesh Chakrabarty.

Notes on Contributors

Matt Foley is Lecturer in Modern and Contemporary Literature at Manchester Met. He is the author of *Haunting Modernisms* (Palgrave, 2017) and co-editor, with Dr Rebecca Duncan, of *Patrick McGrath and his Worlds* (Routledge, 2019). His main research interests are in modernism, the gothic, and literary acoustics.

Rodge Glass is the author of the novels *No Fireworks* (Faber, 2005), *Hope for Newborns* (Faber, 2008) and *Bring Me the Head of Ryan Giggs* (Serpent's Tail, 2012) as well as a graphic novel, *Dougie's War* (Freight, 2010, written with Dave Turbitt), *LoveSexTravelMusik: Stories for the EasyJet Generation* (Freight, 2013) and *Alasdair Gray: A Secretary's Biography* (Bloomsbury, 2008) His work has been nominated for numerous awards, and he won a Somerset Maugham Award for Non-Fiction in 2009. Rodge has also written for The Guardian and The Paris Review and his various fictions have been widely translated. Rodge is a Senior Lecturer in Creative Writing at the University of Strathclyde in Glasgow, also the Convener of the MLitt in Creative Writing.

Oliver B. Langworthy is associate lecturer in Patristics at the University of St Andrews and an academic editor with the St Andrews Encyclopaedia of Theology. His research interests include Patrististic theology and Biblical reception, later Patristic reception, Pneumatology, and deification.

Rebecca Langworthy's doctorate was awarded in 2019, and her thesis examined the development of adult fantasy as a sub-genre in the work of Scottish author George MacDonald. Her current research interests include Scottish Victorian literature, the Gothic, religion and literature, and fantasy literature. She has recently published on George MacDonald's short story 'The History of Photogen and Nycteris', and the literary psycho-geography of the Aberdeenshire town of Huntly.

Kristin Lindfield-Ott is an independent scholar based in the Scottish Highlands. She has published extensively on the works of James Macpherson (1736–1796) and on contemporary Scottish fiction. Formerly Programme Leader for Literature at the University of the Highlands and Islands, she now grows vegetables for local communities across Scotland and teaches community groups to grow their own food.

Notes on Contributors

Jim MacPherson is Senior Lecturer at the Centre for History, University of the Highlands and Islands. He specialises in the history and literature of the Scottish Highlands and the region's connections with empire and is currently writing a book (co-authored with Kristin Lindfield-Ott) about James Macpherson (1736–1796) and his history writing, entitled *Macpherson the Historian* (Edinburgh University Press, forthcoming 2021).

Natalie O'Keeffe is a graduate of the University of the Highlands and Islands, holding an MLitt in Highlands and Islands literature. Despite her eclectic interests, she is particularly intrigued by cultural history, transformative storytelling, and the portrayal of gender and sexuality in fiction.

Nicholas Prescott wrote his PhD on authors Thomas Pynchon and Don DeLillo, and has long been fascinated by contemporary and postmodern literature. As well as contributing chapters to Gylphi's Contemporary Writers volumes on M. John Harrison and Michel Faber, Nick has published on Pynchon, David Lynch, contemporary film and the #MeToo movement, among many other topics. Nick broadcasts weekly on the ABC, was a member of the Adelaide Writers' Week Advisory Committee for a decade, and has taught Literature, Film and Creative Arts at Flinders University in South Australia since 1997.

Kate Wilkinson teaches at Queen Mary University of London. Her research focuses on contemporary fiction, and her particular interests include letters in twenty-first-century novels, temporality, technology and communication.

Index

Acampora, Ralph C. 25
Adams, Richard
  Watership Down 18
alienation 2, 52, 59, 83
anachronism 90, 182
anthropology 11, 85, 181–194
anthropomorphism 20, 22, 29, 39, 41, 99
Aristotle 182
Auerbach, Erich 70
  Mimesis 66, 69

Bate, Jonathan 178n.9
BBC 8, 11, 140, 141, 142, 144, 146, 151, 155, 156
Bentham, Jeremy 26
Beville, Maria
  Gothic-Postmodernism 177n.6
Booker Prize 1
Bostrom, Nick
  'Are We Living in a Computer Simulation?' 71, 72
Botting, Fred 172
Bowen, Elizabeth
  Demon Lover and Other Stories, The 177n.8
Brassier, Ray

Nihil Unbound 61, 62
Brontë, Charlotte
  Jane Eyre 167, 174
Brown, Dan
  Da Vinci Code, The 7, 130
Buchan, John
  Thirty Nine Steps, The 7

cannibalism 169
Canongate 129
Carroll, Lewis
  Alice in Wonderland 139
Christie, Agatha
  And Then There Were None 139
cinema 139, 141, 149
'coats of skins' 181, 184, 189, 190
Coetzee, J. M. 37, 38
  Disgrace 37
  Lives of Animals, The 33
Collins, Wilkie 144
colour 103, 153
  perception 22
  use of 61, 152, 154, 156
Conrad, Joseph 8
  Heart of Darkness 88
Crary, Jonathan 82, 85, 87
  24/7 83–84

Danielewski, Mark Z.
  House of Leaves 177n.4
Deleuze, Gilles
  and Guattari, Félix
    'becoming-animal' 37
Derrida, Jacques 2, 18, 64, 73
  'The Animal That Therefore I
    Am (More to Follow)' 58
  'The Law of Genre' 15, 164
  Limitrophy 58
Descartes, René
  Mediations 70
Dickens, Charles 1, 129, 144
  Christmas Carol, A 139
  Dickensian (TV series) 139
Dillon, Sarah 37, 40, 42, 58, 59, 60
Dix, Otto 151, 154
  Brothel Mother 155
  Lady with Mink and Veil 155
  Leonie 155
Doré, Gustav 151, 152
Doyle, Arthur Conan
  Sherlock Holmes 139
dramatic irony 174
Du Maurier, Daphne
  Rebecca 167, 173

Eagleton, Terry 69, 70
Edge Hill University 127, 130
Eliot, George 144
empathy 28, 40, 33–50, 104
Eno, Brian 95, 96
Ernst, Max 151
eschatology 183, 185, 192n.6
ethics 9, 15–32, 33, 34, 36, 37, 40, 42, 169, 171
evolution. *See* Darwinism

Faber, Michel
  adaptations
    See also. Glazer, Jonathan
    Oasis (tv) 52
    Crimson Petal and the White, The (tv) 139–162
  novels
    Book of Strange New Things, The 7, 8, 9, 10, 15, 16, 18, 28, 51, 52, 53, 56, 57, 58, 59, 63, 77–94, 113–126, 127–138, 183
    Courage Consort, The 7, 10, 95–112
    Crimson Petal and the White, The 2, 7, 8, 10, 11, 28, 95, 128, 131, 139–162, 163–180
    Fire Gospel, The 7, 52, 57, 58, 62, 63, 78–94, 128, 129, 130, 131
    Hundred and Ninety-Nine Steps, The 7, 77, 78
    Under The Skin 5, 7, 8, 9, 11, 12, 17, 24, 33, 34, 36, 37, 39, 41, 43, 45, 48, 51, 52, 58, 59, 60, 62, 63, 133, 134, 163, 176n.1, 181–194
  poetry
    'The 13th' 52, 62, 63
    Undying 8, 9, 52, 62, 128, 131, 132
  short fiction
    Apple, The: Crimson Petal Stories 7
    'The Fahrenheit Twins' 95–112

Index

Fahrenheit Twins, The 8, 18, 77–94, 182
'Fish' 8, 9, 67, 68, 69, 74
'Flesh Remains Flesh' 181–194
'Half and Million Pounds and a Miracle' 8
'Mouse' 9, 15, 26
'The Safehouse' 8
'Sheep' 9, 15, 23, 25
Some Rain Must Fall 8, 67, 129
'Tabitha Warren' 9, 15, 18, 22, 27, 78–94
femininity 33–50
feminism 2, 34, 43, 50, 167
fin de siècle 176n.1, 176n.2
Foer, Jonathan Safran
Everything Is Illuminated 33
folklore 102, 103
Freud, Lucian 148
Freud, Sigmund
Das Unheimliche 98
doppelgänger 98, 99
repression 48
uncanny 98

genre fiction 5–10, 12, 15–32, 33, 34, 58, 66, 67, 73, 74, 96, 99, 100, 145, 147, 164, 166, 173, 174
Glazer, Jonathan
Under the Skin (film) 8, 52, 60, 61, 133, 190
Goethe, Johann Wolfgang von 130
gothic 7, 33, 163–180
female 169, 170, 174, 176

iconography 11, 172
parody of 173
Graham, Winston
Poldark 139
Graves, Robert
and Patai, Raphael 103
Gray, Alasdair
Poor Things 130

Hale, Mike 146
Hamilton, A. C. 178n.12
Haraway, Donna 27
Hardy, Thomas 144
Hatoum, Milton
Orphans of Eldorado 129
historical fiction 6, 24, 27, 30, 69, 77, 82, 109, 143, 145, 172
Hofmann, Gert
Unsere Eroberung (Our Conquest) 3
Hurley, Kelly
Gothic Body, The 176n.1
hyperbole 17

Ian St James Award 8
imitation 66, 188, 189. See *also* mimesis

Jameson, Fredric 172, 178n.14
James Tait Prize 1

Kafka, Franz 18
Kristeva, Julia 34
Powers of Horror 48, 49

Lacan, Jacques
  mirror stage 48
late antiquity 181, 182, 184
Lennox, Charlotte
  Female Quixote, The 177n.7
Lewis, Matthew Gregory
  Monk, The 167, 177n.5
Lewis, Michael 93n.2
linguistics 16, 17, 18, 39, 40, 53, 74, 190
Lipman, Maureen 146
literary adaptation 9, 10, 44, 52, 61, 133, 139–162, 190. *See also herein* film, plays, radio drama and tv
London Review of Books 69
Lynch, David 96
  Blue Velvet 96
  Twin Peaks – the Return (tv show) 111n.2

macabre 10, 97
Macallan Short Story Competition 7, 8, 67
Martel, Yann
  Life of Pi 33
Maturin, Charles
  Melmoth the Wanderer 176n.2
McCabe, Eugene
  Death and Nightingales 139
McEwan, Ian 38
metafiction 37, 177n.4
mimesis 66
Minerva 3
misogyny 48, 49
Mitchell, David 7, 11, 12
Montaigne, Michel de 17
Munden, Marc 145

mutilation 34, 48, 100, 103, 169
mythology 10, 97, 102, 103, 116, 129, 130

Nabokov, Vladimir 96
Nagel, Thomas
  'What Is It Like to Be a Bat?' 20
National Short Story Prize 8
Neil Gunn Award 8
neo-Victorian 7, 8, 166, 167, 172, 175
Nietzsche, Friedrich 53, 56
nihilism 9, 51, 52, 56, 58, 59, 61, 62, 63, 64
Nobel Prize for Fiction 1

Orwell, George 41
Ovid
  Metamorphoses 178n.9

Pelevin, Victor
  Helmet of Horror, The 129
Perrault, Charles
  Blue Beard 173
phallocentrism 44
Pick, Anat 26
Plato 182
  'Allegory of the Cave' 70
  Republic 65, 70
Poe, Edgar Allan 10, 97, 100, 102, 109
  'Berenice' 111n.2
  'The Black Cat' 101
  'Facts in the Case of M. Valdemar, The' 101
  'Murders in the Rue Morgue' 101

'The Murders in the Rue Morgue' 99, 111n.2
'The Tell-Tale Heart' 101, 111n.2
pornography 78, 151, 168, 171
Porter, Dennis
   Pursuit of Crime, The – Art and Ideology in Crime Fiction 111n.2
postmodernism 164, 165, 171, 172, 175, 177n.4, 177n.6
prostitution 129, 145, 147, 153, 154, 169

rape 42, 169, 178n.9
realism 27, 66, 67, 69, 70, 74, 99, 102, 108, 145, 177n.4
revenge tragedy 169
   Elizabethan 169
rhetoric 17, 37, 192n.3

Saatchi, Charles 23
Saltire Society Scottish Book of the Year 8
science fiction 7, 10, 17, 27, 29, 33, 58, 66, 74
Science Fiction Studies 37
Second World War 109
Sermon on the Mount 178n.10
Shakespeare, William
   Hamlet 44
   Titus Andronicus 169, 170, 178n.9, 178n.12
Shelley, Mary
   Frankenstein 130
Simondon, Gilbert 85
Singer, Peter 26

Socrates 65
solipsism 25
speculative fiction 34
stereotyping 45, 49
Stiegler, Bernard
   Technics and Time 85
Stoker, Bram
   Dracula 7
suicide 42, 79, 106, 107
Süskind, Patrick
   Perfume 173
Sykes, D. A. 182

Tennyson, Alfred
   'The Lotos-Eaters' 88
Tolstoy, Leo
   War & Peace 139
Tong, Su
   Binu and the Great Wall 129
Trollope, Anthony 144

Uexküll, Jakob Johann von
   Theory of Meaning, A 24
uncanny 10, 107, 95–112, 111, 146, 173, 174

Vila-Matas, Enrique
   There Is Never any End to Paris 132
Vint, Sherryl 37
Virilio, Paul
   Great Accelerator, The 82
Vogue 151
Von Uexküll, Jakob
   Foray into the Worlds of Animals and Humans, A 22

Walpole, Horace
  Castle of Otranto, The 176n.2
Whitbread First Novel Award 8

Žižek, Slavoj
  Violence 178n.13